W9-BRR-815

EVELYN NESBIT

AND

STANFORD WHITE

BOOKS BY MICHAEL MACDONALD MOONEY

Evelyn Nesbit and Stanford White: Love and Death in the Gilded Age

George Catlin: Letters and Notes on the North American Indians

The Hindenburg

MICHAEL MACDONALD MOONEY

EVELYN NESBIT *AND* STANFORD WHITE

LOVE AND DEATH IN THE GILDED AGE

WILLIAM MORROW AND COMPANY, INC.
NEW YORK 1976

Copyright © 1976 by Michael M. Mooney

All rights reserved. No part of this book may be reproduced or utilized in any form or by any means, electronic or mechanical, including photocopying, recording or by any information storage and retrieval system, without permission in writing from the Publisher. Inquiries should be addressed to William Morrow and Company, Inc., 105 Madison Ave., New York, N.Y. 10016.

Printed in the United States of America.

1 2 3 4 5 6 7 8 9 10

Library of Congress Cataloging in Publication Data

Mooney, Michael Macdonald (date)
Evelyn Nesbit and Stanford White: love and death in the gilded age.

Includes index.
1. Nesbit, Evelyn. 2. White, Stanford, 1853-1906.
3. Thaw, Harry Kendall, 1871-1947. I. Title.
HV6534.N5M66 364.1'523'0922 [B] 76-18111
ISBN 0-688-03079-3

BOOK DESIGN CARL WEISS

Dedicated to

THE IDA MAYS—CITY GIRLS

CONTENTS

ACT I

CONFESSION

Then she said to me: "The bitterest woe of woes
Is to remember in our wretchedness
Old happy times; and this thy Doctor knows:
Yet, if so dear desire thy heart possess
To know that root of love which wrought our fall,
I'll be as those who weep and who confess."

—DANTE, *The Divine Comedy*, "Hell,"
Canto V, lines 121-126

CHAPTER ONE

CITYSCAPE:
Topography of Illusion

ONCE UPON A TIME, the City of New York could be located at approximately 74 degrees west, 40 degrees, 42 minutes north —an intersection of navigators' circumferences at a point in Battery Park on the southern tip of Manhattan Island. In the eighteenth century, when the United States was in its infancy and the city hardly more than a village, such navigators' conventions served well enough to locate the Port of New York. When the nineteenth century had passed and the twentieth century began, the city had become a teeming, swarming organism of unknown extent with reasons of its own. By the turn of the century it was not so much a place as the focus for illusions.

Just before the turn of the century, in 1898, legislators of the City and the State of New York met to promote the city's general welfare and to compromise conflicting claims of its jurisdiction. They debated and came to an agreement creating a government they called "Greater New York," which included in the charter the formerly independent cities and boroughs of Brooklyn, Queens, the Bronx, and Staten Island. All these, the politicians finally agreed, would consent to administration by Manhattan's City Hall, and it appeared as if the city had a government.

Yet the new political constituency from which officials would be elected, and budgets voted, and taxes assessed, bore no relation to the city's realities. Greater New York was a government convened a century too late, and a political system whose substantive powers would be limited to inspecting its own anarchy from time to time for the entertainment of its citizens—to their considerable delight—and to the orderly management of parades. The political system of Greater New York ignored the extent to which the city had taken a quantum leap in energies, operating on a scale so magnificent that it was beyond the control of petty magistrates.

Everyone could see that the nucleus of these new energies was centered on Manhattan Island. On twenty-three square miles of rock surrounded by seething tides, soaring constructions of iron and steel thrust up—the skyline, said the city's own citizens, was bigger, better, taller, richer, still growing. The city was not finished yet, they would say, and it would never be finished. Yet no one seemed able to agree on what these gargantuan effects represented, nor what energies were the source of their thrust, nor what might be the extent of their force. For example, in addition to the government device constituted as Greater New York, another system described as "Metropolitan New York" had to be invented, and it was accepted to satisfy the ambitions of the city's shopkeepers. The city's trading area was located by inscribing a circle around a point centered on Manhattan Island, its radius limited only by each shopkeeper's private intuition, and the area resulting—the square of the radius multipled by Pi—designated as "The New York Metropolitan Area." It was an area no one even pretended to govern, a collage of irrationalities, duly noted on cartographer's maps, and including parts of the federal states of New Jersey and Connecticut, and perhaps other states as well.

Beyond Greater New York's political jurisdiction, and beyond Metropolitan New York's trading area, still other energies were obviously focused on Manhattan Island—energies that the city appeared to consume day and night, energies absorbed from the entire American continent, which lay to the city's west, and from the oceans of the world, which began east of Manhattan's Battery Park.

Some of these energies could be traced back to the very beginning of the city's history, and they were energies peculiar to New York's own special inspirations. For example, in a gesture typical of its gaiety, the city had once appointed Captain Kidd to the office responsible for the suppression of pirates. New York always believed it would be best to let Boston enjoy rectitude and Philadelphia measure simplicity.

New York's ship captains had never needed much more than a fair tide to set sail and hazard their fortunes. From their adventures at sea, conducted sometimes as privateers and sometimes as merchant traders—the distinction was often blurred—they returned to heap treasures on the city's docks. In its beginnings the Port of New York always sheltered an astonishing mixture of craft: at first coastwise sloops in from Philly and Boston, gaff-rigged schooners deep on their lines with lumber down from Passamaquoddy Bay, centerboard cotton barques up from Cape Fear, shallow-draft fore-and-afters from the Mississippi sandbars. Later there were Liverpool packets, and clippers from Canton, and there were always tramps arriving, announcing their success: "Brig *Brilliant,* made Isle of May, Rio de Janeiro, New Orleans, Saybrook, and New York."

The city took its first occupations from the sea, each skill deriving successively by complication: the art of ship carpenter first; then riggers, ropemakers, sailmakers, sailingmasters, pilots, shipmasters; then mechanics, boilermakers, and steamboat captains; and commission merchants, insurance agents, brokers and admiralty lawyers, bankers, speculators, promoters, and investors.

Moreover, the sea always provided the city's mainstream of incomes. By 1900 one-half of all revenues of the United States Government were levied as customhouse duties at the Port of New York. These occupations, these salted incomes, accumulated into mountains of capital, were stored as if in middens in the banks on Manhattan Island, and then used as the capital for the development of the continent.

The fortunes of Commodore Vanderbilt, for example, were gargantuan compared to most of his fellow citizens, but the progress of his oceanic career could still be taken as typical for nineteenth-century New York. He was born in May, 1794, on a farm on Staten Island across the harbor from Manhattan. At sixteen Cornelius Vanderbilt went to his mother and asked her for one hundred dollars to buy a boat of his own. With his little yawl, he sailed produce from Staten Island farms to

Manhattan, crossing with floodtide at morning, beating back against the afternoon sou'wester when the tide turned to ebb. He could also carry as many as twenty passengers if he crowded them, and if he could fill his boat with passengers at day, he made his passages with freight at night. During the War of 1812 he won a contract to haul men and materiel to the harbor's forts. He saved the money he earned.

With his savings he built a little schooner—the *Dred*. He built another, the *Charlotte*. In 1819 he became a steamboat captain, carrying passengers to Philadelphia. He always said his business was "boats," and he made himself a "steamboat king." In 1849 Commodore Vanderbilt obtained a charter from the government of Nicaragua for a ship canal across the isthmus and for a transit company. He never built the canal, but he hauled boatloads of Forty-niners across the isthmus and then on to San Francisco for $300 a head. By 1860 he'd built sixty ships, figured he was worth about forty million dollars, and had decided to buy railroads.

Commodore Vanderbilt went down to Wall Street, where railroads were bought and sold. He bought the Harlem, the Hudson River, the Central, the Canadian Southern, the Lake Shore and Michigan. He meant to gain control of every ounce of freight all the way to Chicago. He had to fight piratical railroad wars with Daniel Drew and Jim Fisk and Jay Gould, but he won most of his battles. He had to buy millions in worthless bonds, but he bought them. He had to build Grand Central Depot for his trains, but he said it was just like building a wharf for his ships. He had a statue of himself put up in front of his depot, and he would stand there forever facing south, wearing his overcoat. He always wore his overcoat, winter and summer, and no one ever dared to ask him why. He was six feet one, with a fine large head, a fair complexion, ruddy cheeks, and his hair turned snow-white. Besides boats and railroads, he liked to play cards, to race horses, and to spend time with pretty women. "Don't tell anybody what you are going to do," Commodore Vanderbilt would say, "until you have done it."

In 1877 he was eighty-two and on his deathbed. Around the bed were his son William H. Vanderbilt, his six daughters and their husbands, and a score of grandchildren and nephews and nieces. They all owned real estate on Staten Island, and on Manhattan, and acres of land straight across the continent. They owned railroads and factories and mines. They controlled mountain passes and river valleys. As he was dying he said to them, "I thought you would sing." They sang for him.

He had never set any limit to his ambition, nor doubted his success, nor missed an opportunity, and the energies he exemplified were similar to the city's special powers. In the same year that Cornelius Vanderbilt was sailing his yawl across to the Battery the city's fathers were so confident of their future they mapped out all of Manhattan Island in a rectangular grid of streets. In 1811 there was no one to inhabit the imaginary blocks they traced on their map, but they assumed there would be soon enough. Similarly, in 1825, led by Governor De Witt Clinton, the city's fathers finished digging the Erie Canal through to Buffalo and to the Great Lakes, opening a northwest passage into the immense central river valley system of the continent and then through the Rockies all the way to Oregon's coast. When they opened the canal, the city had established itself as the epicenter of a huge elliptical empire, and if its extent was as yet unknown and uninhabited, that didn't trouble New York at all.

Among others, Mr. John Jacob Astor, an emigrant from the Germanies, seized the opportunity of the new topography. He bought for himself control of a Missouri River trading company and from New York savaged his competition in St. Louis. He stole away the agents he needed on the Missouri from the British Northwest Company. His company hired the mountain men—the legendary men of the West who could stand in Rocky Mountain torrents setting traps scented with castor for beaver. His company engaged the Indian Nations of the plains and mountains in trade.

He sold them blue beads of glass, fired in Venice and then shipped across the Atlantic to Indian squaws—three-fourths pound per string of beads at 37½ cents per pound. He shipped blankets from England's steam looms upriver to Indian chiefs —mackinaw blankets at $9.50 per pair, three and a half points, in blue, green, and scarlet. The chiefs and the mountain men sent John Jacob Astor beaver—about a hundred pounds of beaver to the flat—stinking, greasy beaver skins that were then cured and turned on molds to satisfy fashion's necessities in New York or shipped from New York to London and to Paris and even to Moscow.

To get the continent to deliver up its beaver, Astor sold guns and whiskey to the Indian Nations. To get buffalo hides, Astor built steamboats for the Missouri to carry the hides away. To menace his British competitors out of Oregon, he met them in the boardrooms of their own London banks. It was Astor's company men who opened and secured the trails to Oregon and Astor's system that opened the West for the new nation. Just as Vanderbilt could stand as an example of the city's oceanic energies, Astor could represent the city's continental powers. From New York, John Jacob Astor controlled millions of square miles of western paradise, but he sold it all before he died to buy Manhattan real estate for his heirs.

They prospered. Yet the heirs of Astor and Vanderbilt inhabited a different city from the New York their founding fathers had known. It had grown even beyond the limits of all their ambitions. When the city's fathers drew up their map of imaginary blocks in 1811 the city's population was about 100,000. When Astor died in 1847 the population had grown to nearly 400,000. By the end of the nineteenth century the city housed nearly 4,000,000 souls. As John Jacob Astor had foreseen, Manhattan real estate was a better investment than all the West.

But population was only one measure of the city's quantum change—what had been harvested from the West and what had been seined from the sea was multiplied miraculously by other city inventions: selling immigrants from Europe by the carload to coal mine operators in Pennsylvania; tapping pure Connecticut rivers for water to vulcanize rubber; cornering the wheat crop in Nebraska; squeezing shorts in Minnesota iron shares; ruining apple growers in Michigan with a railway rate; conning inventors out of patents in Washington; laying a million miles of railroad tracks and bankrupting a hundred railroad companies; stringing telegraph lines across the continent and laying cables across the Atlantic's floor; serving as banker to copperworks, brassworks, wireworks, glassworks, naileries, arsenals, forges, furnaces, factories, ironworks, and steelworks, and issuing stocks valued by their assets, and then setting bulls to attack the bears of these stocks, or bears to harass bulls; issuing newspapers to wheel standards of fashion to and fro, and convincing the delighted crowd to run after them—that is, even by convincing ladies which hat to wear.

Of course, such skills had been practiced before, but New York refined them to an art, developed their technique, perfected their details into exquisite skill. To the effects of a national empire expanded across a virgin continent, and with the treasures brought home from the adventurous sea, the city added its genius. The resultant of these vectors was a new force, a new energy, ungovernable by any political system, a style that was peculiarly New York's own—a kind of frenzy.

It was not a city in the sense that Athens was a city, devoted to the glory of man and the study of his politics; nor a city in the sense that Rome was a city, devoted to the glory of God and the worship of His majesty; nor a city like Paris, alternating between gaiety and despair; nor like London, from which an empire won at war might be decently administered. It was a city which, in its startling growth, had abandoned politics, God, gaiety, and even administration of its own empire. It was a city overwhelmed by its own wealth. Lacking any other standard with which to measure the powers of such great wealth—powers that were complex, various, irrational, and sometimes disturbing, New York measured its own power by counting it in money. If its citizens guessed that money might be an unreliable standard, even of wealth, they could not seem to think of any other.

By 1900 this meant New Yorkers still wanted to believe in heroes who would have to choose between moral necessities—between good and evil, and New York wanted to believe in heroines who would have to thread their way through the mazes of social necessity. But these traditional dramas, these evergreen optimisms, could not account for the city's daily spectacle of money—money anyone could see was often made without merit or without effort, more money made in one hour's good luck gambling at some exchange than a million men could make in a year's labor, money that seemed to breed more money silently, even secretly.

The city's spectacle included palaces built along the length of Fifth Avenue that were dedicated as displays of neither power, nor fame, nor honor, nor social standing, but simply as examples of much money. It included corporations that sacked entire blocks to erect skyscrapers as testimonials to money. It included dramas played out every day in the newspapers in which art performed for money, and religion preached for money, and justice was sold for money, and love contracted for money.

Using money for coordinates, a map of the city might be drawn, sprawling along real avenues but without intelligent or comprehensive purpose; a city in which men and women were sacrificed periodically not to any special god at all, not even to Mammon, but to some random ambition, or petty pique, or some momentary and insatiable greed. Showers of luck could be seen pouring down on some mean soul, while another was ruined for what appeared to be no reason at all; a pageant in which it was plain every man must act for himself alone; a morality play for tricksters and traders, performed according to the circumstance in palaces, or apartments, or tenements, but the usual details of domestic comedy had to be worked out with the sulfur of stale banknotes hanging somewhere behind the paper on the wall.

By the turn of the century the city had provided itself—at great expense—with the magic of electric light, and so it glowed, which added to New Yorkers' pride. But it was also a city that loomed with terror: elevated trains rained hot cinders down from their tracks to the avenues beneath them; steam shot up from pits in the streets, colored in rosy tints in towering geysers; immense quantities of coal were consumed to provide both steam and electricity, and the stacks of furnaces sent oranges and a variety of reds against the sky; and the valleys of this strange landscape roared and shrieked and rumbled and wailed. Yet from any distance, as dusk lengthened the shadows into its stone canyons, it gave off a wondrous effect: every window shone some brilliance, and every street had its cones of yellow light, and the Brooklyn Bridge could be seen strung with swaying diamonds, and Broadway—The Great White Way—sparkled with a thousand delights to divert New York's attention.

CHAPTER TWO

TURN OF THE CENTURY: *Evelyn Nesbit*

IN 1901 BROADWAY was still absorbed with all the delights of the naughty nineties. Broadway supplied the songs and invented the jokes. Broadway provided pictures of famous beauties on cigarette cards and stories for the *Police Gazette.* A song written in 1892, and popular at The World's Fair in Chicago in 1893, was still selling tens of thousands of copies in sheet music in 1901, and it was being played by countless roller pianos—"After the Ball." There were other songs like it, semipermanent hits: "My Sweetheart's the Man in the Moon," "Ta-ra-ra-ra Boom De-ay," "There'll Be a Hot Time in the Old Town Tonight," "The Sidewalks of New York," "The Bowery," and "A Bird in a Gilded Cage."

In Broadway's theaters Miss Julia Marlowe was starring in *When Knighthood Was in Flower.* It was not unusual for her aficionados to see her a dozen times. Miss Ada Rehan was playing in *Sweet Nell of Old Drury* to equally ecstatic audiences—the men would stand and cheer her, waving their handkerchiefs to signal their adoration, and the women would weep for her and pitch bunches of violets up to the stage. New York seemed to love young Ethel Barrymore even more: she was playing in *Captain Jinks of the Horse Marines* and was sometimes applauded for no more than entering a salon, and sometimes for just walking along the street. Miss Barrymore was considered a lady.

Miss Lillian Russell was another favorite, but a heroine of a slightly different reputation. She had run through a number of husbands, several notorious consorts, and had even more glorious affairs. Her admirers were said to send her a diamond a week at the Weber and Fields Music Hall at Twenty-ninth and Broadway. Although she was called "Airy Fairy Lillian" by nearly everyone, even her admirers had to admit she had obviously put on a bit of weight.

The Music Hall formula in which she played was a constant: first, a star like Lillian Russell to head the show and to appear in gorgeous costumes; second, a dazzling line of chorus girls with "great legs" and enough beauty or talent to create gossip about the men they were supposed to have captured; and third, some musical nonsense—songs and jokes. Just as songs from Broadway became semipermanent hits, Music Hall jokes would go ricocheting through the city's streets, and "stop me if you've heard this one" was an essential, but politely ignored, requirement of the city's manners. The most successful gag at the turn of the century, according to some Broadway experts, was a Weber and Fields creation that went: FIRST CHORUS GIRL: "I found a pearl in an oyster at Rector's last night." SECOND CHORUS GIRL: "That's nothing, I got a diamond necklace out of a lobster at Delmonico's."

There were other items in the news in 1901 besides the affairs of chorus girls and Music Hall jokes, but nothing half so important. Queen Victoria died in 1901; President McKinley was shot in Buffalo by Leon Czolgosz, and Teddy Roosevelt stepped up to the presidency. McKinley's assassin was tried and sentenced to death in the electric chair, but it took his executioners several attempts before they could electrocute him because their new apparatus didn't work very well.

In 1901 Beaumont, Texas, brought in its first gusher—two hundred feet of oil spouted for ten days; and a Brazilian dandy, Alberto Santos-Dumont, flew around the Eiffel Tower in a dirigible, which caused some seers to predict travel by air in the future. In 1901 Professor Guglielmo Marconi received a signal across the breadth of the Atlantic, which caused the United States Navy to recommend that homing pigeons be discontinued as soon as wireless telegraphy could be introduced. In 1901 J. P. Morgan announced the formation of the United States Steel Corporation, the largest business corporation ever organized. In 1901 men wore derbies or top hats, depending upon their station in life and the occasion, and it was noted that the business suit had not entirely been accepted in place of the cutaway. Women wore their skirts to their shoetops, and the Fashion Institute predicted, "the shirtwaist is here to stay."

Yet the continuing news item in 1901, the source of endless fascination, was the incredible success of a musical—*Floradora.* Everyone had seen it, everyone talked about it, everyone followed the affairs of the beauties in the *Floradora* Sextette. After each performance there were crowds of stage-door johnnies hanging about the Casino Theatre. By 1901 Miss Evelyn Nesbit, age sixteen, had made her way from Pittsburgh, Pennsylvania, to a part as one of the "Spanish Dancers" in *Floradora.*

Backstage they called her "the baby" or "the kid" because she did not look even sixteen. When she sat before the mirrors with the others to get her makeup on, even in all the sweat and smells of powder back there, she could admit the other girls were probably right and guess that innocence was the part that would put her best foot forward. She had an oval face, with a touch of olive in its color that added instead of subtracting from its baby's-milk complexion. Her nose was straight, with a little Irish upward tilt. The mouth was a bit full, she thought, but that might be good, and if she tried a pout before her backstage mirror, she could see how its effect might be devastating. Her body was as slim as a young boy's, with straight legs and good knees, and not even a hint of a married woman's bottom. She knew perfectly well that voluptuous women were the current fashion, but she had already turned her lithesome form to her advantage anyway—she was a famous beauty as a model for artists and fashion photographers. Her best, she knew, was her hair—copper curls, a great mass of them, surrounding the oval of her face and creating a contrast for her hazel eyes. Even back in Pittsburgh she had told her mother again and again that Broadway would serve as the stage of their opportunity. Her part in *Floradora* as a Spanish Dancer was her first chance to turn her innocent hazel eyes on the world she meant to conquer.

Her salary at the theater was twenty dollars a week, and to support herself and her mother she had to keep posing for artists and photographers during the days. Sometimes when she came in from her modeling assignments to the dressing room she shared backstage with eight other girls, all conversation would stop, or she could hear one of the girls whisper, "Nix, nix, the kid!" But she already knew she could wait to hear what they had to say. If her mother picked her up at the stage door every night to take her home, she estimated there would be a time soon enough when her mother wouldn't, and in the meantime she would learn all she could.

During the scenes when she was offstage, instead of going back to the dressing room with the other Spanish Dancers, she would stand in the wings and watch the show. She studied Edna Wallace Hopper, who played Lady Holyrood in a funny little voice and wore smart clothes and what Evelyn knew were her own jewels.

Of course, the big scene every night—a scene that brought a standing ovation before it really began—was the *Floradora* Sextette. Six gorgeous women paraded onstage in frilly pink lace dresses with high collars, the dresses trimmed at their nipped waists with black velvet ribbon. They wore black gloves and big black picture hats with feathers, and each one had a little black ribbon round her neck. Each was a picture of what a Gibson girl was supposed to be.

Then they were joined onstage by six Gibson men—handsome fellows in gray cutaways and black silk top hats and pearl-gray gloves. At their cue the men went down on their knees before the girls and sang:

> "Tell me, pretty maiden,
> Are there any more at home like you?"

Then the girls would twirl their parasols and sing to the men:

> "There are a few, kind sir,
> But simple girls, and proper, too."

Then they joined arms and paraded around together in a very simple step—Evelyn could see it was easy to learn—and marched up to the footlights and took a bow. The audience would stand up and stop the show and demand encores. The

Sextette would run through the part again, picking up where the Gibson men went down on their knees, starting with, "Tell me, pretty maiden."

On the nights that Evelyn Nesbit studied the way the *Floradora* Sextette moved, the six girls were Daisy Green, Clarita Vidal, Susan Drake, Katherine Sears, Florence Clemmons, and Frances Belmont. Florence Clemmons left the company to marry a millionaire, and Broadway gossip had it that every single girl in the Sextette would get herself a millionaire. Florence Clemmons' place was taken by a big voluptuous brunette, Edna Goodrich, who became Evelyn's friend.

Frances Belmont's real name was Fannie Donnelly, and she was big and voluptuous, too, a lovely Irish redhead. She appeared backstage before the show one night showing off a huge three-stone diamond ring as big as the Ritz. Frances told everyone how her admirer had taken her to Tiffany's, and she described how he had asked her to pick out a ring, and what fun she'd had trying on all the different rings the prim and proper Tiffany salesman brought out on velvet cushions.

All the girls wanted to know whom she'd caught, but at first she wouldn't tell them. Finally they got her to admit his name was Harry Thaw. He was from Pittsburgh, Frances said, and crazy rich, and he was going to give her a party at Sherry's in a private room with an orchestra to play and buckets and buckets of champagne. Frances said that Harry Thaw would be inviting the men, "and I'm asking the girls," and of course there would be presents for everyone.

When her mother picked her up that night, Evelyn asked about Harry Thaw from Pittsburgh. Her mother's answer was an excited one. She told Evelyn to have nothing to do with him; that he had a vile reputation; that she was too young to even hear what was said about him back in Pittsburgh. "Florence, if he ever asks to see you, refuse him."

Her mother always called her "Florence," and if the daughter sometimes felt fenced in by her mother's fears, Florence Evelyn Nesbit had learned to respect Mrs. Elizabeth F. Nesbit's practical calculation of the world. They had already come a long way together from Pittsburgh—a very different Pittsburgh from Mr. Harry Thaw's—and most of their journey had been terrifying, made on loose gravel footholds across the slopes above the abyss of poverty.

Evelyn was born on Christmas Day, 1884, in Tarentum, Pennsylvania, a village about twenty-four miles up the Allegheny River from Pittsburgh. She would remember her father as Winfield Scott Nesbit. She would insist that he was a successful lawyer with offices in Diamond Street, Pittsburgh, and that "he commuted." He died when she was eight.

By then the widow Nesbit had two children to raise: "Florence," and her brother Howard—two years and two months younger. Whatever vague hopes there may have been about Howard following in his father's footsteps as a lawyer or of Florence attending Vassar College evaporated overnight. The widow Nesbit moved her children to the North Side, Pittsburgh, sold the horse and carriage they had used in Tarentum, opened a roominghouse on Cedar Avenue, and cooked, washed, ironed, and cleaned rooms for her boarders. She was forced to sell off their furniture and possessions one by one, but the sheriff came nevertheless and put a sign on the door advertising that all the remaining furniture was to be sold. Evelyn remembered that her mother was saved from the sheriff's men at the last moment by the intervention of Mr. Holman, who "came to our rescue and paid this rent that Mamma owed."

But they were forced to move anyway, and Mrs. Nesbit tried to make a success of another roominghouse on South Highland Avenue in the East End. They were edging closer to the districts around Mr. Andrew Carnegie's mills, closer to the rows of grimy tenement houses jammed with "foreigners," Poles, Jews, Slavs, Bulgars, Negroes, closer to the South Side, where it thumped and crackled and clanged day and night and cast up an eerie pulsating orange and red and black into the sky from fifty stacks of open-hearth furnaces along the river.

And so they struggled. Evelyn helped her mother with the cooking, the sewing, and the cleaning of the rooms. They labored, and they humored their boarders and tried to please them, and waited for their rents, and pinched pennies. "Every day," Evelyn would say, "some plan or another of aggrandizement and fame entered my head."

Before she was ten she knew she was pretty. Her mother made every stitch of her children's clothing herself, and Evelyn claimed with a defiant pride that she was the best-dressed girl in school. She remembered her mother had once made a frock out of a sateen bedspread and trimmed it with bands of black, and "it was so lovely that people on the street turned to admire me in it."

With a friend, Evelyn went to the circus. She came home to the boardinghouse to dream of running away and becoming a bareback rider. A boarder gave them tickets to hear Lilli Lehmann sing in *Die Walküre*. She went with her mother, and Evelyn said she had a frantic taste for more opera, "but we could not afford it."

Against the terrors of Pittsburgh and the grim brown world of their boardinghouse, Evelyn began to create another world of her own. She read romances and fairytales "until in my mind the fairies and elves and giants and princes and glamorous thieves . . . had made up a Wonderland." She found a copy of Zola's *Nana* in the room of "a nice old lady while I was making up her bed," and studied the lessons taught by the demimonde of Paris.

The world she invented was something like Tarentum, where a wise, strong father "who commuted" would take her in his lap and sing to her songs in the rhythms of his rocking-chair. They would be sitting there on the porch of their own house and there would be green trees and they could see down to the river. She mixed her dreams of Tarentum with a world she imagined, which was something like the circus: She would stand right up on the horse's back, her right foot tucked up against the heel of her left foot; she would be wearing bright pink tights and a short white skirt that stood straight out. She'd be all spangles, and the band would be playing, and as the horse cantered she would smile and hold the reins in her right hand and wave her left hand way up high at them.

Her dreams would not have been unusual for any little girl, but Evelyn's versions seemed to have a certain urgency to them. Especially when her mother would give way to uncontrollable weeping and in turning to her daughter for comfort would wail, "What's to become of us?"

Early in 1899 they moved to try their luck in Philadelphia. Mrs. Nesbit wanted to get a job as a dressmaker, but despite her skill she could show no experience. When they were at the end of their resources Mrs. Nesbit went to see a Mr. Brewster quite frequently—he was an executive at Wanamaker's—and he finally gave them all jobs: "Mamma as a saleswoman, Howard as a cashboy, and me as a stockgirl." Mrs. Nesbit went about letting down the hems of her daughter's dresses by several inches. Schooldays were over, Evelyn was fourteen, and a working girl wore her dresses to her shoes.

But Howard was only twelve and he did not last long as a cashboy on a twelve-hour day. His health turned delicate, he could not work, and mother and daughter could not make enough together to support him. They had to send him to a farm back in Tarentum, run by his father's sister, and mother and daughter moved into a slightly cheaper boardinghouse on Arch Street.

In the Arch Street boardinghouse the Nesbits made friends with a woman whose brother was a noted Philadelphia artist—John Storm, an elderly, gray-haired, courtly man. He had come over for Sunday lunch and said he was stunned by Evelyn's beauty. He asked Mrs. Nesbit's permission to paint Evelyn's portrait and added that he would pay a small modeling fee for each sitting. Every Sunday thereafter Evelyn went to John Storm's house to pose. She had made her first conquest.

John Storm introduced Evelyn to Violet Oakley, designer of stained-glass windows for churches, and on her day off from Wanamaker's Evelyn was soon posing in Miss Oakley's studio, appearing barefoot, in long white robes, with her copper curls tumbling down around her shoulders. It was as an angel by Miss Oakley that Evelyn Nesbit made her first public appearances, in the stained glass windows of surburban churches.

In Miss Oakley's studios Evelyn met Jessie Wilcox Smith and Elizabeth Shippen Green. In Miss Green's studios she met George Gibbs and Mills Thompson. They were all famous illustrators, and for them, in one fairy-princess costume after another, Evelyn began to appear in books, magazines, and newspaper supplements—illustrating with her innocent beauty the sweet and true and good and beautiful stories being distributed in the millions of copies by steam-driven rotary presses.

"Flattered at having gained the notice of professional artists," Evelyn said, "I began to study my features in the mirror." Her mother would get furious at her fourteen-year-old vanities, and Evelyn would add pepper to their talks by saying that since artists had chosen her as their model, "it seemed to imply that I was pretty." She argued with her mother that she could earn more money posing as an artist's model than she could at Wanamaker's. Since it was true that she could, Mrs. Nesbit's objections, said Evelyn, "crumbled under the force of necessity."

Mrs. Nesbit's objections were that the life of an artist's model was unconventional, that it was Bohemian, and she didn't approve of it. She would go on about how she wished she had the means to send Evelyn to school and she would say she wished there were some way for a woman to survive alone in a commercial world.

Evelyn calculated that her mother's struggle to survive in the economic world was too soft, too sweet, and impractical. Evelyn said her mother should have known the world of competition was a man's world, and she told her mother she was too trusting a soul. Finally, when her mother appeared to be discouraged and unhappy after a year in Philadelphia, when she was exhausted by the tumult of Wanamaker's and unhappy from standing on aching feet at the whim of hard-bargaining women, Mrs. Nesbit said, "All right, let's try New York."

They came across the Hudson River by ferry and awed, but excited, rode the rattling "elevated" up to Twenty-third Street. They had the address of a modest roominghouse at 249 West Twenty-second Street, run by a French family named Bourget. They took a little room in the back on the second floor with its own tiny stove.

Once again Mrs. Nesbit desperately tried to get work as a clothes designer and then as a seamstress, but weeks went by in her futile search. Evelyn argued that she could use letters of introduction she had been given by the Philadelphia artists to get work as an artist's model in New York. Her mother raised all the old objections; she said Evelyn was not yet fifteen and could have no idea whatever what life as an artist's model might mean. When they finally had gone without anything to eat for several days except bread and some coffee, Mrs. Nesbit relented. Evelyn took a letter of introduction to the artist James Carroll Beckwith, and as soon as Beckwith saw her, he engaged her on the spot.

She settled down to posing for Carroll Beckwith two afternoons a week. Then on Saturdays she obtained work posing for Frederick S. Church. She soon had more offers than she could handle, posing for J. Wells Champney, Carl Blenner, Herbert Morgan, George Grey Barnard, and then the famous Charles Dana Gibson. Barnard sculptured her as *Innocence,* and as *Innocence* she would go to the Metropolitan Museum of Art. Charles Dana Gibson did her in profile, in pen and ink, her lustrous thick hair curled down around the nape of her neck, then forward over her shoulders to form the figure of a question mark. Gibson said his sketch of her represented woman as "The Eternal Question."

Evelyn described Mr. Church as a dear, fatherly old man—a gentle idealistic soul, and she said they were soon good friends. At her Saturday posings he would prepare their noon meal, making a salad he had learned in his Beaux Arts student days in Paris. He used *vin rouge* instead of vinegar to cut the oil, sprinkled it with garlic, and served it in a Chinese bowl with ripe Camembert.

As it got dark late on a Saturday afternoon they could look down on Broadway at Thirty-ninth Street from his slanting studio windows, and they would watch the swarms of people and carriages on the way to the theaters. Mr. Church posed her as a shepherdess and as a water nymph and as Ondine with water lilies entwined in her hair and two striped tigers painted at her flanks. She told him of her ambition to go on the stage, and he spoke guardedly to her of her innocence and tender youth. She knew perfectly well what he meant.

Evelyn would explain that Mr. Church gave art a meaning

that "made deserting it seem like a sacrilege," but she had discovered that posing for photographs could be far more lucrative. The *Sunday World* and *Sunday American* had started publishing fashion pages that used living models for the first time to show hats, gowns, shoes, stockings, and sport frocks. The photographs were made in a studio on West Twenty-third Street by Joel Feder, and he paid five dollars and sometimes ten for a sitting. A theatrical magazine picked up two photographs of Evelyn from Joel Feder and published them over the caption: "Evelyn Florence Nesbit, Beautiful Model of New York Studios."

As if by magic, within a week reporters flocked around to the Nesbits' Twenty-second Street boardinghouse to interview the new sensation. Both the *World* and the *Journal* did full-page features—mostly photographs and a little interview. They quoted an artist who said that she was "the most beautiful artist's model in America." Another artist said "she had the most perfectly modeled foot since Venus."

Evelyn guessed her career had been launched, and she saw to it that her picture was seen as frequently as possible. She would admit, if pressed, that she might be one of the reigning queens of beauty. "She is petite," one newspaper reporter crooned. "Her figure is well formed and its natural curves need no artifice to accentuate them. Her hair is indeed her 'crowning glory' . . . thick, long and heavy, with a dull gloss that fits well into almost any pose she need assume."

Lured by the newspaper stories, a flamboyant character appeared at the roominghouse soon enough. He was a bald-headed man, paunchy, with showy diamond rings, a black-and-white-checked suit, and a red tie studded with a huge diamond. He said his name was Ted Marks, he was a theatrical agent, and he wanted to put Evelyn on the stage and capitalize on the publicity.

Mrs. Nesbit said she still objected to the stage, but Evelyn insisted. Ted Marks arranged a meeting for both mother and daughter at the offices of Fisher and Riley, the producers of *Floradora.* When they had been ushered into the inside office, Marks started to explain his discovery, but Fisher interrupted him and began a whispered conference with Riley. The applicants had to wait.

Finally Fisher came over to Mrs. Nesbit and asked her, "Ever had any chorus experience?"

Ted Marks roared with laughter, then explained to the producers their error—it was Evelyn, not her mother, who should go into the show. After another look at Evelyn, Fisher turned to Mrs. Nesbit and said, "Madam, I'm running a theater, not a baby farm!"

Evelyn began to cry, and she could see immediately that tears might be effective.

"Now, now," said Fisher, "we won't spoil your chances on that account—if your mother is willing to let you try."

Mrs. Nesbit explained that she was not willing, but that she could do nothing with Evelyn. With the tears still wet on her face, little Evelyn began to smile, and by that afternoon she was studying the routines of a Spanish Dancer in *Floradora*. Within a week she had learned them.

Watching the show each night and absorbed in her own performance, she said she never noticed a tall, gray-haired man who took a seat in the first row night after night. As she was about to leave the theater one evening, picked up as usual by her mother, she was stopped by one of the show's librettists at the stage-door cubicle. He laid his hand on her arm, then turned her to introduce her to the gray-haired man. "Evelyn, I want you to meet Mr. James A. Garland."

Evelyn stammered some reply. Mr. Garland asked if he could call upon her mother. Evelyn said something indefinite.

Several days passed, and then one afternoon as Evelyn was returning on her own from a matinee she found Mr. Garland sitting in the parlor of their boardinghouse, chatting with her mother. He had invited them to spend Sunday with him on his yacht.

At ten on Sunday morning Mr. Garland called for them in an open landau, drove them west to the Hudson, then took them by motor launch out to the gangway of his yacht. It was, said Evelyn, a lovely morning: They steamed up the Hudson River past the Palisades, through Haverstraw Bay, and past

Storm King Mountain, through Bear Mountain Gorge, and around the bend of West Point, where they went ashore to watch the cadets parade.

When the review was over, the cadets came swooping across the parade ground and surrounded Mr. Garland's party, making eyes at Evelyn and laughing and flirting with her. Mr. Garland did not seem to be pleased and peremptorily decided it was time to return to his yacht. They spent the rest of the day cruising back down the river, and dining—a perfect meal, Evelyn allowed, perfectly served aboard a floating palace.

Her estimation of Mr. Garland's yacht was that it was equal to anything the older showgirls in *Floradora* "were accustomed to enjoying in the gay world they helped to enliven." She measured Mr. Garland, too: a very quiet person, she said, invariably pleasant and engaging; a well-bred conservative and a millionaire many times over; but, she thought, "hopelessly old." Aside from the pleasure she derived from Sunday excursions on his yacht, "he did not interest me in the least."

But she continued to go steaming up and down the Hudson on Sundays. In addition, Mr. Garland escorted Mrs. Nesbit and her daughter to matinees at the Weber and Fields Music Hall. Evelyn was quick to notice that it was a small, intimate theater with an unusual seating arrangement: There was no gallery. Instead, the orchestra floor was surrounded by a string of boxes in such a way that the audience could see each other as conveniently as they could watch the show. The great names of Broadway paraded through the orchestra to their boxes—Lillian Russell, the exquisite Bonnie Mann, the exotic Mazie Follette, the dazzling May Mackenzie. Evelyn told Mr. Garland she saw them through "bewildered, worshipful eyes."

Mr. Garland was not the only escort of the Nesbits. Her mother's old friend from Pittsburgh, Mr. Charles J. Holman, reappeared to visit with them, and this time, with Evelyn acting as her mother's chaperone, Mr. Holman took them to Rector's, which, said Evelyn, was *the* after-the-theater lobster palace. Evelyn noted the restaurant was divided in two, the famous sitting on the right side, the hoi polloi on the left. "And *we* were given a table on the *right!*"

Evelyn said she "couldn't help noticing that men at surrounding tables hardly took their eyes off me." She said she couldn't decide which gave her the greater thrill, "supping at Rector's, or having so many men of the world regarding me with evident admiration. For you see, I was beginning to take a keen delight in such adulation and the pleasurable knowledge that men considered me a theatrical beauty."

At the stage door of *Floradora* she was getting invitations to after-theater parties. Cards were being sent backstage to her with roses, or sometimes, fifty-dollar bills attached. Jewelry began to arrive. She said she refused them all.

One Sunday when Mrs. Nesbit and her daughter were cruising upon the Hudson aboard Mr. Garland's yacht Evelyn remarked on the interesting people she had begun to meet. To her "utter astonishment," Mr. Garland was furious.

He said, "Evelyn, I cannot see you anymore. I have the most serious intentions regarding you. Right now, in fact, I am divorcing my wife. It is a very long story and I intended telling you about it someday. But if you insist on going about with a man like Stanford White, I cannot see you again."

"Why?" was Evelyn's innocent question.

Mr. Garland answered with a set face. "Because Stanford White is a voluptuary!"

CHAPTER THREE

ILLUSIONS OF DEMOCRACY:
"Boss" Tweed

APPARENTLY NEITHER EVELYN nor her mother found it necessary to explain all the details of their association with Mr. Stanford White; nor did Mr. Garland need to say much more about White's reputation, because by the end of the nineteenth century Stanford White was New York's most famous citizen.

He was the city's leading architect, but he was much more than that. He was the city's leading designer, decorator, stylist, and chief arbiter of taste, but he was much more than these. He was the leader of its leading artists, promoter of its best institutions, impresario of its most colorful entertainments, founder and organizer of its leading clubs, and often architect of them as well. He served as a dedicator of the city's permanent monuments and master of ceremony of its celebrations. His immense energies were spent day and night in an attempt to give character to the city's wealth, yet it was said of him that he never did anything for money.

To the extent that New York might realize itself in stone, consecrate itself as an idea as much as a place, Stanford White set the example for all that might have been marvelous along Fifth Avenue. Typically, he designed, then donated the designs, then organized the committees to raise the funds, then supervised the construction at the foot of Fifth Avenue of the Arch on Washington Square—a permanent addition to the city's landscape.

At the intersection of Fifth Avenue and Broadway, where they formed an elongated X on the real estate map, Stanford White promoted, designed, built, and then served as impresario of Madison Square Garden. No matter where it was later actually located, Madison Square Garden kept its name as a permanent addition to the city's landscape.

For these designs he spent masses of the city's money to add to the city's wealth. From the constituency in which most of the city's money was concentrated—the chaotic society of post-Civil War Fifth Avenue, he organized, designed, and built clubs in which, presumably, their members might cultivate the arts of civilization: the Player's Club, the Century, the Metropolitan, the Lambs, the Brook, the Harmonic, the Colony. The architectural firm in which he was a partner—McKim, Mead and White, designed and built dozens of others. He was a leader among his fellow clubmen, and he moved among them, it was said, as if he were Vercingetorix.

In his designs, and by his collaboration with other artists, he showed how money might be used in churches: the Church of the Ascension, Judson Memorial Church, an altar and canopy for the Church of the Paulist Fathers, the doors and porticoes of Saint Bartholomew's, and the most beautiful church, it was said, ever designed in America—Madison Square Presbyterian Church. His masterpieces would be widely imitated, but it would be a sign of his fate that his churches would be abandoned or destroyed because, in effect, New York didn't need them.

Most of the palaces he designed and built for the city's rich would also be wrecked, but he taught the rich what he could of style—the subtle difference between merely spending money and using wealth. At incredible expense, he built and decorated palaces for Astors and Vanderbilts; for the Goelets, the Oelrichs, the Cheneys, the Choates, the Hopkins, and the Whittemores. He gave lessons in style to Henry Villard and William C. Whitney and Whitelaw Reid. He showed his clients how to live comfortably and simply—if simplicity was their preference; or on a grand scale, either in the city, or in the country at Southampton, or in Newport. He was famous for his ability to spend beyond his client's budget and then wheedle and bully for even more to build as he imagined his client ought to live. White tapped money from the rich for his city's improvement, and his abilities at raising funds were described as ferocious. There were some misers who would admit they would rather pay up than suffer a visit from White's exhausting charms.

In collaboration with artists and sculptors, White taught Chicago how it should remember Lincoln—both standing and seated; he bullied New York into learning the difference between classical "junk," and the statue of *Admiral Farragut* in Madison Square; at the same time, he promoted a fountain with a *Boy and a Duck* in Prospect Park in Brooklyn. With his partners, and with his firm's time and expense, he helped lay out the Mall in Washington and the Lincoln Memorial. His firm rebuilt and refurnished the White House, founded the American Academy in Rome to train artists, promoted the World's Fair in Chicago, designed libraries, improved campuses at West Point, the University of Virginia, New York University, Columbia University, and Harvard.

To commemorate Christopher Columbus, White organized and created a city parade. To decorate the Metropolitan Opera for an opening, he arranged twelve thousand roses. He designed magazine covers, book covers, Pullman cars, and yachts. He would stop everything to fix the frames for an artist's show. He created pageants at Madison Square Garden to amuse the idle and he designed a perfect piece of jewelry at a moment's notice for a soprano because, he said, she had a heavenly voice. He backed Broadway shows that he would admit were atrocious because their previews had made him laugh. He would work at his designs straight through the night, littering the floor around his drafting table with masterpieces, bellowing melodies from Beethoven into his empty studio. On the next night the same studio might serve as a salon for the talent he wanted to encourage. At a breathtaking pace he spread out around him his own enthusiasm for anything that caught his fancy; and necessarily, with such energies at his disposal, he loved, as he would any beautiful creation, pretty women.

But New York contained oracles, just as ancient cities were supposed to have, and Stanford White should have taken warning from them of the fate dealt the city's other leading nineteenth-century citizen—Mr. William Marcy Tweed, the "Boss" of Tammany Hall. The city's oracles were issued in newspapers, and their chorus sang something called progress, citing endless facts to support its march. To relieve their readers from so boring a gospel, newspapers spiced their cantatas of progress with titillation—page after page inked in with smirks and sighs and shrieks and giggles. It was a chorus of newspapers who did in Boss Tweed.

Perhaps newspaper editors were jealous of Tweed's success. Just as White attempted to be the architect of the city's wealth—regardless of the cost, Tweed organized the city's politics. Tweed's organization, Tammany Hall, became a permanent landmark of the city's landscape. Just as White's constituency was the city's rich (Fifth Avenue, whatever their actual street address), Tweed's constituency was the city's poor (Broadway), and Tweed organized poor neighborhoods into political clubhouses. Since Boss Tweed died in 1878 at fifty-five when White was twenty-five and barely starting his career, their paths crossed only because they were both maestros of the city's tempo. Curiously, the Arch Stanford White built at Washington Square was a triumphal Roman Arch that spanned nothing whatsoever, an Arch through which no Caesar would ever lead his triumph, but it did span an unused pathway that Bill Tweed had cut through the park for himself.

William Marcy Tweed died a pauper in the city's jail. When he died he stood convicted of graft on a magnificent scale. The newspapers ran column after column of figures establishing beyond any reasonable doubt that the city's funds had been misappropriated. Boss Tweed complained to his judges that he had never done anything for money, but exhausted by their harassment, he offered to explain exactly what he had done for power. They refused to hear his testimony.

William Marcy Tweed was born an Episcopal merchant's son in New York in 1823. He was a contemporary of Stanford White's mother and father and, just as they were, an heir to New York's merchant aristocracy. His opinion of his family's merchant style was that "it was too bland," and he decided to make politics his profession. To see politics as a profession rather than as a civic duty was a revolutionary idea in mid-century New York, an idea that immediately raised the wrath of New York's ministers. If politics could be defined as the art of a city's ethics, the ministers were right to fear losing control of the city's morals. When Tweed sought office it was not as an end but rather as a means, not as a duty but as a privilege, and he never disguised his ambition to use the privileges of moral sanction that once had been reserved only to the ministry.

In his prime, Boss Tweed stood six feet, weighed 280 pounds, trimmed a full red beard and moustache. He never smoked, never drank, and he was a devoted family man. In the style of his day he wore grand English suits, vested, with a railroad watch chain across his belly. In his cravat he sported a diamond stickpin the size of an aggie. He thought himself a poor speaker and avoided it whenever possible. He was an organizer with a big smile, an infallible memory for names and faces, a gruff easy charm, and a financial acumen said to rival Astor's. He listed his occupation as "statesman," and it was said of him he had the will of a Roman disguised beneath the charm of a Parisian. In Tweed's logic, the rules of democracy were simple enough: The majority ruled, and if they won their elections they could do with the city what they willed. It should have been easy enough to see, Tweed explained, that there were more tenants than landlords.

In 1847 events across the Atlantic began to send shock waves toward Old New York. A potato famine in Ireland and then Socialist revolutions in the Germanies delivered shiploads of poor Catholics to New York. They came under the most appalling conditions, but they arrived in the millions, wave after wave of them, to flood the city and be jammed into tenements. Although investments in tenement real estate were remarkably profitable to Old New Yorkers, *The New York Times* warned, "All society was sitting on a volcano, a vast explosive mass of the poor and ignorant—the dangerous classes, who cared nothing for our liberty and civilization."

The "dangerous classes" were the opportunity of Boss Tweed, much in the same way that beaver had been the opportunity for John Jacob Astor, and boats for Commodore Vanderbilt. Tweed saw in the teeming poor the means to control City Hall. He took over one of the city's oldest fraternal organizations, Tammany Hall, changed its symbol to a Tiger, and used it as an instrument of political conquest. He won control of the Board of Aldermen in 1857 and kept control of the city's political apparatus until his indictment in 1872. It could be justly said that he invented his opposition, too. In response to his style the city gathered up forces called "Reform," and, imitating his techniques, Reform finally defeated him in an election. After Tweed it was an established understanding that Tammany Hall, or something exactly like it, would alternate with Reform in the administration of the city's power. Each would customarily charge the other with exceeding the budget and with corruption. "Tammany Hall," the Reverend Parkhurst would preach, "is a form under which the devil disguises himself."

"As if," Tweed replied, "on Election Day, the devil preferred one party's ballots to another."

When the immigrants poured off the ships, the "native Americans"—Tweed called them "Yankees"—were dismayed. They surveyed the rabble coming in at their docks and said, "They are like the frogs of Egypt upon us."

Tweed's men met their voters on the immigration dock, gave them a hot bowl of soup, led them through the formalities, found them a place to sleep, promised them a job. If no work was available, Tammany invented jobs at city expense. At Christmas, Tammany distributed turkeys. "Corruption," said the Yankees.

"As if," said Tweed, "Scrooge came around to being a scoundrel."

The Yankees were appalled. Their attitude, at least until Tweed showed them how to count votes, was that if God had not made the immigrants to be sheared, He would not have made them sheep. The tenements had no water, no sewage, no heat. When it turned cold Tammany Hall often brought around coal, and if the Yankees objected, Tweed's men laughed at them: after all, the city had no source of coal except Yankee coal companies, which therefore were being paid once. How many times would the Yankees like to be paid? "We can spend ourselves rich," said Tweed.

Tweed professionalized the police and the firemen, paying their salaries from the city's treasury. He encouraged unions. He engineered the city's first bill of "Home Rule," removing its offices from the patronage of the state capital, Albany. He changed the laws so that streets could be paved from the city's general treasury instead of from the assessments of the taxpayers who were deemed to use them—which had meant that most streets went unpaved. Naturally, the expense of paving streets sometimes exceeded the cost of labor and materials by spectacular amounts; the profits apparently were entered into the ledgers of Tammany's treasury for the next election and Tweed's Reform opposition given grounds to wail "corruption."

But corrupt or not, the city had to be paved, one street after another, until it was all asphalt. Tammany could say it got things done, and if reformers complained of corruption, or merchants of expense, well, asked Tweed; "What are they going to do about it?" If Reform could not win its elections, it was impotent. Old New York offered nothing but platitudes: virtue, rectitude, and temperance. Tammany offered free beer, free cigars, free coal, free turkeys. Tammany put up bail bonds, Tammany attended wakes.

The city needed sewers. Tammany got them built. The city needed water. A reservoir system from upstate was charged with corruption, but brought down water. In the State Assembly, Tweed arranged the bill establishing Presbyterian Hospital. He encouraged the first experiments with subways. He got the "elevated lines" established, as he explained, so that, "a man without a carriage could get to work as well as a man with one."

When John Roebling proposed a bridge to Brooklyn the merchants opposed it, saying it would siphon off customers to the suburbs. It was, said Tweed's opponents, "conceived in sin, born in iniquity, and would like all similar creations, end in disaster for all concerned with it." But up it went, and Tammany had the city's docks repaired, and the waterfront avenues cleared and broadened, and the avenues above Forty-second Street widened. "Corruption," the reformers accurately charged.

Tweed's Department of Parks was the first such creation in the country. A competition was held for the design of a vast Central Park, running north from 59th Street to 110th Street, west from Fifth Avenue to Eighth Avenue. Olmsted and Vaux submitted the winning design in 1858, and Tammany began accumulating the land. "Corruption in land deals," said the newspapers, quite accurately. For the sake of his opposition, Tweed managed a bill through the State Assembly creating the Metropolitan Museum of Art and consented to its location in Central Park. The museum's Yankee elders also thought they might like to have a restaurant in the park, too, at 59th Street and Fifth Avenue. "No," said Boss Tweed, "the Museum is taffy enough for that crowd."

He had shrewdly assessed the consequences of democratic constitutions, and with less sentiment than his opponents. If Tammany won its elections, it was winner take all. His opposition could not find an easy answer to Tweed's formula, and if at first they imagined they could equate Reform with Virtue, and Boss with Corruption, they soon realized that if reformers were to be elected they would have to become bosses.

They found themselves in an awkward, perhaps even delicate position. They could see that if the logic of Tweed's challenge were carried to its extreme, the wealth they had accumulated would soon evaporate. What they proposed as an answer was an ingenious and generous offer. It was far more complex than meeting the immediate demands of the poor, or the simple extension of paved streets, or arguing over control of the power stations. It was an arrangement legions of German Socialists had never considered in all their tracts. It granted patronage to party without quibble, and income to power without envy, but left the accumulation of capital undisturbed. It included a stroke of genius—an understanding that denied theory and confounded the lessons of history, an idea with a lovely charm that went to the heart of the matter. Tacitly, the merchant aristocracy agreed: that the politics of a city need not be the handmaiden of virtue.

For the protection of their capital they abandoned all the pleasures the city might offer, forever after, on a permanent leasehold to the poor, including, but not limited to, rhetoric, the temples of music, theater, and art, and to a large extent even literature. In addition, they gave up all the inspirations of art, including but not limited to, whiskey, gambling, and vice. As a sign and seal of the easement so granted, the illusions of fame were delivered over to those among the immigrants who cared to reach for them, and with fame went what the city would call forever after, whatever its address, "Broadway."

Old New York would retain for itself "Fifth Avenue." Old New York guessed it could afford to grant the burdens of political administration, and the biannual comedy of the city's elections, to the new democratic powers. Anyone could be mayor, they reasoned; and from their experience they knew anyone often was. But they calculated they could not afford to lose control of the courts, and the problem was that judges were also elected on the same slates as mayors and from the same Democratic clubhouses. In return for giving up Broadway, Capital would want, in case of dire need or in case the expense of the poor came too high, the opportunity to buy the necessary court: not all the courts all of the time, just some of the courts from time to time. That is, Money wanted to limit the power of machine politics by reserving for itself the power to corrupt—if not absolutely, at least occasionally.

Tammany gave over to Fifth Avenue the power to corrupt and kept City Hall. When Boss Tweed lost an election he was tried and convicted of fraud in the millions of dollars and thousands of instances. He said he was innocent and could prove he was a pauper. The reason why his judges would not hear Tweed's testimony of how he had used his power is that his truths would have required indictments of all his opponents.

By the end of the nineteenth century it was an established illusion of the city's landscape that Tammany and Reform would exchange office from time to time and that the administration of the city's offices would be moderately corrupt in most instances. If the city's newspapers pretended otherwise, they must have had their reasons to preach about public virtue. Even the dumbest blonde in a Music Hall chorus could cite a hundred examples that there was no such thing as virtue—public or private, on Broadway or Fifth; and neither Evelyn Nesbit nor her mother could have been confused about the landscape in which they had taken up the opportunities of Evelyn's career.

CHAPTER FOUR

RED VELVET SWING:
Stanford White

BACKSTAGE ONE NIGHT Edna Goodrich—the big, voluptuous brunette in the *Floradora* Sextette—introduced Evelyn to another big, handsome chorus girl who looked much like Edna. When Edna introduced Nell King as her mother, Evelyn said she could not have been more amazed. "Your mother?"

"Right the first time, little girl," said Nell King. "And I still pass on Broadway as Edna's sister."

The Goodrich "sisters" wanted Evelyn to ask her mother for permission to go to a lunch party; Evelyn and Edna would go together to meet some of Edna's "society" friends. "It's all right," Nell King said. "They're lovely people." The upshot of a talk between Nell King and Mrs. Nesbit was that Evelyn could join Edna for lunch on an August day in 1901.

Evelyn's mother dressed her in a little homemade black and white dress. She wore her best hat and tied back her copper curls with black taffeta ribbon so that they hung down her back like a schoolgirl's. "You never would have believed I was sixteen," said Evelyn. "I looked about thirteen." When Edna Goodrich called for Evelyn at the Nesbits' boardinghouse it was already warming up into a hot summer day. Evelyn inspected Edna's big summer hat and Edna's crown of piled-up hair and guessed that anyone who happened to see them in their hansom cab would think they were a chorus girl and her daughter.

Evelyn hoped the hansom cab would be taking them to the Waldorf, which she was dying to see, but instead they turned off Broadway at West Twenty-fourth Street and stopped at an address in the loft district—the last place in the world Evelyn said she expected to lunch with "society" people.

The two girls went up to a dingy doorway next to the entrance to a toy company, and Edna rang the bell. After a moment the door opened automatically. There was no one behind it; the door opened by itself, silently. Evelyn decided it must be electric. "It's all right," Edna said. "We go on up."

They climbed several flights of stairs to the top landing, where a tall, redheaded man was waiting for them. He had a big smile, boomed a cheery hello, and introduced himself as Stanford White. He ushered them from the stairway landing into what Evelyn described as a breathtaking room.

It had been done in different shades of red, and there were heavy red velvet curtains that shut out all the daylight. There was a soft light, but Evelyn could not see any direct light anywhere—electric bulbs had been concealed so that only their reflected glow lit the room. There were tapestries and fine paintings on the walls, and Evelyn was startled by an exquisite nude, lit by one of the hidden lights from overhead. The furniture was Italian antique, she thought, and there was a table set for four.

Edna Goodrich seemed to be perfectly at home. Evelyn followed her lead, took off her hat, sat down on one of the Italian chairs, and tried to act as nonchalant as Edna was. Another man came up the stairs and into the room. He was introduced as Mr. Reginald Ronalds. He was very cheery and full of little jokes, but Evelyn thought he was disappointingly old, and not a bit handsome like Mr. White.

She guessed Mr. White was in his forties, which was old enough she supposed, but there was a wonderful corona of energy around him. His red hair stood straight up from his head like a brush, and somehow his moustache had been electrified, too. When he laughed he threw his head back and his teeth flashed. His eyes were a distant blue and they gathered up in them whatever they saw. His gaze delighted her so much she was afraid to meet it too often, but she watched him avidly. Every part of him was in constant motion. As he talked his eyes moved over what he imagined as he described it, his hands and his shoulders and head moved with what absorbed him. As he talked one hand came down like a lion's paw on Mr. Ronald's forearm to emphasize some enthusiasm

—it was an easy gesture, both careless and intimate at the same time, and Evelyn could see his touch had warmed old Mr. Ronalds.

Lunch was served by Mr. White from a portable cabinet such as the service hotels used—with a little charcoal heater at the bottom to keep it warm. The food was delicious, and there was champagne on ice in a bucket. Evelyn told them it was the first time she had tasted champagne, and they said she should have no more than one glass. Everyone laughed a lot at nothing at all. Both men fussed over her, and their admiration, their frank gazes, made her feel grown-up. After lunch Reginald Ronalds said he had to leave because he was a stockbroker.

When he had gone Mr. White took them up another set of stairs that began from inside the apartment and led to the top of the building, where there was a marvelous studio which must have been more than two stories high. Busts, paintings, and drawings were lying about, and there were etchings of nudes on the walls. At one end there was a gorgeous swing hanging from the ceiling on red velvet ropes, with green smilax wound around the ropes and trailing down from its red velvet seat. Mr. White said, "Let's put this little kid in the swing first."

What fun it was, said Evelyn, to swing higher and higher out across the studio's floor. If she kicked her feet hard and pulled back on the ropes, she could get way up. Mr. White gave her extra pushes to help her fly. He had rigged the swing so that at its highest arc she could kick her feet through a paper Japanese parasol hung almost at the edge of the ceiling. The big parasol could be rotated by pulling on a string. Mr. White told Edna to pull the string as Evelyn swung high near the ceiling, and a fresh section of parasol would be presented as a new target for Evelyn to kick. She kicked it in, section by section, and she laughed so hard her sides ached. When it was time to stop it took her a long while to catch her breath.

At about four o'clock Mr. White said he thought the girls should be going home. As they were putting on their hats in the vestibule he said Evelyn should visit his dentist. He wrote the address on a card and told Edna she should take Evelyn there. They could go this afternoon. He could see one front tooth that needed professional attention. He said to Evelyn, "It's your only defect, and it spoils your smile."

Mr. White's chauffeur would have driven them in his electric hansom, but they didn't go to the dentist because Edna didn't want to go. She ordered Mr. White's chauffeur to drive them around Central Park instead. In the park Edna Goodrich gave Evelyn one or two nasty looks, but Evelyn thought that was just too bad for her: Edna Goodrich wasn't going to spoil the wonderful time she'd had.

At the boardinghouse Evelyn told her mother that Mr. White was a handsome, charming, splendid man, thoughtful and kind, a brilliant conversationalist, and that he had an extraordinary magnetism. Within a few days a letter came from Mr. White asking Mrs. Nesbit's permission for Evelyn to come to lunch again, saying he would send the electric hansom to pick her up.

Edna Goodrich had not been asked to the second lunch. Instead a blond girl—Elsie Ferguson, who was in *The Strollers* at the Knickerbocker Theatre—came with a Mr. Thomas Clarke. Mr. White explained that Mr. Clarke was a very famous dealer in Chinese porcelains and antiques. He had white hair and walked with a cane. Evelyn said he looked as old as Methuselah to her, which made Mr. White laugh.

Once again after lunch Mr. Clarke said he had to leave, and Elsie and Evelyn and Mr. White climbed the stairs to the big studio. Once more Evelyn played with the red velvet swing. Mr. White pulled the string himself to rotate a new parasol. Once again as they were leaving he asked about getting the tooth capped, and he was surprised Edna Goodrich had not taken Evelyn to the dentist as he had asked. He said he would see Evelyn's mother about it. He wrote down an address on a card and asked Evelyn to have her mother call on him at his office so that he could make all the necessary arrangements for the dentist.

For some reason, Evelyn's mother delayed going to Mr. White's office. Then a letter came from Mr. White, saying that he was asking Mrs. Nesbit up to his office in her daughter's behalf, and the letter went on about the dentist, and the tooth spoiling her smile. Evelyn couldn't see why her mother shouldn't go.

Mrs. Nesbit returned the next afternoon to say that she had found Mr. White utterly charming, and she soon sent Evelyn off to have the tooth fixed. Within a week they moved from the boardinghouse on Twenty-second Street to the Audubon Hotel at the corner of Broadway and Thirty-ninth Street, directly opposite the Casino Theatre where *Floradora* was playing. Evelyn and her mother agreed they were more comfortable at the Audubon than they had ever been. They had a sitting room, an alcove bedroom, and their own private bath, and Evelyn's mother said she thought it was wonderful to live in New York.

Mr. White sent them flowers every day, and one day a package was delivered. When they opened it they pulled out from its tissue paper an English-tailored cloak in American-beauty red with long, flowing lines and a boyish satin collar. When Mr. White called upon them late that afternoon Evelyn modeled the cloak for him. He said he thought "it was just bully." He asked her mother if Evelyn didn't look just like Little Red Riding Hood, and her mother said she certainly did.

Mr. White was even more generous about Howard. Because Mrs. Nesbit told him that the health of Evelyn's younger brother was a constant worry to both of them, Mr. White made arrangements for Howard to be admitted to Chester Military Academy, just outside of Philadelphia. As fall came on and the leaves from the city's sycamores began to litter the gutters in the sidestreets and the air in New York turned sharp and clean Mrs. Nesbit said she would like very much to go to Philadelphia to see what the new surroundings had done for Howard's health. Then perhaps she would continue on to Pittsburgh to visit her fiancé, Mr. Holman, but she said she was afraid to leave Evelyn alone in New York. Mr. White assured her it would be quite safe for her to go; he promised to look after Evelyn in her absence. Mr. White and Evelyn went together to see Mrs. Nesbit off on the train. They barely had time to wave her good-bye because Evelyn had to rush back to make the *Floradora* curtain.

Mr. White sent a Union Club cab to the theater every night to pick her up, just as her mother had done, even though the Audubon was across the street. He never met her himself. So many Union Club or Racquet Club cabs waited for girls in *Floradora* that the assistant stage manager had to have the girls paged: "Racquet Club cab for Miss So-and-so. Union Club cab for Miss Nesbit." The news that Stanford White's Union Club cab waited every night for Evelyn caused a sensation backstage. Evelyn soon sensed a change of attitude—no one laughed at her anymore as "the kid." As the days passed the atmosphere backstage became deadly. The Goodrich "sisters" snubbed her.

Within a few days of her mother's departure Mr. White sent his electric hansom to bring Evelyn to the offices of his firm, McKim, Mead and White, at 160 Fifth Avenue. He spent much of the afternoon escorting her through the several floors and explaining to her how they made the drawings for people's houses. He brought her into the office of Mr. McKim, his partner and his dearest friend, and introduced her.

"This little girl's mother has gone to Pittsburgh and left her in my care," he explained.

"My God!" said Mr. McKim, but Evelyn thought Mr. McKim had a friendly laugh.

After the show that night the driver of the Union Club cab gave Evelyn a note from Mr. White instructing her to meet him at the Twenty-fourth Street place. It was the first time she had gone there at night. He met her as usual at the top of the stairs, on the landing. He took her Little Red Riding Hood cloak, and as she took off her hat she could see the table had been set for supper, but just for two.

During supper Stanny told her funny things about what people wanted in their houses, and she told him the gossip from backstage at *Floradora*. She had several glasses of champagne. After supper he took her on a tour through the whole place, showing her rooms she had never seen before. There was a tiny little room, no more than ten feet square, its walls and ceiling all made of mirrors, and even the floor was like glass. Indirect lighting cast a soft glow over everything. Along one side there was an immense couch, almost too large for such a small room, covered in moss-green velvet. He left her there, returning in a moment, with a gorgeous yellow satin Japanese kimono embroidered with festoons of wisteria. While he went to get more champagne, she tried it on.

They sat on the green velvet couch sipping more champagne, and Evelyn was thrilled by her own reflections and the sight of herself nestled next to Stanny. He seemed to be trembling. Then they stood up again, and he led her back through the room where they had left their supper to a bedroom in the back.

It had a log fire flickering in the fireplace. There were red velvet draperies from ceiling to floor. There was a four-poster bed draped with heavy velvet curtains that drew apart or came together again by pulling a cord. Stanny showed her how the cord worked. Evelyn tried it.

The headboard of the bed, and the dome of its canopy, and the wall next to the bed, were all mirrors. Hidden around the top of the bed, up in its canopy, were tiny electric bulbs that could be regulated by pushing different buttons for different effects. Evelyn pushed one button, which gave an amber glow to the mirror in the canopy overhead. She could see herself as an amber woman in a yellow kimono, her copper hair unfastened and spread across amber pillows. Another button produced a soft rose effect and another produced a soft blue, which was the color she would remember later around Stanny's huge shoulders.

She said that when she woke up she started to cry. Stanny was lying there beside her, and he turned to her and petted her and kissed her, and said, "Don't. Please don't. It's all over. Now you belong to me."

He got up and put on a robe and gave her the yellow kimono, which had been tossed across the back of a chair. He removed the telltale sheets and took her to an armchair and held her on his knees and soothed her, and she quieted. He told her he would come to her again that afternoon, but he was going to drive her back to the Audubon now.

It was in the early hours of the morning when she returned

to her rooms at the Audubon. She said she felt utterly confused, and a bit dizzy, and terribly embarrassed and afraid, and excited all at the same time. She sat in a chair by the window, assailed by new emotions, absolutely sleepless. "This was what people made such a fuss about. This was what love meant."

Evelyn would sometimes describe the night in the fall of 1901 "when she became a woman" as a sweet dream, as if she were remembering a sixteen-year-old girl's drama of a poor butterfly. But there would be other occasions when she would recall that night somewhat differently. It all depended upon who her audience might be. She would claim that a man nearly fifty had drugged her with champagne or with an opiate in the champagne, which had a bitter taste. She would say she had lost consciousness; that when she awoke and discovered she was no longer a virgin she began to scream. She would say Stanny came over and asked her to please be quiet and not to make so much noise, that he had said, "It's all over; it is all over."

She would remember she had got out of bed and begun to scream even more, but then she would admit that if there were any cries at all, perhaps she had let out "one suppressed scream." She would not be able to remember how she got her clothes on or how she got home, yet she would describe how he went away and left her, and how she sat up all night.

Later she would insist that Stanford White had forced his attentions upon her, that she never loved him, that everything went black that night, that she hated him, that she felt outraged when a "big yellow brute drugged and wronged her." She would admit she often "drank to excess with White." She would say she never told her mother about it, that she always resisted him and never submitted willingly. "I always resisted. I didn't like it."

But Evelyn always offered a number of versions of everything that happened to her. She would accurately say of herself that "calmness was one of my traits; I was not given to fainting or hysterics." Every version she told agreed she was a tired butterfly the next day because she didn't go to bed at all.

She was head over heels in love with Stanny, and she waited by the window of her rooms in the Audubon until she heard Stanny's familiar drumming at the door.

When she had let him in he got down on his knees and picked up the hem of her skirt and kissed it. He was trembling violently again. She did not look at him but stared out the window. After a while he put his arms around her and asked her, "Why don't you look at me, child?"

She said she couldn't, and he began to talk to her. He told her that everything was all right. He said she had the most beautiful hair he had ever seen. He said he was going to do a great many things for her. He declared everybody did these things. He said she was so nice and young and slim, that only young girls were very nice, that the thinner a woman was, the prettier she was, that nothing was so loathsome as fat, and that she must never get fat.

She looked at him and asked, "Does everybody you know do these things?"

He said that was all anyone ever lived for.

She asked him if the girls in the Sextette did these things. He sat down and started to laugh, and "laughed and laughed and laughed."

The winter of 1901-1902 began to creep in on fall, and as the weeks passed Evelyn said she couldn't help but marvel at the strange effect she had on him. Whether they met at his office or after the show, whether they went to his Twenty-fourth Street place or to his studio in the Tower above Madison Square Garden, when he first put his arms around her, or only touched her, he would begin to tremble. She was fascinated by the power she could apparently exert over so strong a man. She was, she estimated shrewdly, a constant thrill to him. She decided she must be the kind of woman he "adored and fell slave to."

At the Twenty-fourth Street studio he would sometimes put her in the red velvet swing stark naked and send her soaring toward the ceiling. As she kicked in another Japanese parasol with her bare feet he would roar with delight. Sometimes he loved to hoist her up on his shoulders; she would hold a glass of champagne in one hand and a bunch of grapes in the other, and he would study the effect in one of the mirrors and then march around the studio, leading some parade he imagined, singing the march at the top of his lungs.

He wanted to have her photographed and he took her to a house on East Nineteenth Street. Externally, it looked like a typical brownstone, but inside it had been completely transformed. As in every one of Stanny's places, daylight was completely shut out by drawn dark shades and thick velvet curtains. There was a large studio room on the second floor, with a stone-carved Norman fireplace from floor to ceiling. He said the fireplace had been brought over in sections from an ancient castle. He showed her the fantastic bedrooms above and below the great studio room. He had brought with him his most gorgeous kimonos, some of them, he said, worth two thousand dollars. When she had changed and was ready she should come down to the second-floor studio where the photographer Rudolf Eickemeyer would pose her.

She modeled in one kimono after another, and as a Greek goddess, patiently obeying orders for more than an hour. She finally tired of it and flopped down on the white bear rug in front of the fireplace, curled up, and pleaded with them, "No more. I'm tired."

"Hold that!" cried Eickemeyer. "Don't move!"

He rearranged the lights, drew the slide from the plate, and tripped the shutter. The photograph became Eickemeyer's best known work. He called it "Tired Butterfly," and it was sold all over the world by the Campbell Art Studios, even on the backs of postcards.

At supper one night Stanny explained to her that some girls in the theater were very foolish and got talked about, but that people should not talk about these things and should never tell about them. He said the girls in the theater ought to realize that society women understood that the great thing in this world was not to get found out. He told her stories of society women who were not discovered. But Evelyn knew that Edna Goodrich had some damning letters written to her from Stanny, letters in which he had referred to Edna as his "bride."

Evelyn thought her lover was "amazingly careless," and involved himself unnecessarily by writing so many letters—he seemed to be an incurable letter writer. At the theater Evelyn had picked up the story of how Edna Goodrich and her mother had brought suit against him, and how Stanny had hired a lawyer named Abe Hummel to represent him, and that Hummel was able to manage a settlement out of court for the letters for five thousand dollars.

Nell King was still furious about the whole thing. She had told everyone that Evelyn was "a menace." One night backstage she had even threatened to give Evelyn a beating, so Evelyn was not dissatisfied to learn that Stanny and his crowd had stopped speaking to Edna and her mother and that the Goodrich "sisters" soon found it was "no easy matter to get jobs on Broadway." Their behavior, Evelyn sniffed, had put them "outside the pale."

Within the pale she went with Stanny to his brilliant parties at his suite in the Tower of Madison Square Garden. His private parties were famous, but he was very cautious about them. The food was always sent over from the exclusive Manhattan Club—canvasback duck in orange sauce, partridge, or quail, and it came in cabinets to keep it warm. The waiters had their instructions to leave the food in the kitchenette, which had its own entrance just to the right of the elevator in the Tower. They were never permitted to see the guests. Stanny passed the champagne himself, and there were always showgirls to help.

The guest list for Stanny's Madison Square Garden Tower parties—not at West Twenty-fourth Street, mind you, only the inner circles of his men friends were asked up to his "hideaway"—was a glittering list of the wealthy and powerful, the talented and successful. Stanny's "celebrities" were the ranking artists mixed with the important figures from both Broadway and Fifth Avenue. At different times at Tower parties, Evelyn met the sculptors Augustus Saint-Gaudens and Frederick MacMonnies, actress Ethel Barrymore, playboy Jimmy Breese, author Mark Twain, publisher James Gordon Bennett, Jr., corporation lawyer Joseph H. Choate, and United States Vice President Levi P. Morton. There were, as one gossip column reported it, "numberless others who were then suns in their chosen spheres or on the way up over the horizon of fame." The Tower parties would sometimes last all night.

Invitations to the Tower were envied, said one newspaper account, as if they were invitations to the Garden of the Gods. The Tower studio high above Madison Square Garden was described as Stanford White's "second home." It was horseshoe-shaped, modeled around the elevators and stairway, and two doors led to it off the elevator—the kitchenette by which the unseen waiters entered on the right, and the main entrance on the left. Evelyn described how one whole wall of the apartment, the broad end of the horseshoe, was mirrored, with a green couch stretching along its entire length.

No daylight ever entered the room; the windows were heavily curtained, the walls covered with priceless tapestries. There were gorgeous Oriental divans and exquisitely carved antique chairs from Italy and Spain; in one corner a particularly lovely tapestried couch and opposite a large round table at which the suppers were laid out. All the divans were covered with bear, tiger, and leopard skins. Magnificent carved pillars reached from floor to ceiling. Scattered here and there were artificial orange trees and in them electric light bulbs, shaded to resemble oranges, shed a warm, diffused light into the room. In the center of the room Stanny had hung a cardinal's red hat upside-down and put light bulbs into it to send a rosy glow over the long divan. When all the lights were on, said Evelyn, it was a scene from the *Arabian Nights*. "It would take Scheherazade herself to describe it adequately."

Evelyn said many nights, "or I should say mornings—around three o'clock," Stanny would give her a ride in the elevator to its last stop, and then they would climb the spiral staircase to the top of Madison Square Garden's Tower, three hundred feet above the streets of the city. Above the Tower, Stanny had placed a statue of *Diana,* sculptured in copper-bronze by his friend Augustus Saint-Gaudens, thirteen feet high and set on ball bearings to move as a weather vane. Evelyn loved to climb up there and, holding tight to *Diana*'s heel, gaze out over the city. It was, she said, an enthralling sight on clear nights when the moon was full. "Often we would stand there for a long time, holding hands and softly talking."

By Christmas of 1901 Mrs. Nesbit apparently trusted her sixteen-year-old daughter's virtue to the forty-eight-year experience of the fatherly Mr. White. Her mother no longer believed it necessary to meet Evelyn backstage after the show. Instead Evelyn would take a Union Club cab directly from *Floradora* to the Tower and meet Stanny there. He would often return from the opera or a theater opening, serve late supper for his celebrities with Evelyn at his side, and then when their guests had finally left, turn to his drawing board —still in his evening clothes—and begin to sketch. Evelyn loved to watch him working late at night on his designs.

His pencil would fly across reams of tracing paper. Although she could understand a sketch for the top of a pillar, or the facade of a building, most of the things he finished looked, she said, like "abstruse hieroglyphics." He drew plans and perspectives and details, pedestals for Saint-Gaudens and MacMonnies, office-building details for press lords, parts of churches and altars, decorations for restaurant tables, a fireplace for editor Richard Watson Gilder, a monument for Consuelo, Duchess of Manchester. Everything done so swiftly, and so surely.

Evelyn would wrap herself up in one of the animal skins and fall asleep on the long green divan. When morning came a messenger would come in from the offices of McKim, Mead and White, then tiptoe to his drawing board where the designs that had been satisfactory were left, and signed "SW" in the corner. All around the board there would be a snowfield of abandoned paper, many crumpled up, others skimmed into oblivion.

The messenger would pick up the sketches and assignments for the draftsmen in the office to finish. Stanny would still be in his opera clothes, sleeping off his exhaustion on the small divan. The messenger would tiptoe out, leaving behind new piles of office memoranda, correspondence to be answered, finishes to be examined and approved; setting them on the drawing board and then departing through the soft orange lights of the Tower's "Oriental" studio.

Stanny seemed to think everything out to the last, minute detail. He said he planned to move Evelyn and her mother to an apartment in a new hotel that had gone up on Seventh Avenue, the Wellington, but he would not let them see their new place until it was completely ready. When they did finally get to see it, he had completely furnished the rooms, even to the toothbrushes in the bathroom. Evelyn had her own bedroom in red and white—white satin walls, red wool carpets, a white bearksin on the floor, ivory-white furniture, and a bed draped in ivory-white satin covered with lace. The canopy of her bed was also in white satin, and above the canopy Stanny had put a huge crown of five thick white ostrich plumes. He had placed white swans around the apartment, fashioned of wood, and there were plants in them. There was a white piano, and he told her he had hired a piano teacher for her so that she could study and learn to play Beethoven for him.

For Christmas in 1901 he gave her a large pearl hung on a platinum chain, a set of white fox furs, a ruby and diamond ring, and two solitaire diamond rings. She told him she loved him with all her heart.

By early 1902 there were dozens of men sending flowers backstage at *Floradora* to Evelyn. Some sent her jewelry. Some sent money with their flowers, enclosed in their cards. Others lay in wait for her at the stage door and shouted her name, and others maneuvered introductions through the showgirls. Evelyn told Stanny she turned them all away, because "I loved Stanford White. I wanted only to be with him."

She continued to go to his brilliant parties at the Tower, and there were parties at Jimmy Breese's studio. Sometimes Stanny's friends would play host—Tommy Clarke, or Charles MacDonald, or Freddie Gebhard. But Stanny spent every weekend with his family in Saint James, Long Island. Sometimes he was away for a week or more because of his work, and when summer came around, he went off to Europe on one of his trips to buy things for his clients' houses. He always took his wife with him. There were times when Evelyn fretted about her inactivity.

She had an explanation, of course. She had asked about him backstage right at the very beginning, and they had told her that he was married. She knew he constantly worried about any scandal that might stigmatize his family and that although he lived "his other life" in the city, he never neglected them. He told her how much he respected his wife and how much he valued his son's love, and she estimated that he must have been a marvelous and understanding father because "he was always the patron saint of anyone in distress." He told her once, "You are the only girl in the world who can point her finger at me."

Evelyn was not so sure about that. Certainly Edna Goodrich had pointed a finger at him and collected five thousand dollars for her letters, and she guessed there might be many others. She came across a little black book in which he had recorded the birthday of every pretty woman he knew. There were names she knew on Broadway, and others she recognized from Fifth Avenue. She would explain later that despite all his attentions, she suffered jealous pangs, and she would say she acted the silly child to make him jealous of her. Eventually she would realize how much he had risked for her. She said she always managed to conceal "any visible signs of my heartaches" from Stanny.

But she would have a variety of other explanations, too, artful variations that depended upon what her audience wanted to hear. She could say, as if she were finally revealing the secret truths of a schoolgirl's diary, "I foolishly longed for an opportunity to make him really jealous of me." She could also say, as if the facts spoke for themselves, that Stanny never seemed to get jealous, never rebuked her, because "he appreciated my love of play and respected my love of freedom." He was enough of a sophisticate, she justly pointed out, "to apply no hard and fast rules of right and wrong to me."

An anonymous man bombarded her at *Floradora* every day for a week with Japanese lotus flowers from the shop at the Waldorf. Her admirer managed an introduction by bribing one of the other girls backstage, and Evelyn accepted his invitation for supper. At the restaurant he laid out on the table a fortune in diamonds and emeralds: a dazzling necklace, a bracelet, two rings, and a brooch. She refused to accept them and laughed at him, and he was stunned. It made a great story backstage, and Evelyn passed him on to another girl.

Another man sent her a pearl-and-diamond lavaliere with his card. She promptly returned them because he was too ugly and too old, and for years afterward she would still laugh about him. Wherever and whenever he saw her he would stop in his tracks and stare at her with a puzzled expression on his face.

At Stanny's parties she had met dozens of men who interested her, and at the parties she had a better chance to size them up. She was particularly fond of what she called the *jeunesse dorée,* the boys who belonged to the Racquet Club, because they were young and gay and full of fun, she said, and "more suited to my age than Stanford and his friends." She was particularly attracted by Monty Waterbury, a handsome polo star, and Bobby Collier, son of the publisher of *Collier's Weekly.*

A group of them hired a private room at Rector's, invited Evelyn to be their only guest, crowned her their princess, and gave a dinner in her honor "with a colored orchestra to entertain us." They made up a game in her honor in which she sat on a chair behind a partition, and as each young man fed her bluepoints over the top of the screen, he had to describe his love for her. In turn she had to guess the identity of the man whose hand was feeding her. There was a great rivalry over which one would escort her home. With all the ceremony of a queen at a French court, she chose Bobby Collier.

Evelyn had supper with Bobby Collier from time to time, because, she said, he wrote beautiful verses to her and stared at her "with absorbed tender eyes." Bobby Collier tried to convince her she was wasting her time on the stage, and he proposed to send her to art school in Paris. He kept insisting she had a great talent for drawing. She told him he would have to send her mother with her, and he agreed to that.

She told him he was a sweet and endearing man. They made an appointment to discuss the question "seriously" at lunch in the Garden Room of the Imperial Hotel. She refused him as gently as she could. He said anytime she wanted to go to Europe, he would send her, and her mother, too. Evelyn would recall he was one of a half-dozen millionaires who proposed to her in 1902 when she was seventeen.

When *Floradora* was coming to the end of its run, neither she nor her mother had to worry about money because by then Stanny had opened accounts for them at the New Amsterdam Bank and at the Mercantile Trust Company. He gave the Nesbits a weekly allowance of twenty-five dollars, but in addition he paid all their bills.

As *Floradora* was closing, one of the best-known producers on Broadway, George W. Lederer, came to talk with Mrs. Nesbit at the Wellington. He had been Lillian Russell's producer, and after several long conversations with Evelyn and her mother he said, "I think I can make a star of your daughter." He thought Evelyn could play the part of a gypsy girl in a new musical he planned "if she could only sing."

Mrs. Nesbit assured him that Evelyn had had a lovely voice as a child but lost it when she was about twelve. Undismayed, George Lederer arranged for a voice teacher to give Evelyn three lessons a week. Mr. Lederer was very attentive, and his encouragement once again fired Evelyn with ambition for success on the stage.

Mr. Lederer announced to the newspapers that he was naming the musical after Evelyn. It was going to be a gypsy musical, and Evelyn reminded him of a wild gypsy rose. When *The Wild Rose* opened in Philadelphia the show was an instant success. The day after it appeared on Broadway, "Nancy Brown," a song Marie Cahill sang, became the most popular ballad in New York. Within a week every orchestra in town was playing "My Little Gypsy Maid," and Eddie Foy was hailed as a new comic star for his routine, "I'm Unlucky."

The musical earned additional pages of publicity because on the day the show opened it was discovered that Mrs. George W. Lederer was suing her husband for divorce and Mrs. Lederer named the wild gypsy rose, Evelyn Nesbit, as corespondent—which Evelyn said was nothing but a vicious slander.

One summer weekend George Lederer shipped the entire company and all the sets by boat to Newport to play *The Wild Rose* for a party on a temporary stage at Beaulieu, the summer palace of Cornelius Vanderbilt II. Evelyn said there were dozens of familiar faces in the audience, members of the Racquet Club and the Union Club, sitting there stiff and starched and embarrassed in their evening clothes. Only after supper, and plenty of champagne, did they finally loosen up and begin to have a good time, and go around introducing the girls to the society women. "Countess, I should like to present my friend Mazie Follette."

During the same summer Evelyn began a passionate affair with John Barrymore. She had met him at one of Stanny's Tower parties, and he was introduced to her as Ethel Barrymore's younger brother. He was twenty-two and a cartoonist on the *Evening Journal*. While supper was being served he kept tugging at his moustache, and Evelyn thought he had an incredible profile and she could not keep her eyes off him. He kept throwing admiring glances at her, and their eyes were constantly meeting. When Stanny left the room to answer a phone call, Barrymore leaned forward and whispered to her, "Quick! Your address and telephone number!" He wrote them on his shirt cuff and sent her violets that very night.

Stanny went off to Canada on his annual summer salmon-fishing trip, and every night Jack Barrymore called for Evelyn at the stage door of *The Wild Rose*. They would go to Rector's for supper, and Evelyn said they always had lots of fun. Jack would order a glass of milk, set a rose leaf floating on its surface, and say, "That is your mouth." He always called her "Eve," and he told her she was "a quivering pink poppy in a golden whirlwind of space." They would laugh so much at each other that people at nearby tables stared at them. The news of their affair made the *Morning Telegraph*.

If Stanny knew about it, he said nothing. When *The Wild Rose* closed in the fall, Evelyn rehearsed with a show called

The Silver Slipper, which barely managed to open, then lasted only two weeks. During its brief run Evelyn stayed over one night in Jack's apartment. He lived, she said, in an ugly, poverty-stricken firetrap, but he wrapped her in the cloak his father, Maurice Barrymore, had worn as Romeo. They didn't wake up until eleven the next morning.

When she walked into her own apartment at the Wellington, her mother and Stanny were waiting for her. There they stood—Stanny was white-lipped and gray; her mother was shaking with anger, weeping and wringing her hands. Evelyn said her mother's face was distorted "by an expression of hatred I had never seen there before."

Stanny kept bending over her mother solicitously, trying to calm her, assuring her everything would be cleared up, and that no further harm would come to Evelyn. He had apparently won her mother's consent to what had to be done. "Come along, Evelyn," he said, and taking her by the arm, he led her out. They drove to a street in the West Thirties, off Fifth Avenue, where he left her in the offices of Dr. Nathaniel Bowditch Potter.

Dr. Potter kept her locked in a room all day. He asked all sorts of questions, examined her, and made tests. Dr. Potter would not let her out of the locked room. She had nothing to eat until a maid finally brought some food on a tray late in the evening.

Then Stanny reappeared, got a report from the doctor, and took her to the Tower. He explained to Evelyn that he felt he was responsible for her, that her mother was threatening to make a fuss because her mother thought she might be pregnant, and that he didn't want any scandal. Evelyn said that if she was pregnant, she would be happy to marry Jack Barrymore.

Stanny explained, in his kind fatherly way, that her mother had been adamant: her mother would not under any circumstances allow Evelyn to marry John Barrymore. Stanny explained that perhaps her mother had a point when she said marriage to John Barrymore would ruin Evelyn's career and name, and demolish her mother's hopes for her daughter.

He had told her mother he would square things, and there

would be no need for any scandal. He told Evelyn he had sent for John Barrymore, and when Barrymore came to the Tower, he wanted them to sit still and listen.

When Jack arrived he explained to Stanny that he had already taken Evelyn to a Dr. Carlton Flint on the West Side and that if Dr. Flint was correct and Evelyn was pregnant he wanted to marry her.

Stanny said they had been very foolish and that if they got married they would have nothing to live on and would probably quarrel and separate, and end up getting a divorce. They were too young. It would be much better for Evelyn to continue on the stage and try to be a great actress.

Jack didn't seem to be listening, so Stanny tried a new tack. He turned to Evelyn. "Besides, John is a little bit crazy, the whole family is a little bit queer. His father—Maurice Barrymore—is in an insane asylum on Long Island, and on that account alone you should not marry."

Evelyn said she didn't care, that she liked him very much and she would marry Jack if she wanted to.

Jack asked her, "Eve, will you marry me?"

Evelyn said she didn't know, she had to think about it, which made Stanny's face turn purple.

Jack asked her to marry him again, and again she said, "I don't know," which for some reason made her laugh and laugh and laugh.

Again Stanny demanded, "If two kids like you get married, what will you live on?"

Jack said, "On love!"

Evelyn thought Jack had such an impish grin. Stanny said he had to make a phone call and stormed out of the room.

In the long mirror across the wall at the end of the room Evelyn could see herself sitting in a big carved Italian Renaissance chair. She thought she looked so tiny. She could see how the soft glow from the hidden lights overhead fell across her hair and heightened its coppery tones. She decided she looked as if she were wearing a burnished tiara. It would be fun to have a real tiara.

"Don't move, Eve. You look beautiful there." Jack's voice was soft and sweet and far away. "Why not marry me, Eve?"

She looked at him. He was so beautiful, so disarming, but he was still just a boy—so romantic he would fling everything to the winds for love.

Stanny finally reappeared and said Jack should go home now, that he would drive Evelyn to the Wellington. When they arrived at the apartment, Stanny told Mrs. Nesbit not to worry about Evelyn any longer. He had arranged for Evelyn to be registered at a school in Pompton Lakes, New Jersey, which was quite secluded and very nice. He said he would drive her there the next day.

The DeMille School was far from Broadway, a large yellow structure in the Ramapo Hills. In late October the hills were still glorious in all the reds and yellows and oranges of fall. Mrs. DeMille explained there were fifteen girls at her school, and she ran it "just like a home." They would be studying literature and music and French. Evelyn could learn to play tennis, and there would be skating in the winter on Pompton Lake. She took Evelyn to an annex of the main building, a small yellow cottage across the road, and introduced her to her roommate, a girl nicknamed "Prunes."

The room she shared with Prunes had Japanese paper on the wall, said Evelyn, and contained "two virtuous white beds." Evelyn wrote in her diary, "I suppose I will be a noble character before I get out of here," and she drew a sketch of a nun beside her entry, followed by three big exclamation points.

She spent the Christmas holidays alone at Mrs. DeMille's and went skating in January, 1903, with a handsome young man—Robert Fulton. In her diary she noted they skated hand in hand and she wore a gray skating costume—a short skirt, a fuzzy sweater with a cap to match, and angora gloves. Her mother had sent them to her from the Algonquin, where she had moved because the apartment at the Wellington, all done in red and white satin, had been closed.

CHAPTER FIVE

ILLUSIONS OF BONDS:
Henry Villard

WHILE EVELYN WAITED for spring at Mrs. DeMille's school, Stanford White continued to pour his energies into designs—shaping from his Tower the proceeds of the city's heaping wealth into style. A simple listing of his efforts, even a partial listing, even a listing restricted, as if it were a parenthesis, to the same seven months Evelyn waited at Mrs. DeMille's would still give only an approximation of the range of White's influence or his importance as a tutor.

For example, in the latter half of 1902 his firm was absorbed in designs for: Mrs. William Astor at Newport, Rhode Island; Mr. Charles T. Barney at 67 Park Avenue; a set of gates for Bowdoin College in Brunswick, Maine; the Army War College, in Washington, D.C.; the Committee for Improvements of the District of Columbia—especially the Mall; gates for the classes of 1857 and 1880, and the Harvard Union, in Cambridge, Massachusetts; the Institute of Arts and Sciences, Central Wing Number 1, Brooklyn, New York; a house for George Gordon King, Newport, Rhode Island; a building for the Phelps Association, New Haven, Connecticut; homes for Philip A. Rollins, Madison Avenue and Seventy-eighth Street, Robert B. Van Cortland in Mount Kisco, New York, and R. Dudley Winthrop and William C. Whitney in Westbury, Long Island.

During 1903, while Evelyn went skating with a handsome young man, McKim, Mead and White were redoing the White House for President and Mrs. Theodore Roosevelt; they were also working over the drawings of the Officers' Messhall at West Point; competing for the commission of the West Point General Improvement Plan; building the First Congregational Church, and a house for Harris Whittemore, in Naugatuck, Connecticut; a house for A. Cass Canfield in Westbury, Long Island; designing the powerhouses for the Interborough Railway Company at Eleventh Avenue and Fifty-ninth Street; opening the new store of the Havana Tobacco Company at Broadway and Twenty-sixth Street; designing for the New York Public Library its Carnegie Branch, Number 2; and for Rhode Island, the State House in Providence.

In 1903 McKim, Mead and White also worked on the government's buildings on Governors Island, New York. White was absorbed with the porch and doors of Saint Bartholomew's Church, which were to be paid for by Mrs. Cornelius Vanderbilt and on which he worked in collaboration with the sculptors and artists Daniel Chester French, Andrew O'Connor, Herbert Adams, and Philip Martiny. During 1902 and 1903, while Evelyn waited out her seven months, Stanford White was busy doing a house for his friend—the artist who had sketched Evelyn as "The Eternal Question"—Charles Dana Gibson, at 127 East Seventy-third Street. Gibson's house was simple classic New York townhouse. At the same time White was building a great Renaissance stone mansion at 7-11 East Seventy-third Street for Joseph Pulitzer, the strange publisher of the New York *World*. Evelyn had posed in the *World* in shoes, stockings, and hats.

White was also collaborating with his friend Augustus Saint-Gaudens on the base and setting of the *Shaw Monument* in Newport, and on the monument to *William Tecumseh Sherman,* on his horse and led by *Victory,* on the Plaza in New York. In 1902 and 1903 Stanford White designed, built, and decorated a palace for Mrs. Hermann Oelrichs in Newport—a palace, and a setting, on a scale so magnificent that its splendor would permanently tantalize the dreams of the ambitious; an icon for success with money. In 1902 and 1903 Stanford White was also designing, building, and decorating a palace for Clarence H. Mackay in Roslyn, Long Island—a château like those near Paris, designed to impress the peasantry of a duke's unrelenting power.

Clarence Mackay's father had struck it rich in the Comstock Lode, but the son seemed frightened by White's schemes for decoration. Mackay wrote White, "In regard to the remaining mooseheads which you strongly advise me to buy, and of which I understand you made a hurried inspection, you seem to forget the main point, viz: the price."

In the end the price for Mackay's Roslyn château came to more than one million dollars. There were, for example, wine racks for 21,900 bottles in the cellar. White scoured Europe in an "endless quest for ideal chairs and irreproachable tapestries." He wrote the heir of a Comstock Lode fortune, "Although it may be a calamity to you, you must acknowledge that, in the end, you will get a pretty fine château on the hill."

Just as he scoured the Continent for Mackay's furnishings, White continued to tour Europe for furnishings for Mrs. Whitelaw Reid. He put over one million dollars of "decorations" into Mr. and Mrs. Reid's palace at Fiftieth Street and Madison Avenue. Mrs. Reid was the heiress of Darius Ogden Mills, who also had the luck to strike it rich in the roaring camps of the West, and the Reids bought their palace already built—constructed in 1883 and 1884, the first major palace designed by McKim, Mead and White.

Despite the Reids' occupancy, New York would always refer to their residence as "the Villard houses," not only because the complex of houses designed around a central courtyard in flamboyant Renaissance style were permanent landmarks of the city's history but because their original owner, Mr. Henry Villard, exemplary journalist and typical financier, was both legend and example of the city's determination to embrace the illusions of bonds.

He was born Heinrich Gustav Hilgard in Speyer, Bavaria, in 1835. He was typical of the emigrants from Germany's revolutions. With dreams of adventure and freedom promised by America and stifled by his family's measured world of petty officialdom, and angry at his father, he borrowed the passage money from relatives in Wachenheim, sailed from Hamburg on the bark *Nordamerika.* He landed in New York on October 18, 1853, could not speak a word of English, brought no more with him than the clothes on his back, and had to borrow money from a fellow traveler for his first night's lodging.

He estimated the population of the city to be about 500,000 when he landed. He was one of 400,000 immigrants to America that year and one of 119,000 Germans to arrive in New

York. An equal number of Irish came, moving into tenements and joining Boss Tweed's new political machine. Most of the Germans traveled farther west into the continental heartland, and Henry Villard went to Cincinnati and from there to the farm of an uncle in Belleville, Illinois.

He began to learn English. By March, 1855, knew it well enough to obtain a job copying deeds into the records of the circuit court clerk of Clinton County, Illinois. He thought he might take up the study of law. In 1856 he abandoned law for journalism. He covered the campaign of the first Republican candidate for President, John C. Fremont. In August, 1858, journalist Henry Villard was in Ottawa, Illinois, to report the first of seven Lincoln-Douglas debates. He met Lincoln for the first time at the Freeport debate, and when it was over they shared a boxcar on a railroad siding as a shelter from a thunderstorm. Abe Lincoln told him that Mary Lincoln insisted that he was going to be senator from Illinois, "and President of the United States, too." Henry Villard reported the idea made Lincoln roar with laughter, his arms around his knees, shaking all over at his wife's ambition.

When the campains of 1858 were ended, Henry Villard rode the first stage across the plains to the Rockies. He was the first to report for the papers back East the Pike's Peak gold discoveries and the subsequent gold rush in Cherry Creek and Denver. In 1860 he covered the Republican Convention, and after Lincoln's election was confirmed he rode with Lincoln's train from Springfield to Washington.

Lincoln issued his first call for volunteers against the rebellious South on April 15, 1861. For the New York *Herald,* Henry Villard reported the early isolation of the capital, and the Battle of Bull Run in 1861. He rode back through the Union rout to bring the first news of the disaster to Washington and President Lincoln. War correspondent Villard campaigned with Sherman in Nashville, reported on Shiloh, Memphis, and Perryville. In 1863 he went aboard the ironclads when they attempted to bombard Charleston Harbor. He covered Morgan's raids, Chickamauga, the bloody battles in the Wilderness, Lee's surrender, and Lincoln's assassination.

During a lull in the war he fell in love with and married Fanny Garrison in Boston. She was the daughter of William

Lloyd Garrison, and Henry Villard's marriage joined him with one of the famous American families of the Abolitionist aristocracy. Her brother, Wendell Phillips Garrison, married Lucy McKim, the daughter of Miller McKim, secretary and field general of the Quaker opposition to slavery. Miller McKim's son, Charles Follen McKim, was the partner of Stanford White in McKim, Mead and White.

After the war Mr. and Mrs. Henry Villard lived at the Garrison home in Roxbury, Massachusetts. A daughter and a son were born, and Henry Villard was elected secretary of the American Social Science Association. By 1870 he was a widely known and respected journalist, a Republican liberal or "mugwump" in his political hopes. He wrote and worked for Civil Service reform, and he was appalled and disgusted by the antic piracy surrounding the Grant Administration.

Just as war correspondent Henry Villard had habitually ridden out to the forefront of battle to report the details of victory and defeat, he inevitably took up the enthusiasms of peace along its front lines. Typically, he began by thorough study, then turned a clear eye to the march of events, then seized opportunity with goodwill and for sound reasons. By 1870 he was thirty-five, his brow was wide, his hairline just beginning to recede, his deepset eyes seemed to possess distance and experience, a coolness perhaps, or the perspective won by having been witness to the bloody scenes of war. In comparison, everything else could be taken in its proper place. He stood as straight as the cavalryman he had been, and everything in his manner spoke of practical knowledge and of rectitude. He appeared to be a man who would do the right thing.

As secretary of the American Social Science Association, Henry Villard began to study both public and corporate financing. He knew the geography of America better than most men because he had ridden out across the plains and up into the canyons of the Rockies. He understood American politics and the national sense of continental union, and he could explain to doubtful Europeans that the national wealth of the union would be more than enough to pay for the war. In February, 1873, he joined a group of bondholders to investigate the value of the bonds they had bought in an Oregon railroad company. They had paid eleven million dollars for these securities at 7 percent, and banks in Germany, London, and New York had subscribed to the Oregon bonds for themselves and their customers. For the benefit of the bondholders, Henry Villard went out to Oregon in the summer of 1873 to investigate "firsthand" the value of their investments. He returned to report the bonds worthless and to explain how the company's promoter had dispersed the faith of his investors.

Henry Villard knew, however, that in the mood of national exhaustion that followed the Civil War, and the boredom and distaste that prevailed for the windy cant of politics, only one topic caught the public fancy, what was called "The Winning of the West." From the Civil War until the turn of the century the march of the railroads, the great iron highways designed to unite at last one nation indivisible, were the constant delight of the national imagination. Railroad news was reported daily, miracles discovered, then announced and broadcast as little creeks were bridged or long tunnels cut. Each benchmark was celebrated with countless parades, marching bands in gold uniforms, howling gales of oration, and hosannas sung in thanks to Divine Providence and the Union Pacific.

The Winning of the West was a morality play upon a continental stage, the consummation of the central element in the national faith—the drama in which Nature was met and conquered in snow-covered passes, according to telegraphed reports hot off the presses, by engineers leading divisions of heathen Chinee laying down iron at a rate of up to eight miles in a single day. The pageant included scenes of spectacular grandeur—golden spikes and Custer's stand and cattle drives to the dusty railhead at Dodge City and Jesse James and homesteaders stringing barbed wire and range wars. Railroads were the means by which miraculous fortunes were assembled, and the building of the railroads was the odyssey from which the heaping riches of every client of Stanford White could be traced.

There were parables in the legend that would need exegesis forever after. There would be considerable debate about what actually happened, and there were disbelievers who would assert the national inheritance had been raped for the pleasures of the few. Whatever lessons might later be learned from their example, certain elements of the railroad miracle were indisputable. The most significant of these lessons was that railroads were amoral legal persons, who could never be consigned to heaven or hell for their sins or their virtues, but only to Delaware or New Jersey where their securities were probably registered. The routes of railroads were never meant to be competitive, but arrangements undertaken that would hopefully lead to monopoly. To the extent that any railroad had to compete with another, both would be ruined.

Despite advertisements to the contrary, the hauling of freight or passengers was immaterial to a railroad's success, except if it were necessary to the maintenance of the railroad's franchise—a concern of every railroad's depot clerks, but immaterial to railroad directors. Railroad prosperity depended not upon profits, but upon the excess of assets over liabilities on the balance sheet, and the excess so calculated was usually a matter of fiction—figments of an accountant's imagination. One calculation estimated that three-fifths of all costs of building the railroads was borne by the national, state, and local governments—$707 million in cash and 335 million acres in land. Against these assets delivered over by the citizens' governments, railroad companies issued mortgages on the land, mineral rights, company towns, miles of tracks and tunnels and bridges, and rolling stock. These mortgages were called railroad bonds, and in fact were systems of paper franchised by government—what ordinarily is called "money." It was the poetry of bonds that Henry Villard, journalist exemplary, took up as his study.

Once it was understood that everyone—judges, legislatures, town boomers, wheat dealers, boilermakers, cotton kings, newspapermen, ministers, and even bankers—would approve of every railroad adventure, no matter what happened, then it could be understood that railroad bonds were a kind of magic money. Bonds could be printed endlessly, issued, sold, abandoned, pooled by bulls, shorted by bears, run up or down in price at the pleasure of their creators. Bonds could earn, in interest, money that operated by magic numbers—double the investment in seven years; bonds could be defaulted, and the assets upon which they had been issued declared bankrupt, and precisely by such definitions be more valuable than the bonds upon which their creators had witlessly paid the interest due. Bonds were an invention for making money not from nature, nor from art, but from money itself, and it was a necromancy practiced exclusively by an ordained priesthood. When Henry Villard became an initiate in bonds it may have seemed an odd conversion for a respectable journalist of fabled rectitude, but the opportunities of Villard's new faith similarly dazzled most of Villard's friends—the leading men of Boston, Philadelphia, and New York. All of America, in the adventure of Winning the West, was enthralled by railroad bonds. The assets created by the national enterprise were financed by bonds floated in cascades, but entailed generations to pay the mortgages.

Although Henry Villard reported to the Bondholders Protective Committee that their Oregon Railway bonds were worthless, he returned from Oregon to New York entranced by Portland, by the Yoncalla and Willamette valleys, and by the operations he had studied in California—especially the Central Pacific. By 1876 Henry Villard had arranged to have himself appointed as receiver of Jay Gould's bankrupt Kansas Pacific Company. He then bought for himself shares at ten cents each against the assets of a railroad with empty and rusty tracks and six million acres of federal land. He added to his portfolio other bankrupt properties: the Wabash, the Missouri Pacific; the Saint Joseph and Denver; and the looted and defunct Texas Pacific, which had thirteen million acres of federal land. He bought the lost savings of widows and orphans and he sold out his shares of the Kansas Pacific at about $140 apiece, with six years bank interest due. Henry Villard, journalist, was recognized by everyone as Henry Villard, financier.

He purchased the Oregon Railway and Navigation companies he had reported as valueless and opened negotiations to connect Oregon to the Northern Pacific in a transcontinental trunkline. Since he was a rich man, he did his duty and bought *The Nation* and the *Evening Post,* journals of liberal opinion, devoted to the "advocacy of truth, regardless of party and of all other considerations." He organized "a blind pool" of forty million dollars, obtained control of the Northern Pacific, and said he would push the line through to the coast, uniting the nation from Maine to Oregon. He engaged McKim, Mead and White to design and build a grand hotel at the western terminus in Portland.

Under Henry Villard's leadership, twenty-five thousand men, including fifteen thousand Chinamen, pushed the Northern Pacific west to the Columbia River Valley. They built branches into Minnesota, North Dakota, Montana, and Washington. Villard set up "immigration bureaus" in Europe to bring the poor, hungry, and hopeless into New York and then by rail to the Northern Pacific's lands—forty-seven million acres of federal lands, which he sold to the faithful on easy terms, one-sixth cash and the balance in five equal payments.

On September 3, 1883, as the sun abandoned the coronas it cast along the mountain ridges and the long chill shadows of Rocky Mountain dusk reached out across the desert, baby Hilgard Villard touched an ordinary iron spike with his pudgy baby's hand, and the spike was then hammered down into the final tie connecting the Northern Pacific to Oregon. An artillery battery roared salutes. The head chief of The Crow, assembled with two thousand of his tribe, ceded his Nation's ancient hunting grounds to Henry Villard's railroad. Cheers were shouted by the assembled Chinee, a brass band struck up, and champagne from Bavaria was popped open and passed all around.

As Henry Villard smiled and nodded and shook hands with ministers of Great Britain, Germany, and the Austrian Empire, with seven governors assembled, with flocks of judges, senators, representatives, mayors, and newspapermen reporting the great event, only Villard knew that his Northern Pacific, his Oregon Transcontinental, and all his subsidiaries were bankrupt. Only Villard knew all his bonds were worthless, and that Henry Villard was broke.

The complex of houses—the Renaissance palace on Madison Avenue always called the "Villard houses"—designed for him by McKim, Mead and White, had to be purchased by Mr. and Mrs. Whitelaw Reid for $400,000 to satisfy Villard's creditors.

He sold them unoccupied to the Reids, a family also preoccupied with journalism and finance, and Stanford White decorated and furnished them for Mrs. Reid.

Henry Villard sailed for Berlin in 1884 to recover from his reverses, but his bankruptcy was, in its way, his consecration in the priesthood of money. He would return to New York within a few years with a new insight. He would repeat his former successes all over again, even improve on them, including regaining control of his Northern Pacific, but he had learned that he never need go bankrupt himself while serving the magic illusions of money. He would once again be president of the Northern Pacific, and it would once again default its bonds, but Henry Villard would emerge unscathed. He would be president of the Edison Electric Company, and the General Electric Company, and his private brokerage firm of Decker, Howell & Company, and they would all go under, and Henry Villard would smile and be praised for his contributions to the American Museum of Natural History and to Harvard.

What he had learned was significant, and simple, but understood by only a few: Under the laws of the United States of America—particularly by interpretation of the Fourteenth Amendment and the laws of the State of New York and the City of New York—corporations could be bankrupted endlessly, their bonds defaulted regularly; indeed, the legal fictional person of a corporation could commit any crime whatever without penalty. According to the laws of the land, Henry Villard as a director of a corporation could never be held responsible for more than a limited liability for his corporation's actions, and his corporations could, like angels, dance by the thousands on the head of a pin.

The city of New York became the place where corporations preferred to perform their dances. It was the temple in which the magic of money was best understood, the stage on which it was easiest to earn the applause of newspapers, and except for the comedy exchanged between Tweed's successors and Reform's buffoons, no laws of any kind to limit the results of illusory bonds were even discussed, not by serious men.

CHAPTER SIX

GROWING UP IN PITTSBURGH:
Harry K. Thaw

"I AM HARRY THAW of Pittsburgh," he would say, as if he meant to signal to the discerning a host of associations. He was the son of William Thaw who had died in Pittsburgh after accumulating a fortune in coal mine leases, franchises in railroad feeder lines from minehead to hearthpit, and extraordinary success with his capitalized stocks and bonds, and maneuvers, in the Pennsylvania Railroad.

His son, Harry Thaw, remembered the summer of 1877 when the Great Strike was called against all the eastern trunk railroads. The railroad corporations had declared a 10 percent wage cut for all employees. With the support of a huge army of hungry and desperate unemployed men, the strike developed into what appeared to many as a general national rebellion.

In Pittsburgh there were pitched battles between troops of the Pennsylvania National Guard and the mob, and order could not be restored until the President of the United States sent federal troops. For three days Pittsburgh was a battleground. Scores of men died, one hundred sixty locomotives were burned, and every railroad shed put to the torch. From the Thaws' palace on Beechwood Boulevard they could see a wall of flame almost three miles long down by the river. Foreign agitators were said to have been responsible. Young Harry Thaw remembered that many shareholders of the Pennsylvania Railroad "became alarmed," and when the stock had been driven down to twenty-five, his father "bought all in sight day after day." William Thaw made a fortune in the Pennsylvania Railroad, and his son Harry was the beneficiary of forty million dollars in bonds.

Evelyn Nesbit said that long before she even met Harry Thaw a bitter hatred of Stanford White "seethed in the weird, unfathomable labyrinth of Thaw's brain." Actually, said Evelyn, it all started with the party Frances Belmont had told the girls about backstage at *Floradora.* Harry Thaw was going to invite the men to the private dining room at Sherry's, and Frances had picked out the girls. After the show on the night before the party Frances walked into Sherry's main floor with her boyfriend Frank Crowninshield, who would be editor of *Vanity Fair.* They passed a table where Harry Thaw was drinking with some of his society friends.

Frances said hello, but Thaw snubbed her, turned his head away, and looked off into space, pretending he didn't know her. Frances had an Irish temper and always believed she was at least a duchess in the natural aristocracy, and she was furious.

Before the show the next night, the night the dinner was to take place, Frances told everyone backstage the story of Thaw's snub, called Thaw every name she could think of, and plotted revenge. All the girls agreed that Mr. Harry Thaw from Pittsburgh could not be very sure of his social position if he was afraid to talk to a chorus girl in front of his smart-set friends. Frances gathered about her the girls she had invited to Harry Thaw's party, and they worked out their plan.

When the curtain came down at the end of *Floradora,* Thaw took his men guests to the private dining room at Sherry's. They were supposed to wait there for Frances and her girls to change after the show. Thaw had arranged carriages to bring them over. While Thaw and his friends dawdled at Sherry's, and the orchestra played, there was no sign of Frances or her girls. Harry Thaw's hired waiters stood around, and Harry Thaw's champagne started turning flat in its buckets. When midnight had come and gone Harry Thaw told his friends he'd telephone to see what the trouble could be. He phoned all over town, trying to locate Frances and her girls. In vain.

Frances Belmont had stood him up. She took her girls to the Tower at Madison Square Garden, where Stanford White served them a grand supper, and they all got quite drunk and did a lot of singing. The next day everyone on Broadway had heard about it. By the end of the week *Town Topics* printed the whole story, playing up Stanford White as the hero of the evening and portraying Harry Thaw as a fool: "Floradora beauties sing for their supper in White's studio, while Thaw's orchestra fiddles to an empty room at Sherry's."

According to Evelyn, from that day on, Harry Thaw hated Stanford White. Not much later, in January, 1902, *Floradora* moved from the Casino Theatre to the New York Theatre, and flowers began to pour into Evelyn's new dressing room. The flowers came with a card signed "Mr. Monroe," but none of the girls backstage could tell Evelyn who the mysterious Mr. Monroe might be. There was much curiosity about his identity because the flowers were spectacular: masses of American Beauty roses, milk-white gardenias, and every variety of orchid—mauve orchids, purple orchids, green and yellow orchids. Sometimes there were fifty-dollar bills in the envelope with the card from "Mr. Monroe."

At about the same time one of the girls—Elba Kenny—began to press Evelyn with an invitation to take tea at Rector's at four in the afternoon. Evelyn said she thought Elba Kenny's invitation a strange one because Rector's would be deserted at that hour, but Elba kept asking her, and Evelyn finally accepted.

Rector's was practically empty as Evelyn and Elba sat there fiddling with their teacups. Then a man came up to their table and asked if he could join them. Elba Kenny stammered introductions, and he revealed that he was the mysterious Mr. Monroe. He sat down without either of them actually asking him to.

He appeared to be in his thirties. He was tall, with coarse black hair combed almost straight back, and he was clean-shaven. He had a short, wide nose, and Evelyn thought his eyes had a wild look—"he glared," she said. There was something about him that was frightening. He spoke in short, clipped sentences. "He talked so rapidly that I could barely understand half of what he said."

Mr. Monroe told her she was the prettiest girl in New York, and when Evelyn played modest, saying she knew lots of girls just as pretty, he insisted on it. His insistence was peculiar—not so much a flattery as a demand. He said that if she didn't believe she was the prettiest girl in New York, she was a fool. He glared at her when he said fool—as if he wanted to get into an argument over it. He seemed to want her to admit: Yes, I am the prettiest girl in New York. When she would not submit, he abruptly announced that he was not Mr. Monroe at all. "I am Harry Thaw of Pittsburgh."

Backstage, she'd heard plenty about Harry Thaw of Pittsburgh, and she thought that in person he was too eccentric for her taste. She got ready to leave. As she stood and offered her hand, he remained seated, refusing to take it, and said: "Why does your mother permit you to know that beast?"

"What on earth are you talking about?" Evelyn demanded. "What beast?"

"Stanford White!"

Evelyn ignored him and excused herself. As she swept out of Rector's she saw that Elba Kenny stayed, playing with her teacup. Evelyn guessed that Harry Thaw had paid Elba to get her to Rector's. Backstage Evelyn told the other girls she liked Harry Thaw even less than she did his reputation.

But Harry Thaw continued to hang around the theater, sending flowers and invitations, polite at first, then increasingly insistent. Unable to get by the stage door, Harry Thaw turned up at the Wellington Hotel "to pay a call," as he put it, upon Evelyn and her mother. He came on several afternoons, but each time Evelyn would hide in the bedroom, and her mother always told Mr. Harry Thaw that Evelyn was out. Once Frank Crowninshield saw Harry Thaw enter the Wellington, demanding to see Evelyn, and Crowninshield apparently told Stanny about it, but Stanny just shrugged his shoulders.

When Evelyn repeated to Stanny the story of the tea at Rector's and the Mr. Monroe who was really Harry Thaw, Stanny recalled that Mrs. Hamilton Fish had brought Harry Thaw to one of his supper parties at the Tower. They had come uninvited and created a rude little scene, which was largely Mrs. Fish's fault, but Stanny said that Harry Thaw was well known along both Fifth Avenue and Broadway. He told Evelyn to keep away from him. "He's a bounder, and worse."

Thaw announced to everyone, "I am Harry Thaw of Pittsburgh," as if an heir to forty million dollars in Pennsy bonds was entitled to at least a mental genuflection—as if the Pennsylvania Railroad in some self-evident way could confer grace upon nature, and as if it should be obvious that a society devoted to money would honor those baptized at their birth in money's blessings. Harry Kendall Thaw was born February 12, 1871, in Pittsburgh, Pennsylvania, in Lyndhurst, his family's castle out on Beechwood Boulevard—Pittsburgh's own Fifth Avenue.

Evelyn Nesbit—who was also from Pittsburgh, but a different Pittsburgh from that of the Thaws—could remember that as a child her mother's boardinghouse was not so far from Beechwood Boulevard, and that as a young girl she had watched the carriages of the mysterious rich roll by. She remembered catching a glimpse once of what must have been a rich lady settled back against her cushions, gazing out from behind the curtains of her carriage, her matched pair of gray horses jingling in harnesses of silver and gold, her carriage box painted with what must have been her own coat of arms, and sitting up on the box, her own footmen dressed up in her own livery.

Evelyn could recall walking on a Sunday along the avenues of the rich, where there were ornate street lights, and the avenues were lined with trees. She had seen long driveways curving through the gates up to the castles of success. She remembered how each castle had its gardeners, who could be seen trimming the green lawns and clipping the hedges and weeding the flower beds and digging—there was always a gardener digging something—along the landscaped edges of the gravel walks.

The castles were surrounded by walls of Allegheny granite, or maybe a wrought-iron fence as much as nine feet high. After the Homestead strike there were guards posted at each castle's gate—men in blue or brown uniforms with leather belts and guns and sometimes fierce dogs by their sides. Her mother told her that according to the newspapers Mr. Carnegie, and some of the others, had fixed up their fences with electricity—anyone who tried to climb over their walls would get electrocuted. Out along Beechwood Boulevard was where Mr. Andrew Carnegie and his family lived, and Mr. Henry Frick, and people like the Phippses, the Olivers, the Peacocks, the Morrisons, the Lovejoys, the Thompsons, and Mr. Andrew Mellon, and the William Thaws.

Within walking distance of the Thaw's castle "Lyndhurst," were the boarding houses on Cedar Avenue and South Highland Avenue in which Evelyn and her mother had scrubbed and scoured and dreamed of escape. From beyond the guarded gates of landscaped Edens, the Nesbits had admired the rewards of Pittsburgh's success in oil, coal, iron, steel, and Pennsy bonds. Unfortunately, the Nesbits were also only a few steps from the mills on the South Side, from which they could always hear thumping and crackling and clanging, the incessant din of the poor condemned to their labors.

Trains were being made up, or sorted out, their couplings crunching into each other as they were rammed together. Cranes were being swung up and over, screeching along their rails. The hearths were constantly being bunkered down or charged back up, their steam hissing and coiling in displays of vicious anger. The rumbling and wailing, the sirens and whistles, went on around the clock, day and night.

When the sun went down, a rosy glow was cast up against Pittsburgh's surrounding mountains, flickering against the ridgelines and along the shoulders of the valleys. Even from the East End, the Nesbits could see more than a mile of the Monongahela River catching the images from fifty stacks of open-hearth furnaces and reflecting them up in eerie, pulsating oranges and reds. Down at the center of that infernal scene, men would be discharged in battalions through the gates long after sunset. When the shifts changed, their sentence suspended, the men poured out, silently—as if stultified by all the clamor, passing those going in without even a nod to their fellow prisoners.

The men trooped back and forth from their gray tenements, rows of houses as grimy as they were themselves, and indistinguishable one from the next, except by number. Their tenements were uniformly three stories high, built of wood around a common courtyard, with perhaps ten apartments to the house and as many as seventy souls competing for a place at the only pump of water. After the Homestead strike, the tenements were increasingly jammed by "foreigners," men rounded up by steel-company agents, shipped in past the Statue of Liberty, unloaded like sheep from special Pennsy trains, sent to Pittsburgh as replacements for the Homestead strikers and the Homestead union men.

Foreigners and union men alike worked twelve hours a day, for about nine dollars and sixty cents a week: loading and unloading the trains in the switching yards; standing to their knees in the cinder pits; passing red-hot metal from puddlers to roughers and catchers in pools of their own sweat. It was work for the young and agile and strong because one false step meant death, or worse—a crippling injury. Every day the newspapers reported some of the accidents: "A train of hot metal, being hauled from mixing house to Open Hearth No. 2, was sideswiped by a yard engine near the 48-inch mill. The impact tilted the ladles of some of the cars and the hot metal spilled in a pool of water along the track. Antony Brosak, Constantine Czernik, and Kafros Maskar were seriously wounded by the exploding metal."

Out along Beechwood Boulevard, of course, there could not have been any way for Harry Kendall Thaw to know that Constantine Czernik had been wounded by exploding metal. Harry Thaw would say that his earliest memory of Pittsburgh was the winter he was four and looked into the fireplace in Mrs. Herron's drawing room "when my mother and she started the Pittsburgh Poor Association." The Thaws of Pittsburgh were intimate friends of the Scotts of the Pennsy and the Carnegies of Steel, and like their peers, the Thaws accepted with a practiced modesty the praise of Pittsburgh's newspapers for their generous endowments of art and education. The Thaws were the source of scholarships in science at Princeton and Harvard, and after Mr. William Thaw died, Mrs. Thaw was frequently noted for her good works in church charities. She did her very best to involve her daughters

Margaret and Alice Cornelia Thaw in such charities, and to require of her sons—Josiah, Edward, and Harry—at least the appearance of piety.

Mrs. William Thaw would recall that Harry had been a difficult pregnancy for her, that he seemed normally healthy until he was three months old but then had an attack "of congestion of the lungs, involving the brain." He was a very nervous child, his mother said, often troubled with sleeplessness, and he would sometimes go without sleep for "so long a time on a stretch that he would wear out both his nurses and myself."

His mother recalled that from the age of three Harry "was of very frail appearance." When he ran she thought he had "an unsteady gait." When he was excited she described how he would scream loudly and throw himself on the floor, and his "forehead would become very much flushed, and he would hide his face on a couch." His mother said he had these "periods of excitement" until he was twelve or thirteen years old, that his attacks occurred frequently, and "almost anything would make him nervous." The family's doctor, Dr. Charles Francis Bingamon, agreed the boy had "a neurotic temperament," and Dr. Bingamon recalled that Harry once had "an attack of Saint Vitus' dance lasting four weeks."

On Harry's first day at kindergarten he screamed until he was taken home, "although," he would remember, "I saw a very fine layer cake which I was to have for my lunch." The next winter, January, 1877, he was entered in Mrs. Belle Morehouse Lawrence's private school for his first years in the elementary grades. Mrs. Lawrence would recall that Thaw seemed to have a language of his own, that at first his speech "was absolutely unintelligible," but that she was eventually able to understand him. There was hardly a day when he didn't cause a scene. The classroom would be quiet and peaceful, when Harry would suddenly jump up and run around the room "with a fixed stare in his eyes." He would scream for no apparent reason or crawl under a desk, refusing to come out. Mrs. Lawrence would have to pick him up bodily, carry him to the bathroom, and pour cold water on his head and wrists.

From Mrs. Lawrence's school, Harry was sent at ten to a boarding school in Lititz, Pennsylvania, owned and run by Mr. Abram Beck. At the time, according to Mr. Beck, there were fifteen boys enrolled in his school, and he remembered Harry Thaw as mostly "sullen, unreasonable, and unhappy." Harry Thaw said Mr. Beck's school was "barren" and that he was homesick and wanted to go home to his mother's house. His mother took him back.

At fifteen Harry was sent to Wooster College in Ohio, a strict Presbyterian school, because his mother thought that might be just the thing for her son. He was boarded with the family of the Reverend Dr. Davis, who had courted Mrs. William Thaw's favor for the good works of the church. While at Wooster, Harry paid the girls of a visiting leg show in town to wear garters in Wooster's school colors, a prank that outraged the Reverend Dr. Davis. Harry again said he was homesick and again returned to his mother's house.

In due time Harry Thaw was enrolled in the University of Pittsburgh, and he announced he would indeed study law, but since he lived at home, his father could see that his studies took none of his time. In fact, Harry apparently was not inclined to work for long at anything. He was, in his father's opinion, "an idler," and when Harry's father died and the will was read, his father's opinion from beyond the grave was reasonably clear: "with great regret and reluctance and solely from a sense of duty, I hereby cancel and revoke any and all provisions of my said will directing payment of money or property to my said son, Harry Kendall Thaw."

Instead of an inheritance Harry Thaw was to have his money managed by a trust fund "for his maintenance during his minority," and then when he was twenty-one, the trust was to pay him no more than $2,400 a year at $200 per month for the rest of his life. If his father had planned to guard Harry against folly by having a trust dole out the money, it soon turned out in practice that the trustees would always see it as their duty to do whatever Mrs. William Thaw wished. Mother Thaw soon raised her son's allowance to a more comfortable $80,000 a year.

From the University of Pittsburgh, Harry was sent off to

Harvard, where, he said, he studied "poker." He also would admit he drank "a good deal," went to cockfights in Cambridge, wrote a poem to a girl that was published in the *Lampoon,* and chased a cab driver down North Avenue in Cambridge with a shotgun, because said Harry, the driver had cheated him. Harry Thaw claimed the shotgun was not loaded and that it was not his fault the driver didn't know that. Having been presented with charges reported as "moral turpitude," President Eliot later gave Mr. Harry Thaw of Pittsburgh three hours to pack.

Back in Pittsburgh once again, Harry Thaw continued his study of poker. One of his games of five-card draw became a legend because it went on without interruption for sixty hours, and the stakes were reported to run into the tens of thousands of dollars. Harry insisted he came out a winner, and said he kept a couple of uncashed checks from the settlement, "as souvenirs." He claimed he never again played poker "seriously," except with John W. ("Bet-a-Million") Gates, Tom Scott, president of the Pennsylvania, "and with the Carnegies," in their castle in Scotland.

He spent a summer riding through his family's sixty thousand acres of ranchland in North Dakota. He spent a winter trying to start a polo club with some friends in Pittsburgh. With another group of friends he was a founder of the Allegheny Country Club, and they were successful at building a golf course for themselves in Homewood Park. His mother took Harry and his younger sister Alice Cornelia Thaw on a tour of Europe in the summer of 1892. They believed that they had been to all the best places.

When he was not in Pittsburgh, Harry Thaw spent a good deal of his time at what he called "studying" in New York. His electives included a fight in Mollie's with Jim Hall, an Australian middleweight. Harry explained that his friend Morris Carnegie liked to go around hitting people first, with no warning, and Harry tried imitating Morris Carnegie, but Harry Thaw was not a success at barroom brawling. In one case he got knocked cold by a bartender who conked him on the head with a bottle. By 1894 Harry decided he was bored with "studying" and that he would travel. He sailed in December from New York for London; he was almost twenty-four, and he would continue his education in Europe.

"I'm Harry Thaw of Pittsburgh," he would say, and it often was good enough as an introduction. At Christmas in London he had dinner with Sir George Lampson, financier of London's merchant banking society. There were several other stockbrokers there, Harry recalled, and Harry advised them all to buy shares in Canadian Pacific. "They never got over it," said Harry, "for it rose and rose."

His American dollars were the only *passeport* he needed, and he went on tour to Vienna, Budapest, Bucharest, Varna, and Constantinople. He sailed by steamship back through the Greek islands to Cairo, then to Naples and to Rome. Fortunately, in Rome he discovered the Phippses from Pittsburgh were also stopping at the Quirinal, and after running into them, Harry Thaw said his tour of Europe was "a round of meeting with friends in different places."

He attended endless dinners and excursions and teas, although, as Harry explained, "no one actually drank tea." A bicycle-drive-lunch was given by J. J. Van Alen, which Harry thought was grand fun. "Lady Mary Montague," Harry reported, "was lovely—she and her sister used to drive around in Prince Colonna's carriage."

Harry filled his diary with the details of pointless excursions, and if "pointless" seemed a pejorative judgment of his aimless sorties such a judgment would have mistaken the reasons for his hegira. Harry Thaw was enjoying the fruits of his inheritance, and since there was no "point" to it all, and there never would be any point to its mysterious anointment, he therefore traveled from Rome to Monte Carlo, then on to Spain, and to Seville for the fiesta. "All sorts of Andalusians bring you into their tents and they really had charming entertainments, but you must not eat cooked food for they use some cheese for everything." In Seville he had the good luck to meet up with the Duc and Duchesse d'Uzes, "who were so cheerful," and at the end of the fiesta in Seville he went off to Tangiers with them.

From Tangiers he traveled back through Madrid to Paris, where he attended the races at Longchamps and at Auteuil, and dinners. "And no matter if a hundred or alone," said Harry Thaw, "dinner is worthwhile." He had dinner with Lady Randolph Churchill—she was the daughter of Leonard Jerome of New York, and though she was in mourning, "she was charming." He ate with Count Boni de Castellane and his wife Anna—she was the daughter of the "Mephistopheles of Wall Street," Jay Gould—and though she was furious most of the time at her wastrel husband, "she was charming." From Paris he went to London again, then Hamburg, then Saint Moritz. He spent five years on tour "completing his education," which consisted for the most part of dinners and banquets and balls, in Europe and in New York, among heirs like himself of America's empire.

He said he fell in love in Paris in 1896 with a poor French beauty—Augustine—but he left her to tour Russia, or to climb Swiss mountains, or whatever. His love for her "might have lasted forever," he said. When he left her, he noted with a certain pride, at the end of their affair, "she had all sorts of money." With an equal intensity, he also grieved the death of his butler Drews in Rome in 1898, and he buried Drews, he noted with a certain pride, in the Roman cemetery where Shelley and Keats were also buried.

By 1900 he could number among his friends Lady Churchill and General Brackenbury, the Marquis and Marquise Rudini, the Count and Countess Potocki, Prince Egon von Furstenburg, Baron Rothschild of Vienna, Prince Radziwill of Berlin. Every one of them had bought into American railroad bonds or married into their American securities.

In Paris, Harry Thaw gave a dinner for his friends, and among his celebrated guests were Mrs. Potter Palmer from Chicago, Mr. and Mrs. Townsend Burden from New York, Mrs. Arthur Paget, the Vicomte Charles de la Rochefoucauld, the William Burdens, the Bradley Martins, and Lord Lonsdale. Every one of them had a house on Fifth Avenue; that they were in Paris was, more or less, an accident of their occupation. At Harry Thaw's dinner the band was John Philip Sousa's, playing "The Red, White and Blue," and "Stars and Stripes Forever," and Harry thought "Sousa's own 'Overture' and the *William Tell* 'Overture' were played with remarkable vigor, and Liszt's *Second Rhapsody* lifted the roof off, as it were."

In Paris, Harry Thaw gave another kind of dinner, and he would always deny the exaggerated accounts of its extravagance with a proud smile. He would never admit it had cost him anything near fifty thousand dollars; he would characterize as exaggeration invitations to one hundred beauties of the stage; he had certainly not spent seven to eight hundred dollars for jewelry to be set beside each beauty's plate. He had to admit, of course, there was perhaps a "beauty" dinner; there were perhaps a number of the most beautiful demimondaines present; each one did perhaps find some small "favor" in the napkin on her plate. Yes, Harry Thaw, would admit, he was the only man present.

In New York he could not deny that he had tried to ride a horse into the Union Club after he had been refused membership. He admitted he had perhaps driven an automobile through the display window of a shop whose salespeople had affronted him—it was just a good joke and he had paid all the damages. It made for topical conversation at the dinners he attended in New York, "with all the better people": the Lispenard Stewarts, Miss Mabel Gerry, the Harry Havemeyers, Mrs. Towney Burden, Jimmy Cutting, Jimmie Gerard, Mrs. Hermann Oelrichs, Mrs. William Astor, Mrs. Ollie Belmont, Mrs. "Corneel" Vanderbilt—the society of Fifth Avenue.

Along Broadway there was also the story that Harry Thaw of Pittsburgh was being sued by one Ethel Thomas for thirty thousand dollars in damages, the suit alleging that Thaw had enticed Miss Thomas to his apartment at the Bedford Hotel, locked the door, and beaten her with a dog whip until her clothes hung in tatters. And along Broadway there was a rumor that Susie Merrill provided girls in her brothel on the West Side for Harry Thaw to whip. But at the turn of the century there was often that sort of gossip in New York about anyone who had a few dollars to his name, most of it malicious, and a great deal of it nothing but attempted blackmail. Harry Thaw's reputation might be explained as "apparently no exception."

In April, 1903, the most notorious story about the Thaws

of Pittsburgh was the gossip of Harry's sister Alice, and her marriage to His Grace, the Earl of Yarmouth. His Grace had arrived in the United States in 1899 and gone directly to Newport to spend the summer with Mrs. Astor, as her protégé. Mrs. Astor found His Grace "charming" and saw to it that he "got around" to the dinners in New York during the winter of 1900-1901. At the dinners to which he was invited, His Grace often explained he was busy organizing a new theatrical company. In fact, his time on Broadway was spent as an actor in Frohman's stock company under the stage name of Eric Hope. His Broadway salary paid for the costumes he needed when he was invited for dinner on Fifth Avenue.

At one such dinner His Grace met Harry Thaw of Pittsburgh. His Grace was delighted to discover what a charming companion Harry Thaw could be. His Grace was also surprised to learn that Harry had an unmarried sister, Miss Alice Cornelia Thaw. According to Harry, Alice had not got about much in society because she had steadfastly associated herself with her mother's charitable and church work. His Grace had the good luck to be on the very same train leaving Washington for Palm Beach that Alice Thaw and her mother had booked, and in no time at all it was said that His Grace had won Alice's heart. In any case the Earl of Yarmouth was an acquisition that both Harry and his mother apparently thought might do.

When the engagement was announced of Miss Alice Thaw to His Grace, the Earl of Yarmouth and heir to the title of Marquis of Hertford, Miss Alice's two other brothers—Josiah and Edward Thaw—were understood to be enraged, but Harry stood by her. His Grace sent a solicitor from London to help arrange the financial settlement and the contracts of marriage, and the solicitor made what seemed to everyone, including Mrs. Thaw's lawyers, a suitable arrangement. Unfortunately, His Grace was arrested in Pittsburgh on a writ from a London court for a debt of three hundred pounds sterling on the very morning of the wedding.

The warrant, of course, had been served beyond its effective jurisdiction, but the Earl said he had little choice but to ask for more cash in advance—to settle some similar matters that were pressing. He upped his price to over one million dollars, and he refused to appear at the church until a new agreement was signed.

By the time the new agreement could be drawn up, by the time all the lawyers were satisfied, by the time the new contract was actually signed and then witnessed and notarized by all interested parties thereto, the ceremony at the church was late starting by forty-five minutes. Guests and bride alike were forced to dawdle until business was finished. The last-minute delay, the new demands, the sheer affront of His Grace in keeping guests and bride waiting, so incensed Harry Thaw that he refused to give his sister away as they had rehearsed. Before the ceremony began he stalked out and took the train for New York, explaining that he had "some business to attend to."

The scandal of Miss Alice Cornelia Thaw and her marriage to His Grace, the Earl of Yarmouth, was gossip for a day or two during April, 1903, but forgotten soon enough because, perhaps, it was understood that what the Pennsy had joined in holy matrimony, no man could put asunder.

CHAPTER SEVEN

ILLUSIONS OF OPPORTUNITY:
"I Want You, Honey, Yes I Do"

"NO MARRIAGE OF THE ORIENT where brides were merchandise ever presented so bewitching a picture," said Joseph Pulitzer's New York *World.* Between 1900 and 1910 nine million immigrants arrived in the land of golden opportunities, but Pulitzer's *World* was reporting a special day. The *S.S. Baltic* docked in New York with an unusual cargo of 1,002 unmarried maidens looking for husbands. They were met by a fine band, which played "I Want You, Honey, Yes I Do," and by reporters from all the newspapers, and the girls had their pictures taken. It was exciting and grand fun, and a thoroughly charming story.

"They just stood there," the *World* reported, "fascinated by their first glimpse of the New World. . . . colleens from Ireland, lasses from Scotland, maidens from Wales, girls from England and blondes from Scandinavia, rosy, dimpled and roguish-eyed, marriageable every one."

All their pictures showed them smiling. Miss Ann McGirr from Edinburgh said she wanted a man with dark hair: "A city man? No, a farmer. A man who is making one thousand dollars a year will do. That isn't too much to ask in this country is it? How old? Thirty. He has some sense by then."

The *World* reported all the girls could "cook, sing and play the piano, scrub, take care of a house and mind children, milk cows, raise chickens, weed garden beds, go to market, sew, patch and knit, make cheese and butter, pickle cucumbers, and drive cattle."

"I like tall men and blonds," Susan Thompson said. "I have read much about Americans making good husbands," and then her companions all screamed, and Susan laughed with them until she could hardly speak.

"They tell me," said Nellie O'Brien from Loch Crae, Tipperary, "that there are no men in Pittsburgh but millionaires. I am going there, and it's soon I'll be riding in my own carriage, I suppose."

CHAPTER EIGHT

PRINCESS PRO TEM

IT TURNED OUT that the business Harry Thaw had in New York—the excuse he gave for abandoning his sister's wedding in April, 1903—was actually at Mrs. DeMille's school in Pompton Lakes, New Jersey, just outside the city. He had discovered Evelyn Nesbit's residency there and bombarded Mrs. DeMille with flowers and gifts, ingratiating himself to such an extent that Mrs. DeMille came around to Evelyn for a serious talk. "This wealthy young man is madly in love with you, Evelyn. He tells me he wants to marry you." Evelyn said she was afraid of Harry Thaw, that there was something about him "that almost scares me to death."

By April, 1903, Evelyn had been at Mrs. DeMille's school for a term of approximately seven months, and her diary reported the subsequent events approximately as follows: she said that one morning as she was about to report for classes she was seized by a savage attack of abdominal pains. Dr. Colfax was called from the village of Pompton Lakes to attend her, and he drove over to the school's infirmary in his buggy. The school also telephoned Evelyn's mother at the Algonquin Hotel, who in turn called Stanford White, and in his turn White phoned Dr. Nathaniel Bowditch Potter, who went to Pompton Lakes by train with Dr. John B. Walker.

It seems that while Evelyn was at Mrs. DeMille's school, Harry Thaw had also made friends with Evelyn's mother. When the news of Evelyn's spasms reached Mrs. Nesbit at the Algonquin, she not only telephoned Stanford White, but also called Harry Thaw, explaining she was desperate to reach her daughter's bedside. "Let me take you out to the school," said Thaw to Mrs. Nesbit. "If I cannot arrange for a special train, we will drive there together in my motorcar."

The last thing Evelyn remembered before succumbing to the ether was her mother, Mrs. DeMille, white-robed doctors and nurses all standing around her bed, and Harry Thaw on his knees beside the operating table, kissing her clenched hands. Then blankness. If any child was born that day to an eighteen-year-old mother, no one seemed to remember it, and every doctor in attendance agreed that Evelyn Nesbit had probably had an attack of "acute appendicitis."

When consciousness returned, the thing Evelyn would remember was Stanny sitting at her bedside, saying, "Poor kiddie, poor little kiddie." After consultation with her doctors, Stanny arranged to have her moved from Mrs. DeMille's to a private sanatorium in New York. In the city Evelyn was much happier. Visitors came to see her in an endless stream during her confinement, and Stanny had a telephone installed in her room—a rare luxury.

While she recuperated, Stanny and Harry Thaw visited her continually, but somehow managed never to meet at her bedside. "When one visited me in the afternoon," Evelyn said, "the other came after dusk." Harry Thaw was so careful of his behavior that she began to doubt all the stories she had heard about him. She thought Harry had "a rare characteristic: a sudden, charming, and completely disarming smile." She told him she liked his wrists and hands—he said he thought his wrists should be thicker, but she said she liked them as they were.

Harry Thaw saw to it she had everything she might want. He paid the famous Oscar Tschuerke of the Waldorf to stand ready day or night to satisfy Evelyn's "wildest gastronomic whim." He presented Evelyn's day nurse with a Tiffany diamond brooch. When Dr. Potter estimated that Evelyn had recovered sufficiently to leave the sanatorium Harry Thaw suggested a sea voyage as a program of recuperation—a trip to Paris: no dancing, no theatrical work, no parties until she was strong again, and then a grand tour of Europe. Evelyn's mother objected; she still did not like Thaw's reputation and they had done very well under Mr. White's wing. But

Evelyn countered, "What difference does it make, Mamma? We'll stay in Europe until I am well again. Then we can come back to New York and I'll get a job in some show."

Evelyn and her mother were already aboard the *S.S. New York* in May, 1903, about to sail with Harry Thaw for Paris, when Stanny came to see them off. At the last moment Stanny gave Evelyn a letter of credit drawn on Cook's for five hundred dollars—as a bon voyage gift or in case an emergency arose and she might need it.

In Paris, Evelyn and her mother discovered that instead of putting them up at a hotel, Harry Thaw had rented an apartment in the Avenue Matignon. The apartment was divided into two sections by a large salon, decorated in the style of Louis Quatorze. Evelyn and her mother were to occupy a suite of two rooms separated by a bathroom at one end, and Harry Thaw and his valet, the ubiquitous Bedford, occupied the suite on the opposite side, next to the kitchen. Mrs. Nesbit had expected they would be living in a hotel by themselves, and Evelyn had to argue with her—Evelyn told her mother she was being too straitlaced, and they should try to enjoy Paris.

Harry Thaw was willing to take them wherever they wanted to go, and with Harry's money to spend, they soon would have exchanged Paradise for Paris. Mother and daughter shopped every day along the Rue de la Paix. They swept up closets of clothes and discovered scarves that would match and tried on shoes and hats that were just perfect. They had linens and laces and silks spread out before them and brought to the sunlight for an examination of their colors. They tested soaps and powders and bath oils, and perfumes that made them blush. As they left the little shops, always promising to return, they would have the doors to the street held open for them, because it was understood that *"La Bébé"* was *la protégée* of an American from Pittsburgh and the other one was her mother.

The clothes Evelyn had in profusion, the new costume she could choose each night, the brooches and necklaces and rings she wore like spangles, led her to the serious study of menus at Voisin, La Pérouse, Le Petit Paillard, at the Laurent and the Marguery. She would stage a little drama indicating her appreciation of the dishes set down before her—making a careful selection after a long review of all the delicious possibilities, savoring the first taste of the attendant maître's presentation, deliberating long enough over its delights to create the suspense, then giving the knowing nod and receiving in return the answering bow from the staff. She played her part to the hilt, as if she were a natural princess approving once again this year her crops of milk and honey.

Mother and daughter rode through the Bois in their own carriage and acknowledged tactfully with a gloved hand the hats that were gallantly raised to them along the Champs Elysées. At the races at Auteuil or at Longchamps every Sunday mother and daughter took their seats in Harry Thaw's box and kept a loose count of how many heads turned. They were never entirely uncomfortable if they spotted a pair of field glasses trained on them. They went with Harry Thaw to the Latin Quarter, to cafés like The Dead Rat and watched with wide eyes cancans, and cakewalks, and the *apache*. Their excursions gave them just exactly the right things to talk about at the dinner parties Harry constantly arranged.

They went to Les Invalides, and took the carriage to Père-Lachaise, and spent a day at the Louvre. Evelyn said she was spellbound before the *Venus de Milo* and the *Winged Victory* —which "Stanny had taught me transcended all other sculptures." She also saw living kings, Russian grand dukes, South American millionaires, English lords, and the Aga Khan. And, more important, they all saw Evelyn and were obviously intrigued by her—they too called her *"La Bébé."* She discovered that when she made the most of her innocence to her admirers, she could make Harry Thaw insanely jealous. Soon Harry would not let her out of his sight, which was, she considered, "an infernal nuisance."

They were not in Paris for long before Harry Thaw proposed. As tactfully as possible, she told him she would never marry, that she was going to devote her life to the stage. He was flabbergasted. He claimed all sorts of women had thrown themselves at him—actresses, lonely widows, debutantes, women of all ages. "Give me a reason," he demanded, "some definite reason why you refuse to marry me! Don't you realize what marriage to me would mean? Why—if the United States were a monarchy, I would be the Prince of Pittsburgh and the Duke of Allegheny!"

She fended him off, but he would not drop it. "You can't go on like this," he argued. "Do you want people to think you are a cocotte?"

That made her laugh, and she made him see that he could laugh, too, and when he sent ambassadors to plead his case—expatriate heiresses such as Elsie de Wolfe and Elizabeth Marbury—she put them off with more laughter. But Harry kept it up, night after night. He would start to pace the floor in his pajamas and robe, biting his nails, weeping, storming, pleading, threatening. She said it really began to wear her.

Then he refused to leave the apartment for days. Food would be sent from a nearby restaurant, and the three of them would eat in a strained silence. Her mother began to loathe him, and she told Evelyn she wanted to go home. "We must get out of here," she said. "Please, please, come home, Florence—we have Stanford White's five-hundred-dollar letter of credit."

Evelyn protested. They hadn't seen London yet, or Berlin, or Vienna. She didn't want to go home. Despite Thaw's "peccadilloes," she was having a marvelous time. He was odd though, she had to admit that. For example, he flew into a rage when a waiter brushed crumbs from the tablecloth. One night he jerked the tablecloth off the table, showering the dishes and food and wine all over the floor, shrieking, *"Arretez, arretez, arretez!"* Another night when they were having supper at the Café de Paris and Evelyn had gone to the ladies' room, he stood guard at the entrance and gave a huge bribe to the woman attendant so that "no strange woman could talk to her."

If Harry saw another man looking at Evelyn in admiration, he would charge at the poor fellow and start a fight. One day in the apartment Bedford was rearranging a bowl of fruit on the table in their salon, causing Harry to fly into a fury. He broke open a package that had just arrived from the perfumer's and began throwing cakes of soap at his valet. Just as suddenly, Harry calmed down and smiled as if nothing had happened, and no one dared refer to it. Bedford quietly picked up the shattered soap.

Sometimes Harry would sit in one of the Louis Quatorze chairs for hours, biting his nails, staring off into space. Then a fit of rage would seize him. After it had passed he would suddenly drop down on bended knee, smother Evelyn's hand with kisses, and plead with her: "I'm sorry, boofuls. Her so boofuls. Please forgive." Every now and then he would disappear for the day, and when he returned he always seemed abnormally quiet and, in some strange way, relieved.

Then he would begin again the cycle of his marriage proposals. Late one night when Evelyn had been exhausted by him, he asked her in a low, hoarse voice, "Are you a good girl? Pure?"

She said she didn't understand.

"I mean, are you a virgin?"

She said she was exhausted, that she wanted to go to her room, that she had to get to sleep, that she didn't want to go on with these exasperating discussions any longer, and that she would go crazy if he continued talking like this.

He seized her by the wrists. "You've got to tell me! I won't let you go until you do!" His grip upon her wrists was hurting her, but he would not let go. "If you're not a virgin," Harry said, "we won't get married, but we'll live together. I'll always take care of you, I can't live without you, but I've got to know. I won't let you go until you tell me!"

Evelyn asked him to stop shouting—he would wake her mother. She promised to tell him everything he wanted to know.

He asked, very quietly, "Was it Stanford White?"

She said it was and began to describe how White had seduced her in the studio at Twenty-fourth Street. As she added first one detail and then another she could see Harry Thaw's eyes begin to glitter. Her story excited him. It was delivering him over to her powers.

She told her story with a new abandon and devised variations of its meaning for him. She said she could never consent to marry him because so many people knew she had been

White's mistress, that if Harry Thaw married her it would cut him off from his family. She told him she realized what a good thing it would be for her to be the wife of the Prince of Pittsburgh, but she cared so much for him that she knew marriage would not be for his own good. She emphasized what a humiliation their marriage would be for him—for everyone to know that he had married one of Stanford White's virgins.

She made him weep. He marched up and down, wringing his hands and sobbing. He kept saying, "The beast! The filthy beast! A sixteen-year-old girl!" And he pleaded with her for even more details of the studio at Twenty-fourth Street and the parties at the Tower. She obliged him with all the little things she could remember, and he would repeat, "Damn him, damn him, damn him to hell." Evelyn talked on and on, calmly, in a steady voice. Harry Thaw would remember her eyes as she talked—"as sable and soft as death."

When dawn lit the windows of the salon, they were still sitting there in their Louis Quatorze chairs. Harry's eyes were red and swollen. Evelyn was exhausted, and at breakfast her mother asked her what had gone wrong. Evelyn said she had had a quarrel with Harry, but they had patched it up. They all went to the races at Auteuil that afternoon.

Thereafter, Evelyn studied Harry's melancholia, as they continued their drives down the Champs Elysées and in the Bois, their shopping, and their rounds of suppers and parties. Then at night, after Mrs. Nesbit had gone off to bed, Harry would ask Evelyn to tell him the story again. With the appropriate reluctance, she would allow him to drag new details out of her, perhaps embroidering the tale of her ruination just a little here and there, until the illusion she created for him had him marching up and down, wringing his hands and shouting, "The filthy beast, the filthy beast!"

She tried a divertissement one night. She said he should not call Stanford White a beast, that Stanford White was different, that he could not be compared with other men, that he was above them. Her sortie threw him into the most incredible rage, and whenever he would remember what she had said—"that Stanford White was different, that Stanford White was above other men"—he would go on a rampage, even if they were in a restaurant, turning over tables, scattering dishes, smashing glasses. Fortunately, they were in Paris and such scenes could be explained; the witnesses to his outrageous behavior would whisper to each other that he was an *Américain* of Pittsburgh, crazy rich, and they would go on with their dinners, their talk, and their flirting as if they had not noticed anything of any importance. *Mais, bien entendu,* all rich Americans were *gauche, n'est-ce pas?*

If Harry saw a young girl on the street, he would say, "That's what you were like before you met the beast." It got so that anything might touch off his mania. Evelyn began to tire of their game, so she explained to him how much she and her mother would like to visit—just for a few days—Boulogne-sur-Mer. It would be good for them to get away. At first Harry would not hear of it, saying he wanted them to go with him to London to meet his sister Alice, the Countess of Yarmouth. He would insist upon it. But Evelyn's powers over him were growing, and she promised they would meet him in London and that she would write him twice a day. Harry said she would have to write him six times a day, to which she could easily consent, and he went off to London ahead of them.

In a shop in Boulogne Mrs. Nesbit saw some lingerie that she thought Evelyn should have. Since Evelyn had lost all the money Harry had given them for their trip by playing *petits chevaux* in the casino, mother and daughter went together to Cook's and cashed a check for two hundred dollars on the letter of credit Stanford White had given them.

They left Boulogne in a gay mood, crossed the Channel to London, and discovered that Harry Thaw had arranged for them to stay at the Claridge Hotel. He occupied a separate suite for himself at the Carlton—an arrangement of distances much to Mrs. Nesbit's satisfaction. They visited Alice Thaw in Berkeley Square, and Evelyn thought the Countess of Yarmouth bore a striking resemblance to Harry, yet there was a wistful, unhappy expression behind her eyes. Despite the illusion of a brilliant marriage, Evelyn concluded Alice Thaw had been thwarted socially, spiritually, physically, and "that she must have been a tormented soul."

Perhaps it was the result of their separate suites, but in

London, Harry seemed to be on his best behavior as once again they began a round of suppers and parties, of restaurants and shops. Harry would not let Evelyn go anywhere unaccompanied, and once again she began to tug on her leash. One afternoon she asked Harry to take them to see the famous Tower of London. He refused; he said she should be ashamed "at the very mention of a tower." Then one afternoon Harry spotted the lingerie they had ordered in Boulogne. It had finally been delivered to their suite at Claridge's and was lying there in its tissue paper on a small settee. "What's this stuff?" he demanded. "Where did it come from?"

Evelyn said they had bought it in Boulogne.

Harry said he thought they had no more money—Evelyn should remember that she had lost everything playing *petits chevaux*.

Evelyn stammered out that "Mamma had a little extra money."

Harry pursued the subject relentlessly, and when Evelyn was finally exasperated with him, she admitted they had cashed a small check at Cook's. There was soon no way to avoid explaining that Stanford White had provided them with a letter of credit. Harry demanded to see it, and he screamed and raged at Mrs. Nesbit because she was the one he assumed had hidden it from him. They finally handed over Stanny's letter, and he tore it up in pieces.

Harry then disappeared for a day. Her mother was exasperated. She shouted at Evelyn that she was sick of Harry Thaw, his tantrums and his rages, and she would never speak or have anything to do with him again. Evelyn argued that Harry would calm down, but her mother said she would stay in bed whenever he was around. Within a few days Harry suggested, "If your mother is so homesick, I will get somebody to take her home and will find you a suitable chaperone, and we can make a tour of all the cities you long to see."

Harry offered to pay for her mother's voyage. He said he had arranged to have Ida Vera Simonton accompany Mrs. Nesbit back to New York. He promised Mrs. Nesbit that he had engaged a chaperone for Evelyn, but in the meantime Evelyn could stay on at the Hotel Claridge and have everything she wanted. Mother and daughter argued about it late into the night. Her mother was adamant—they must go home together, and the time to leave was now.

The next morning Evelyn packed her bags and took them by carriage to a suite in a hotel near Oxford Circus. She moved in with Harry Thaw. They went to lunch at the Savoy, where Harry introduced Evelyn to a man Harry claimed was a well-known doctor. Evelyn asked the doctor why her hair had thinned and had started to fall out. The doctor explained it was a result of her operation for "appendicitis." According to Evelyn, it was the well-known doctor who recommended that she shave all her hair and then let it grow back again. In any case, the doctor would serve as Evelyn's excuse: "I was willing to try anything to save my hair."

Immediately after lunch Harry took her around to Clarkson's, the famous wigmaker, and Harry stood guard over her as Evelyn's copper curls fell around her on the floor. He watched until she was shaven bald. At Clarkson's they fitted her with "a gorgeous blond wig." Harry then instructed their driver to go to Tiffany's, where Evelyn waited in the cab until Harry came back with a long white leather box in his hands. It contained four diamond brooches, flawlessly matched, set in platinum, graduating in size. The cab drove them to the boat train, where they waited before boarding until the very last minute, but unfortunately the chaperone Harry had promised failed to show up. "Never mind," he said. "We'll get one in Paris."

On the French side they went straight to an apartment on the Avenue d'Antin that Evelyn said was even larger and more sumptuously furnished than their previous suite. They took up another round of theater parties and suppers. To Evelyn's relief, Harry had not mentioned Stanford White. One afternoon Evelyn saw a small oblong metal box resting on a table in their salon and, idly wondering what it could be, opened it. There was a hypodermic syringe and several needles in it. As she was staring at them Harry walked into the room.

He started a terrible row, "like a man gone berserk." He rushed into the kitchen and called Bedford every filthy name he could think of, demanding to know why the box had been left lying around. Bedford kept saying, "It's your own fault, Mr. Thaw. You left it there yourself, sir. Don't blame it on my carelessness, sir, when it's your own fault." They were yelling at each other, Evelyn said, "at the tops of their lungs."

The next morning Harry announced it was time to start their tour. They would not need Bedford with them. They went by motorcar up the Rhine, then along the Main to Munich, where they stopped for several days. They drove south by the Tagensee, pausing for a lunch of brook trout in a tiny restaurant overlooking the lake. The following day they climbed part of the Unset then went on to Innsbruck. They gave up the motorcar and went by carriage into the Austrian Tyrol, through the village of Meran, then along a valley road to the foot of a mountain, where they had to stop and continue the rest of the way on foot. "I have rented an old castle for us," Harry said, "the Schloss Katzenstein." Porters followed them, bringing their luggage up the path to the castle. Evelyn said she felt she had arrived in a dream world.

Evelyn could explore after Harry had dismissed the porters. The Schloss Katzenstein was a small castle nestled against a wooded mountainside, its towers jutting out over a romantic valley scene. From the windows of the watchtower Evelyn had a magnificent view of the village of Meran far below and of the stream that ran through the valley between mountainsides. On its way to the village the stream looked like a silver ribbon curling its way through square patches of green vineyards. The castle had a vine-covered balcony—the vines were so thick they must have been three hundred years old, and the balcony overlooked a rose garden. Evelyn discovered she would sleep in an ancient bed, high off the floor, its posts carved like the beds she had always imagined for the princesses in the fairy-tales.

They had been there a week—taking walks along the mountain paths, breathing the sharp mountain air, everything scented with pine, divorced from all reality—when late one afternoon a black thunderstorm gathered at the head of the valley. Evelyn watched it from a casement window, fascinated by the zigzags of lightning exploding on the flanks of the mountain ridge across the valley, the thunder rumbling through their castle's stone walls. They were almost alone in their magic castle—the only other humans Evelyn ever saw were the caretaker and his Frau, who cooked and served their food and banked down the fire in the hearth at night and then disappeared.

On the night the thunderstorm had passed down the valley Evelyn woke in terror. The bedcovers had been swept from her bed, and a naked Harry Thaw stood over her, tearing off her nightgown. She started to scream, but he clapped his hand over her mouth and hissed at her, "Keep quiet!" His eyes were glassy, his pupils dilated, his nose flaring, his face flushed, his lips drawn back in a thin, strange smile.

She struggled, but the more she fought, the more violent he became. He clawed at her when she tried to defend herself, his nails digging into her arms and raking them. He finally succeeded in tying her hands behind her with a strip of cloth. She had to be quiet, but she thought she still might have a chance to talk to him. Then Evelyn saw he was holding a dog whip in his right hand. Down it came. A thin stream of fire seemed to burn into her. She screamed.

At first he covered her mouth with his hand, his fingers choking her. She twisted and turned, but her body was being lined with livid welts. After a while he didn't bother trying to silence her, and she screamed and screamed and then began to cry. She begged him to stop, sobbing and pleading with him. Every few minutes he would pause but then he would begin again.

She lost track of how long she had been sobbing. She couldn't think clearly. After a while Evelyn could only whisper; she whispered promises to him—if he would only stop. He asked her to beg him for things, and she begged him for whatever he asked. He suddenly seemed to wilt, like a punctured balloon, and in a strange hoarse voice, said: "Stay there. Don't move. Don't move!"

He left the room, and while he was gone she stayed on her stomach, trembling in pain and despair, her knees drawn up into her belly, her bald head against the pillow, her eyes shut tight against the tears and whatever else was to come.

Afterward he was exhausted, and she said he seemed to be a totally different person. He dressed in his pajamas, robe, and slippers, and seemed composed and sympathetic as he untied her hands and brought her a small glass of brandy. He said she ought to drink the brandy, speaking to her as if nothing had happened. He drew the bedcovers over her bleeding body ever so gently. Tears were still streaming down her face as she fell asleep.

It would be three weeks before Harry Thaw decided they would abandon the Schloss Katzenstein. Evelyn would later say she made all sorts of plans to escape, but could not devise a way to get down the mountain without him knowing about it. Her explanation was that Harry watched her the way a cat watches a mouse. She said she had to stay in her bed, in pain and anguish, her spirit broken, for one solid week before the welts began to heal. "I suppose you hate me now," Harry said to her.

"Yes," she said, "I hate and detest you." He got down on his knees before her, and apologized and pleaded with her for forgiveness. She was very careful not to give it to him. As she recovered and her strength returned, she began to demand that he explain why he had to do these awful things. He would say he just had to. She said she didn't understand his explanation—it wasn't good enough. He would get down on his knees, and beg her to forgive him, and say, "Please, boofuls, please." But she would just smile at him from far away.

He showed her reproductions of exotic paintings of Persian and Turkish slave girls. "If we were living in ancient times," he would explain, "you would be my slave. I would be a prince and you would have to dance and serve me, wearing bracelets and anklets." Evelyn noticed how his eyes would change when he talked that way. Then he would start to bite his nails and stare off into the distance.

They finally left the Schloss Katzenstein and drove past the peak of the mountain Ortler, where Italy, Switzerland, and Germany joined; then to Santa Maria in Switzerland; and then to Zurich, to Lucerne, and up into the valleys at Interlaken, and stayed beneath its spectacular falls. It might have appeared that their continued touring gave Evelyn increasing opportunities to escape, but of course she had no money of her own. As they traveled Harry brought with him a locked bag in which he kept the reproductions depicting the slave girls of ancient times displayed on the auction block. In the bag he carried all his other paraphernalia—hypodermic needles, various kinds of drugs, and different kinds of whips.

He would decide from time to time that she had been "too impudent," and he would tie her hands and stuff a napkin or a scarf into her mouth and use the dog whip on her, or the rattan cane. On the backs of her calves the rattan cane, she discovered, was by far the worst, and every one of her screams for mercy was real.

She tried to reprove him for the cocaine, saying that if he kept on using it he would go insane. He compelled her to submit to it herself, saying she would be "impudent" if she would not and then using the dog whip until she begged him for cocaine. Actually, she liked its effects, but she feared she would lose control of Harry when he had taken the drug. On the other hand, his pleas for her absolution were always more fervent after the cocaine had in fact made him lose contact.

Toward the end of September they were back in Paris, and Evelyn had Harry doing everything he could to amuse her. He put on an incessant round of dinners, operas, theater parties, and picnics for her. They lunched in the trees at Robinson's, climbing the steps around the trunk of an ancient elm to a large platform in the lower branches where their table was set. They ate while gypsies sang love songs to Evelyn from down below. They drove through the Bois in a big blue victoria, which Evelyn insisted they should always have on call. Anything Evelyn saw in the shops was hers for the asking, and she collected treasure with a vengeance: she bought rare perfumes, a silver fox and an ermine, and real diamond buckles for her black satin evening slippers. She bought two wigs in her natural color of copper and various falls to add as her hair grew back in. One afternoon they took tea with Elizabeth Marbury and Elsie de Wolfe in their flat. Evelyn learned they were sailing on the *S.S. New York* within the week, and she got Harry to consent to allow her to join them. He said he would follow in a few weeks.

Three days after she arrived in New York, at about seven o'clock one evening, she heard once again—with a tremor of joy, she said—the familiar drumming signal of Stanford White on the door of her hotel room. Her heart almost stopped beating when she saw him standing there in the doorway, his eyebrows arched, studying her Paris outfit and her Tiffany brooches. After what seemed a long minute he came in and sat down and drew her to him. "Oh kittens," he sighed, shaking his head, "kittens, where have you been?"

During the next few weeks she told Stanny where she had been, or some of it, a little bit at a time. He began asking her to lunch and to supper parties at the Tower, but Evelyn complained that she seldom saw Stanny alone. She said several weeks passed before "we did manage to have several long talks." When she was finally able to indicate to him an approximation of what she described as her nightmare with Harry Thaw at the Schloss Katzenstein, Stanny boiled over with anger. Evelyn would have expected no less of him.

He arranged for Evelyn to hear some of the stories about Harry Thaw that were common gossip on Broadway: Harry Thaw had tied a girl to a bedpost and whipped her until she was bloody; Harry Thaw had put a girl in a bathtub and poured scalding water on her; Harry Thaw took morphine; Harry Thaw was crazy.

In addition he made an appointment for her to meet with Mr. Abe Hummel, a famous lawyer. He asked her to take with her Edna McClure—a very pretty girl he admitted he was devoted to. Stanny had also had Edna photographed by Rudolf Eickemeyer and Edna was a girl whom Harry Thaw also was attempting to see. Stanny wanted Edna McClure to hear Evelyn's testimony to Abe Hummel, Esquire.

Stanny told Evelyn and Edna that they must not be frightened when they saw Abe Hummel, that "he looked like an abortion," with a tiny little body and a very large head. He also had warts on his face. But he was a famous lawyer, and Abe Hummel would fix things, said Stanny, so that Evelyn would be spared "any further contact with that lunatic."

On October 27, 1903, Evelyn Nesbit and Edna McClure went together to Abe Hummel's office. Evelyn stared at the pictures of actresses "all over the walls," and Abe Hummel explained he "got divorces for them." He began to ask Evelyn questions about how she met Harry Thaw and how she happened to go abroad with him and about the quarrels with her mother in London and about what happened at the Schloss Katzenstein. Her answers had him shaking his head. He said it was absolutely terrible, especially since she was a minor and not of age. He said that Harry Thaw was certainly a very bad man and that he had other cases against Harry Thaw in his office. Then he sent for a stenographer.

Evelyn Nesbit, being duly sworn, said she resided at the Savoy Hotel, Fifth Avenue and Fifty-ninth Street, in the city of New York, and that she was born on Christmas Day in the year 1884. To the stenographer, she described leaving for Europe in the company of her mother in June, 1903, and she described where and when she had stayed with her mother in London and Paris. Mr. Hummel led her up to the events in a castle rented by Harry Thaw in the Austrian Tyrol, said castle known as the Schloss Katzenstein. She then described the manner and circumstances of repeated wrongs by the said Thaw.

Her affidavit was filed with the Supreme Court of the State of New York and stated that she had been repeatedly told by said Thaw that he was "very inimical to a married man whom, he said, he wanted me to injure; and that he, Thaw, would get him into the penitentiary; and the said Thaw has begged me time and again to swear to written documents which he had prepared, involving this married man and charging him with drugging me and having betrayed me when I was fifteen years of age. . . ."

For preparing the aforesaid affidavit of Miss Evelyn Nesbit, sworn to and signed by her, and containing her deposition against Mr. Harry Thaw of Pittsburgh, the partnership of Howe and Hummel, Attorneys, charged Stanford White one thousand dollars. In addition they secured from Miss Nesbit a packet of letters written by Harry Thaw, and they telephoned Mr. Thaw's attorney, Mr. Frederick Longfellow,

Esquire, informing him of their possession of Miss Nesbit's affidavit and Mr. Thaw's letters. They explained to Mr. Thaw's attorney that Miss Nesbit had said she was a minor and would not reach the age of eighteen until Christmas Day, 1903. Until then, Mr. White's attorneys pointed out, it would be in the interest of Mr. Longfellow's client to keep clear of a minor.

However, according to the testimony of her sworn affidavit, Evelyn Nesbit was already eighteen in 1903 and would be nineteen on Christmas Day. But on advice of counsel, Harry Thaw kept clear of Evelyn until after midnight on Christmas Eve, when the protection guaranteed to minor females by the laws of the State of New York would expire. Then they had supper at Rector's.

While Harry and Evelyn celebrated at Rector's, Stanford White played host at his annual Christmas Eve party in the Tower at Madison Square Garden. According to Edna McClure, who was there with him, all the famous and great of the city came to Stanny's Christmas Eve party.

ACT II

MAZE

"Did any ever, descending from that place
Where loss of hope remains their only woe,
Thread to its depth this hollow's dreary maze?"

—DANTE, *The Divine Comedy,* "Hell,"
Canto IX, lines 16 19

CHAPTER NINE

CITYSCAPE:
Theology of Illusion

BY CHRISTMAS DAY, 1903, Stanford White had lived past fifty. He was born in New York, November 9, 1853, the same year eighteen-year-old Henry Villard arrived from Germany along with nearly half a million other immigrants, and the same year William Marcy Tweed, at age thirty, completed his first term as alderman from the Seventh Ward. In 1853 the city was busy extending gaslight north of Eighteenth Street, both along the avenues and into the houses; the Croton Aqueduct was opened to bring water to the "Egyptian Reservoir" at Forty-second Street and Fifth; and the Crystal Palace was opened in the park behind the reservoir to display a continuous fair of industrial inventions. In 1853 the city was already the focus of empire, but its citizens were still faithful to the manners they had practiced in an eighteenth-century village.

Stanford White was the second son of Alexina Black Mease White and Richard Grant White, and his family were accepted members of the society of Washington Square, a community organized "uptown" in the "Village." The Whites' house at 121 East Tenth Street could be taken as typical of the style of the city's merchant aristocracy, and it stood just down Tenth Street from Grace Church, Protestant Episcopal. The solid pews in Grace Church were rented annually, and could be inherited, by Old New York's society, and the graceful spire of Grace Church was a landmark of Old New York's faith.

There were, of course, other churches in Old New York besides Grace Church. At the foot of Wall Street the spire of Trinity Church rose 294 feet. The Church of the Ascension at Tenth Street was the first church constructed on Fifth Avenue—built "uptown" in 1841. The First Presbyterian Church arrived on Fifth Avenue in 1846 between Eleventh and Twelfth streets, and the Fifth Avenue Presbyterian Church was located at Nineteenth Street in 1850. Among others, the Marble Collegiate Church, the South Dutch Reformed Church and the Church of the Transfiguration moved uptown and into the "Village" neighborhood in the 1850's. In 1853, when Stanford White was born, each church was singular because each one expressed, without doubt, the manners of a distinct congregation—the particulars of their faith and the history of their prosperity.

In 1853, each of the city's principal churches could easily be identified by its spire, rising above the rooflines that sheltered the city's other activities. Taken together, however, they were significant because halfway through the nineteenth century, church spires were still the only landmarks on the city's horizon, indicating a certain community among them all. Collectively their spires were signs of the city's theology.

Ministers were still the unquestioned arbiters of social behavior, and the faith they preached was supported from the pulpit both by general acceptance of its truth and by the strength of the ministers' personalities. The accepted faith of Old New York might be summarized as founded in duty—duty owed to God, to family, and to city. Salvation was to be achieved by performing these duties in accordance with moral imperatives, which were the virtues of temperance, fortitude, prudence, and justice.

Much the same faith had been the source of Boston's style, but in Massachusetts there seemed to be a grimness to it. In Philadelphia the articles of the same doctrine carried with them an earnest quality. In New York the lessons were applied with a certain gaiety: hymns were sung lustily and the feasts of the liturgical calendar were always celebrated with enthusiasm. The prosperity of Old New York seemed to indicate that in addition to its advantageous geography, its leading citizens might well be among God's elect. The most popular ministers in Old New York emphasized the amazing possibilities of creation, and since they had never been troubled by narrow researches, nor by spiritual struggles, nor by any morbid introspections and since progress could be seen just around the corner, Old New York's ministers could preach by example of the diversity and richness of life.

Their theology of progress assumed a society composed of the right-minded, and therefore manners were important. Although it was rarely said in so many words, the source of good manners was without question good family—a genealogical claim to distinction, reinforced by activity "for the good of the community." The women of Old New York devoted themselves to reinforcing their family's distinction by a lovely gregariousness. During Lent they met in sewing circles for the poor. On Easter Sunday they trooped from house to house with their families in tow, leaving their calling cards on silver trays set out to receive them. They organized church bazaars, and church teas, and choir practices. Their social season was calculated as beginning at Epiphany.

Entertainment was done at home in drawing rooms and at dining tables, exchanged from house to house. Although there were servants "to help out," a revelation that the recipe for the oyster stew had been handed down to the mistress of the house from an even more virtuous grandmother would carry with it an unquestioned cachet. The talk at the table was never about money because money was never discussed, and in any case, rent rolls were expected to be profitable and ships docked every day loaded to the gunwales with capital returned. The talk at the table in Old New York was about breeding horses, about a church bazaar, sometimes even about Whigs and Democrats.

The aristocracy of Washington Square allowed themselves a few moderate ostentations, but nothing that might outrage the moral imperatives of temperance or prudence. Mild luxuries such as a fine pair of horses or a quick sloop for racing down the bay might be allowed, but nothing out of scale with the determined simplicity of their faith—the source, they correctly guessed, of their success. Any actual devotion to physical beauty, even to its imitation in art, or in music, any ecstasy of any kind, was viewed with righteous suspicion. They guessed that decoration, ornament, the complex adoration of image, might be dangerous—it would smack of Rome. They admired achievement in the arts, therefore, as they would sin: at a distance. If they admitted any acquaintance to art's pleasures, they would do so only in intimate circumstances, among close friends, and then suggest they had their information by inference, or as a result of a trip to a museum, or as an incident of European travel.

But the Washington Square into which Stanford White was born lived in a deceitfully permanent present. The sexton of Grace Church, Isaac Hull Brown, had made himself useful to his congregation by becoming the social arbiter of what he imagined to be the entire city. He was a huge, gregarious man, described as "skilled at psalms, punch, and cricket." He collected a stock of intimate information from every household in the parish and then advised its ladies on whom to invite and whom to omit from their entertainments. He compiled a list of presentable young men who would appear, as necessary, in black swallowtail coats, white vests, and white cravats, prepared to eat supper and dance, and whose good manners were more or less guaranteed. But the village of New York had become a boom town, and Sexton Brown was soon complaining, "I cannot undertake to control society above Fiftieth Street."

As the city grew, its ministers could feel their control slipping. Membership in the community was no longer restricted to ownership of a pew; order in society was no longer dependent upon genealogy; and, evidently, celebrity could be substituted for manners to gain acceptance. The repetition of the Psalms, the readings from the Book of Wisdom, and the singing of hymns were being replaced by galas, extravaganzas, and balls. Dinners were being held in public places. The very progress the ministers had preached, the unlimited possibilities of life they had extolled, had expanded beyond any stable limits. The stories they had retold from the gospels were being replaced in the city's imagination by dramas presented on stages.

In 1863, when Stanford White was ten, P. T. Barnum advertised the banns of marriage between Mr. Charles Sherwood Stratton and Miss Lavinia Warren. The announcement declared they would be married in Grace Church on February 11. The society of Washington Square was scandalized; Mr. Stratton stood two feet ten inches in his socks, and he was popularly known as General Tom Thumb. His bride stood two feet eight. The newspapers reported that Commodore Nutt, Lavinia's former suitor, would serve as best man despite a broken heart. They said Lavinia had rejected Commodore Nutt for General Tom Thumb because "she could not resist the taller man."

Fifteen thousand New Yorkers sought invitations, but Barnum, acting as the father of the bride, said it would be a small family affair. He would extend only two thousand invitations to "the elite, the crème de la crème, the upper ten, the bon ton, the select few, the very first families of the city." He put a public notice in the newspapers as a warning to the frantic uninvited. "The wedding is no more a money matter than is that of any of the readers of this notice, and therefore money will not purchase wedding cards."

When Barnum's wedding carriage approached Grace Church, Broadway was blocked from Ninth to Twelfth streets by a crowd estimated at fifteen thousand. The city's police had to clear a path through barricades. As the bride was lifted down from her carriage the crowd cheered. Inside the church thousands of tulips had been banked around the altar and down the aisles. Jammed into Grace Church's pews were Astors, Vanderbilts, Belmonts, and Roosevelts, grinning recognition of each other, waiting for the wedding march. The New York *Herald* reported: "Here was the carnival of crinoline, the apotheosis of purple and fine linen. Never before was the scarlet lady seen to such advantage. Babylon was a rag fair compared to it."

The organ struck up the wedding march, and from the pews a shout went up, "Here they come!" Washington Square stood on the seats of their inherited pews to gain a better look. Mrs. Astor, only twenty-three in 1853 but already the successor to Sexton Brown in attempting to control society above Fiftieth Street, had arrived at Grace Church equipped with a stool for her pew. With some help to keep her balance, she put the stool on the pew and stood upon it. From there she could see the Reverend Dr. Thomas House Tyler give the benediction, and the general kiss his bride. From her advantageous height, Mrs. Astor could report the proceedings to her giggling fellow parishioners.

But Barnum's triumph was only a minor shock to the city's former rectitude compared to the raucous march of progress: the millions of Catholic immigrants; the extension of the roaring elevated lines; the paving over of the old skating ponds and the filling in of the brooks and meadows; the transformation of the city's landscape by steam, iron, coal, steel, and finally electricity; the introduction of telephones and elevators; the constant construction of buildings until by the turn of the century not a single church spire could be seen on the city's horizon. The faith of Old New York must have continued, guarded by a blessed remnant, but if it did, no sign of it could be seen.

The orderly society of Washington Square had to adapt itself to living and working in the shadows of canyons, to the sight of uncollected garbage, to newspapers blowing in the gutters, to paupers settled in doorways. In the incessant roar of the city, in the screech of elevated trains on a bend and the screams of sirens in the dead of night, the voices of ministers grew faint. Ministers no longer preached of life's infinite possibilities, but did the best they could to teach an abhorrence of social cruelty.

By the turn of the century the pride the city had once expressed in its own beauty was noticeably changed; the plans and maps it once habitually drew up for its future were abandoned. The gregariousness shared by the city's old congregations was transformed in the city's manners to an obvious contempt of one's neighbors. Under the impact of Tammany's administrations—or Tammany's nemesis, Reform—the administration of justice was most often presented as a spectacle of revenge. The modest dinners made from inherited recipes were supplanted by immense banquets at which hosts rivaled one another in the presentation of gluttony. The virtuous women of good family had to stand aside while young women were pursued to the extent they had a reputation for vice.

In Old New York profit was assumed to be the product of labor or genius. By the turn of the century profit was calculated from the balance sheet and was most handsomely converted when fraud accompanied the bonds issued. In Old New York, invention was praised and Science understood to bring power over Nature. By the turn of the century, especially after the discoveries of radium, it appeared as if energy might drip from every pore of matter, and Nature was increasingly feared. In Old New York the ministers had preached what they believed to be a continuous truth, a vision that had endured for at least two thousand years, and in the end a truth that would last as long as the world itself. By the turn of the century ministers had been replaced by newspaper editors as the sources of wisdom. Editors were men with habitual squints who worked in their shirtsleeves and wore green eyeshades—bitter, cynical men with manners so vicious they were fortunately never seen by their congregations.

These new ministers worked in buildings whose towers loomed high above any church spires on the city's horizon. They spoke as ancient cardinals must have spoken to a faithful numbered by the millions. Editors received their truth, however, not from any blessed text preserved over centuries, but from clattering teletype machines—an incessant rattle of printed words punctuated every so often by the sounding of the machine's little bells to announce in the midst of blather some solemn item. They tore this processed truth from their machines in swatches of paper, parsed it with sharp pencils, then sent it forth by rotary presses, arranged on a front page—a revelation that was instantaneous, and a witness that was always new.

The city which in 1853 had located its center in the mannered virtues of Washington Square and which could identify every church spire on its horizon had by the turn of the century abandoned its old moral imperatives—temperance, fortitude, prudence, and justice—as irrelevant to salvation, or for that matter, as measures of success. The work of Stanford White, therefore, would have to be considered not only by aesthetic standards—whether, for example, his renderings of Renaissance detail pleased the eye, but as expressions of the city's theological preoccupations. Acting as the city's architect, Stanford White would attempt to improve chaos with the illusions of beauty.

CHAPTER TEN

OLD NEW YORK:
Washington Square

IN THE WHITES' HOUSE on Tenth Street in Old New York, Richard Mansfield White, Jr., was the center of his parents' attention for just two years, but then, as sometimes happens for some reason, his younger brother Stanny was born and from that moment was always his mother's favorite.

Stanny was an alert, bumptious, restless, redheaded boy. His enthusiasms could not be contained. He was in and out of every closet. He sorted every opportunity for its curiosities. He picked up on all he heard and he was always the one to volunteer his company for every adult activity. When he was a nuisance, which he frequently was, and had to be chastened his chagrin lasted as long as a summer cloud. His mother wrote a poem in the style of Robert Burns and dedicated it to the ebullient energies of her second son: "His e'e sae blue, his cheek sae red, an old straw hat upon his head, all torn and tattered, O, have ye seen my boy Stannie? Wee busy mannie! . . ."

The Whites sent Stanny to the church schools of Washington Square and then to New York University's grammar school, but the principal elements of his education were inculcated by his father, Richard Grant White, and his mother, Alexina Black Mease White. She was born July 4, 1830, in Old New York when the city's virtues still seemed secure. When she was born open meadowland surrounded Henry Brevoort's house at Tenth Street and Fifth Avenue, Minetta Brook flowed down Fifth Avenue to Washington Square Park, and as a girl she could count at least ten skating ponds in the farmlands that stretched north of Fourteenth Street. She would live more than ninety years—until 1921—and watch her city change: until all of Manhattan was paved over, and there were traffic lights to control the motorcars all the way to the Harlem River, and the imperatives of village duty had been replaced by the necessities of city fraud.

Although she was born in Old New York, her perspective had advantages. She came from an aristocratic southern family from Charleston, South Carolina—from the genteel old South, which disappeared after the Civil War just as completely as Old New York. Alexina Black Mease was one of eleven children, of whom four survived into their majority, three sisters and a brother—a typical statistic of family mortalities in Old New York. Alexina was the eldest of the three girls—Alexina, Frances, and Laura. Their brother, Charles Graham Mease, was always called "Uncle Graham," and was described as a "gentleman" in an era when such an occupation still existed.

Uncle Graham read the newspapers every day to further his education in what he called "political economy," and he was entirely familiar with the writings of John Locke, Thomas Hobbes, John Stuart Mill, Edmund Burke, and many of the lesser theorists of good government. He was devoted to John Ruskin's work, not only for his definitions of the aesthetics of art, but for Ruskin's theory, with which Uncle Graham agreed, that some alternative would have to be discovered to the horrors of industrialism.

Aunt Laura was distinguished among the family for her beautiful singing voice, and she entertained family and friends at impromptu concerts with her repertoire. Aunt Fanny wrote stories for children—*Six Nightcaps* and *The Letter G* by Mrs. Frances Mease Barrows sold hundreds of thousands of copies and in a half-dozen translations all over the world.

Alexina had been named for Mr. Alexander Black, a charming cousin of the Mease family and a gentleman without issue, who had promised as an inheritance to his godchild Alexina a grand plantation outside Charleston. The War Between the States ruined the plantation, but by then Alexina had long since been married to Richard Grant White, a distinguished husband of special talents and an heir to the merchant aristocracy of Washington Square. Alexina Black Mease had been a plain girl, but she was a handsome woman, with a graceful neck, good strong black eyes, forthright and alert, and thick lustrous black hair. As her age advanced, she was embarrassed that her hair never turned white, not even a bit gray, and she eventually added a gray wig to add symmetry to the dignity of her age.

The White family of Washington Square into which Alexina had married could trace its genealogy, and its good manners, to John White, a yeoman from Essex and a member of Thomas Hooker's Puritan congregation. Indicted for treason and sedition by King Charles's wicked ministers, Hooker's Puritans arrived in Cambridge, Massachusetts, in 1632. John White's thirty acres of farmland near the Charles River would one day be the site of Harvard's library, but because of theological disputes with Boston's theocracy, John White sold his farm in Cambridge.

He led one hundred other apostates, men, women, and children—and 160 head of cattle, into the wilderness to a town on the Connecticut River they founded and called Hartford. John White's descendants were Congregationalists, Presbyterians, and Episcopal ministers. To the astonishment of the entire family, one of the Episcopal ministers converted to Roman Catholicism, but otherwise the rest of the family was without blemish. They were founders of many other towns besides Hartford—most of them in New England, but including Whitestone, New York, and Newark, New Jersey.

In New York City, John White's descendant, Richard Mansfield White, grandfather of Stanford White, was urged to the ministry and to Yale, but apparently wanted no part of his family's occupation. Instead, he chose a career for himself at sea, first training as a naval cadet and then serving as a ship captain. He secured a modest fortune for himself in clipper ships, and Captain White believed he was a solid South Street merchant. With the investments he had sailed back from the southern latitudes and applying the experience he had gained off strange coasts, he served as a member of the Diocesan conventions of the city's Episcopal Church. He was credited with establishing the first Episcopal Sunday Schools in both Manhattan and Brooklyn. In 1845 he was driven bankrupt—

ruined, it was said, by the advent of steamships and the competition of piratical men like Commodore Vanderbilt. He retired from any active life, moved to Orange, New Jersey, was cared for by his son, and died there soon afterward in 1849.

Captain White's son, Richard Grant White, father of Stanford White, was born in Old New York, May 23, 1821, and he was said to have been the despair of his ship-merchant father. He was not interested in either Episcopal devotions, nor the opportunities of the sea trade, but only in music—not just church music either, nor choir practices, but the cello and the violin: "fiddles and foreign music."

When Richard Grant White's voice had settled to a fine bass he sang in the choir of Saint Ann's Church, of course. Yet to his father's despair, he spent hours practicing on his cello. When the family moved across the river to Brooklyn he would take the ferry to Manhattan to play with orchestras in the city. He organized his own string quartet and at the age of nineteen gave a concert in his father's house with "music arranged by Richard Grant White." The program included *Le Nozze di Figaro,* Mozart; "Overture" from *Oberon,* Weber; and "Allegro and Presto," *Symphony No. 7,* Beethoven. If the program was a success in its performance, suspicions lingered that music so complicated might be the near occasion of sin. Moreover, the captain's son was soon wearing his hair long, as if he were a disciple of the arts.

Richard Grant White was graduated in 1839 as a Bachelor or Arts from New York University. During his residency, with his long hair tumbling down over his shoulders, he gave an oration on "Government," arguing from Tory principles that the Constitution was faulty, and the outcome of American democracy would be "corruption and disintegration." After his graduation he studied medicine under Dr. Alfred C. Post, advancing sufficiently to be appointed senior walker in New York Hospital; then he decided he would be better off as a lawyer, studied in the offices of Judge Woodruff, and was admitted to the bar in 1845.

That was the year his ship-merchant father went bankrupt. Richard Grant White discovered at the age of twenty four that he was responsible for his father and two sisters. In 1845 he also composed a sonnet to George Washington, sent it to William Cullen Bryant's New York *Evening Post,* and his sonnet was acclaimed throughout the United States as the equal of Wordsworth's work. The fame of his sonnet won Richard Grant White an appointment as music and drama critic of Henry J. Raymond's *Courier and Enquirer.* The reviews of the twenty-four-year-old doctor, lawyer, and amateur cellist soon commanded respect. He was thereafter a leading citizen of Old New York.

He published the first critical work in English on Beethoven in *The American Review.* He wrote on Shakespeare, edited and published a standard edition of the Bard's works, discoursed on Christian art, and guarded, in essays and books, the purities of the American language. He wrote for *Harper's Weekly,* and the *Atlantic Monthly* when it was edited by William Dean Howells. He helped James Gordon Bennett found the New York *World,* and he was a founding editor in 1865 of E. L. Godkin's *The Nation.* As a member of *The Nation*'s board of editors and its first critic of the arts, he was New York's link to the Abolitionist aristocracy of Boston and Philadelphia—the men who had worked against slavery for more than a generation, had taken the Civil War in their stride, and expected the fruits of their victory would be decent government.

Richard Grant White was described as a man who "walked Broadway like an active transitive verb looking down on a rabble of adverbs and prepositions and other insignificant parts of speech." He could be seen lunching at Delmonico's, a man of the world, an epicure, "an amateur, a gallant, almost a coxcomb," dawdling over his *oeufs en miroir,* six feet three, a striking man with a ruddy beard and moustache, a voluptuous mouth, and what appeared to be listless, self-complacent eyes.

As opera was introduced to the city he was tutor and critic, and he knew his operas from the scores. As painting began to fascinate collectors he was consulted because his perception of color was said to be so accurate he could remember for weeks the difference between two shades of pale lilac. He was scholar, essayist, arbiter, poet, admired citizen; the familiar and friend of William Dean Howells, James Russell Lowell, Ralph Waldo Emerson, Charles Dickens, and Robert Browning. He was a lover of controversy and disputation, a man of both great obstinacy and overwhelming charm. He tutored his city's eye in Shakespeare and theater and trained its ear to Beethoven and music—against the suspicions of the city's ministers; and he defended Miss Lydia Thompson's Burlesque and her "Quartette of English Beauties," against the righteous complaints of the city's bluenose culturati.

Every Thursday evening at eight o'clock sharp the Richard Grant White String Quartette rehearsed in his dining room. Its membership varied over the years and its principal audience was its own membership and their families. Its leader had five cellos, including an Amati, a Bergonzi, and a Gagliano. During an evening of the Quartette's rehearsals Richard Grant White would shift from one cello to another while he played, comparing their tones. He collected instruments of all kinds to test their timbre against his jewels, and he kept a workshop where he could take apart his minor acquisitions—cellos, violins, or violas—to make "repairs." According to his son Stanny, the "repairs" often required experts to be called in to repair the damages of his father's curiosity.

But Stanford White would always remember his father's house as a home full of melody—music all day and all night; his mother and Aunt Laura singing duets together in the kitchen or with the Quartette on Thursday nights in the dining room. Stanny grew up believing it was as natural to sing as to breathe—or to whistle, hum, or bawl if necessary, selections from Beethoven or *Le Nozze di Figaro.*

Besides music, there was always literature in the house, and talk of it: the editions of Shakespeare edited by his father; a history of their great-grandfather Calvin White written by Richard Grant White for his sons; letters from Mr. Howells or Mr. Dickens or Mr. Browning to be read and argued over; and the topics of criticism available from the White family's own house copies of the *Atlantic, The New York Times,* or *The Nation.* From the landscape booming around them, the men and women of the city's preoccupations came to the

Whites' home: the editors, writers, critics, musicians, poets, painters, men of cause, men of genius, men of advocacy, men of prophecy, and perfect fools. They brought into the White household the work they themselves were creating on every street corner—an explosion of their own energies that both delighted and startled. They had been Unionists with Lincoln, and then Mugwumps for Greeley against the robberies of Grant's Republicans. They were appalled by Tweed's majorities and worked with Carl Schurz for Civil Service reform. They were proud of Central Park: Richard Grant White and the park's architects, Olmstead and Vaux, gave free lectures at Cooper Union on the aesthetics of city architecture. They raised money for *The Nation,* for Civil Service reform, for the Metropolitan Opera from Henry Villard and Jay Gould and the Vanderbilts, and then listened in amazement to the details of Gould's gold corner, to the violence of Vanderbilt's war for the Erie Railroad, and Villard's "blind pool" for Northern Pacific bonds. In the Whites' household Stanny's education walked into the drawing room, sat down, crossed its legs, and talked. Stanny grew up thinking it was as natural to talk as he believed it was natural to sing—to gossip, argue, shout if necessary, about the spectacle the city displayed.

By the time Stanny was five Stewart's Department Store, six stories high, had taken over what had been a group of Village merchant houses just down the block from the Whites' house on Tenth Street. Other stores would soon follow "uptown," surrounding what had been a gothic countryside Episcopal parish—Grace Church. As many others soon did, the Whites moved across the river to Brooklyn, where there would be more space for the boys as they grew. By the time Stanny was seven the Fifth Avenue Hotel was being built on Madison Square at Twenty-third Street, where there had been nothing but Corporal Thompson's stagehouse just a few years before. By 1870, when Stanny was seventeen, there were elevated railroads rumbling above what had once been clear avenues lined with sycamores and maples.

Stanny started to draw before he was ten, and what seemed to catch his fancy were the buildings, churches and churchyards at first, then all the energies of the city expressed in stone. Stanny's drawings were extravagantly praised by his mother and his aunts and finally even by his eminent father. The boy tried his hand at watercolor sketches, and the praise increased. Since Uncle Graham pursued his occupation as a "gentleman" in the house of his brother-in-law, Richard Grant White, young Stanny had John Ruskin's books at hand: *The Elements of Drawing, The Elements of Perspective, The Seven Lamps of Architecture, The Stones of Venice, The Opening of the Crystal Palace,* and *Modern Painters.* From Ruskin's works, Stanny could read a defense of the art of J. M. W. Turner as an art "fundamentally true," and there was the suggestion in Ruskin that the principles of art must be understood if the society was to be good.

Ruskin's ideas were not so very different from the faith that had once satisfied Old New York: that art was a duty and carried with it moral imperatives; that art should be "true," and to the extent that art was true to its traditions, society would be improved. Ruskin preached the Gothic as a style, and Old New York fancied the Gothic for its churches—English Gothic, of course—Episcopalian, not Roman. "We may live without good architecture," Ruskin preached, "and worship without her, but we cannot remember without her."

Young Stanny studied Ruskin's lessons and Ruskin's examples. He could not have been expected to notice that Old New York's village God was a fiercely just God and usually violent, striking with thunderbolts from on high the wicked below, and a male God—usually depicted going about his justice in a full beard. Nor would young Stanny notice that Ruskin's Art, and the deity of good architecture, the inspiration of Art, was undeniably female—never seen with a beard, nor concerned one whit with the niceties of justice, a virgin restless with temperance, prudence, or patience, a "she" full of charms and wiles, absorbed by the possibilities of growth and increase, practicing her graces and keeping her secrets.

In the summers, when young Stanford White visited Aunt Laura's house at Newburgh, on the Hudson, he took his sketchbooks with him to draw the fertile countryside valleys. He tried imitating the Hudson River School in oil, painting the dense, luxuriant and mysterious growths of the mountains. Having studied Ruskin's defense of the Pre-Raphaelites, he searched for the elements of beauty to be discovered in forms, perhaps in the curve of a woman's waist. Having read Ruskin's praise of Turner, Stanny set up his easel and painted the sunset face-to-face, just as Turner had done. His enthusiasms were to celebrate nature, to devote his life to art, and he decided that he would be a painter. He asked his father to arrange an introduction to John La Farge.

His father's generation considered John La Farge a man of protean genius and a master born ahead of his time. In 1872, when eighteen-year-old Stanford White called upon him, La Farge was thirty-seven, lived in the Village on Washington Place, and worked in a studio at 51 West Tenth Street. La Farge was six feet tall, deep-chested, with long slender hands and feet, a magnificent head crowned with thick dark brown hair, a long straight aristocratic nose, and green-gray eyes set in deep sockets. He was the son of a successful French merchant banking family, and his manners were those of a man of the world. He dressed fastidiously in black, as if he too might be a banker, and he carried himself with an Olympian quality—an aloofness, a ceremonial stiffness. Yet with intimates, with his fellow artists, and with young men—with those he considered worth his attention, with the qualified or the hopeful—he knew how to laugh, how to trade limericks and jokes and cigars. His extraordinary imagination, the wide range of his learning and his ideas, and the precise, deliberate, and elaborately parenthetical way he would talk, all combined to make him widely influential.

He abhorred what he called the philistines of bourgeois society, and he detested the dead hand of academicians even more. He could think of few critics who had either talent, or training, or skill, and described them as sheep led by ambitious goats. He had studied in Paris under the academics, worked under the influential Romantics—Ingres and Delacroix. He had been a participant in the stimulating world of the salons of the Bourgeois Empire, in the world of Théophile Gautier, Victor Hugo, and Baudelaire. He had lived and worked with the Pre-Raphaelites and Dante Gabriel Rossetti in England. He had traveled Europe and tracked down Rembrandts,

Velasquezes, and Rubenses. He had published on Japanese art, a subject opened to Americans by Commodore Perry and venturesome clipper-ship captains, and La Farge's works were imitated for the lessons they taught by the court painters of Japan.

He was the world's acknowledged master of work in stained glass, but his paintings had been rejected by the American National Academy because the academics said La Farge painted scenes like farmhouses, topics "too mean and homely" for their grand academic visions. John La Farge said that painting should "indicate very carefully in every part the exact time of day and circumstance of light." To satisfy the perfection of his own new techniques he was engaged in the study of optics, the study of light itself. He had been working on a new philosophy of painting for years before Cézanne had even begun to study in Paris, and the *"naturalisme"* that La Farge advocated would be rejected by both American and French Academies when Cézanne, Renoir, Monet, Manet, and Pissaro developed it. The Impressionists also would paint scenes "too mean and homely" to satisfy academic vision.

John La Farge urged young Stanford White to forget painting. Recognition, even to the best, came slowly and over the opposition of critics and fashion. The rewards of painting would be few—the fleeting embrace of a small public, a few invitations to the drawing rooms of fickle and restless women, and then perhaps a smattering of gratitude expressed posthumously for having left something beautiful to decorate the walls of a philistine, but no money.

Young Stanford White admitted money would be a problem, because his father's occupation as author and critic was not rewarding enough to send a son to study in Paris.

La Farge urged Stanny to try architecture; its principal ingredient was drawing—White's sketches of buildings were his best work. Color and mass and design could be brought to buildings, and not all buildings had to be copies of Ruskin's little Gothic imitations. There were no schools of architecture in America at which Stanford White could learn anything, and in fact there were few trained architects, but there was one genius—Henry Hobson Richardson, who had just opened new offices in Boston and who might need an apprentice who could draw. If Stanny would like to try Richardson, John La Farge would write an introduction for him.

At the age of eighteen, Stanford White set off by train for Boston as an apprentice to H. H. Richardson. On October 29, 1872, he wrote his mother from the Parker House: "Through the goodness of Providence, here I am—with an oversized knee and the influenza. . . . I arrived in Boston from Aunt Laura's in the long-to-be-remembered time of 28 hours 4½ minutes. Truly this is an age of progress and refinement. . . ."

Twenty-eight hours to Boston and a bruised knee were the results of a minor train wreck on the way. When his influenza had diminished to a mere cold Stanford White began five years as the apprentice of one of the most extraordinary men in America. Under Richardson, White would be forced to work in an ecstasy of activity: drawing, sketching, designing, traveling to the sites of constructions, going without sleep for days, choosing materials in the middle of the night, supervising gangs of workmen at sites in Boston, Albany, New York, Chicago, Washington. He was soon Richardson's chief of drawings and often acted as chief of works. He wrote his mother from Boston in February, 1873: "I begin to think that it is my fate to have neither peace of mind nor quiet of body; & both are, I believe, necessary to man's happiness. Shirts—clean ones, that is—are also necessary. I have none. . . ."

He complained by letter to her of train accidents on the road to Albany, of arriving in Buffalo to inspect a site at nearly one in the morning with the temperature at zero, of Albany again, "of all miserable, wretched, second-class, one-horse towns, this is the most miserable." He saw a pastoral valley he wanted to paint at sunset, but there was no time; Richardson's changes in plans, he said, made him feel as if he had been standing on his head all week. "If you don't get another note from me, consider me in my right mind. How Richardson can be, I can't tell; for, setting aside all brandies, gins, wines, and cigars, he seems to subsist chiefly on boiled tripe, which he insists upon calling 'entrails of a cow.' "

In 1872 when Stanford White went to work at eighteen as

an apprentice architect, Henry Hobson Richardson was only thirty-four, but Richardson's reputation had already begun to grow, and clients were beginning to gather at his door. Richardson would die too soon—at just forty-eight in 1886, at the height of his powers and reputation. By the time he died there would be hundreds of imitations or derivations of his designs in every American city, and thousands more would follow his death—private houses, railway stations, warehouses, libraries, churches, state capitols, and armories, all built in a style that could only be called "Richardson Romanesque." He was the advance man for a new American aesthetic, and his work would become a permanent decoration of the American imagination.

Years later historian Henry Adams wondered how reputations, like comets, left trails: "A fair number of men who were born in the thirties had won names—Phillips Brooks; Bret Harte; Henry James; H. H. Richardson; John La Farge . . . but from their school had sprung others, like Augustus Saint-Gaudens, McKim, Stanford White, and scores born in the forties, who counted as force even in the mental inertia of sixty or eighty million people." Henry Adams said Richardson was the only really big man he had ever known, and Adams loved to quote the remark of a German admirer of Richardson: *"Mein Gott,* how he looks like his own buildings."

All reminiscences of either Richardson himself or Richardsonian style struggled with inadequate descriptions: his gaiety, his simplicity, his energy, his influence; but the words most often repeated were *solid, gigantic, titanic, huge, gargantuan.* John La Farge said that "like many other great men, he was a mighty eater and drinker—a pitcher of milk, a pitcher of champagne, a pitcher of water . . . everything was done on a grand scale . . . and his work was of that kind."

In the *Reminiscences* of sculptor Augustus Saint-Gaudens, Richardson's working costume was described as "usually consisting of a black monk's robe, cowled, and roped across an immense belly." Saint-Gaudens recalled being asked to dinner at Richardson's house and arriving to find Richardson dressed in a brilliant yellow waistcoat. "Indeed, it would require a Rabelais to do justice to his unusual power and character.

He had an enormous girth, and a halt in his speech, which made the words that followed come out in a series of explosions. The walls of his dining room he had painted blood-red. It had a low ceiling, and a magnificent oval, black-oak table. To dine with him, with his round-faced expectant children sitting about the table, and charming Mrs. Richardson opposite, furnished the guest with a picture and an honor not to be forgotten."

Saint-Gaudens had been told that Richardson was under doctor's orders prohibiting stimulants of any kind, and absolutely no alcohol. But as Saint-Gaudens arrived at the house in Brookline, Massachusetts, Richardson beamed at the young sculptor. "S-S-Saint-G-G-Gaudens, ordinarily I lead a life of a-a-abstinence, but tonight I am going to break my rule to celebrate your visit."

Whereupon Richardson ordered up a magnum of champagne, which he explained had to be finished between the two of them. The champagne "ought to be accompanied by cheese," which was also proscribed by the doctors but which Richardson nonetheless ate in enormous quantities. Saint-Gaudens recalled the intensity of their talk and that he hardly drank at all, while Richardson poured his way through the whole magnum. Saint-Gaudens guessed "the proceeding occurred every night, as he always arranged to bring home a guest."

Henry Hobson Richardson was born in 1838, a plantation aristocrat in the parish of Saint James, Louisiana. He was the eldest of a family of four, an expert rider, an expert at sword play with foils, and as a boy learned to play chess so well he was able to carry on five games simultaneously while blindfolded. His father hoped to send his oldest son to West Point for a career as an officer in the Army of the United States, but since the boy stuttered, there was no alternative but to enroll him at Harvard.

Richardson was considered the best-dressed man in his class, was a member of the Porcellian, was notoriously fond of the ladies, and was graduated in 1860 an undistinguished student of civil engineering. He sailed for Paris to enroll at L'Ecole des Beaux Arts and to study drawing and architecture. The

Civil War ruined his plantation inheritance, and to continue his studies he went to work as a draftsman in the offices of Labrouste, the architect of the Bibliothèque Sainte Geneviève. After the Civil War he returned to New York, a trained Beaux Arts architect, but work was scarce. His first commission in 1866 had to be won in a competition for a Unitarian church in Springfield, Massachusetts. Despite objections "to an unknown southerner" barely twenty-eight years old, he won the job. Richardson was waiting outside the door of the committee room when the news of his selection was brought to him. Tears filled his eyes. "That's all I wanted," he said, "a chance."

Richardson's contribution to American architecture was to demand that art recognize the scale of the new national forces. At L'Ecole des Beaux Arts he had studied architecture as the art which expressed the ideals of a society—but which society, and what ideals? Richardson refused to transplant French architecture to America. "It would not cost me a bit of trouble to build French buildings that would reach from here to Philadelphia, but that is not what I want to do." He said the things he would most like to design were American symbols, "a grain elevator and the interior of a great river steamboat."

He insisted on large, expansive designs, examples of mass and volume, vigorous, balanced on the land but varied in their shapes, and in earthy colors—reds and yellows and browns. He wanted boulders, not stones, for building materials—specimens of "boisterous, titanic gamboling." He wanted Americans to build lusty constructions, because that was what the American experience called for. He labored at his sites alongside his masons and artists and workmen, organizing them into cooperative gangs. And he would happily modify his designs or decoration to incorporate the inspirations of his fellow workers, because democracy was our national temper.

His style was called Romanesque because it was a style he thought easy for Americans to identify. It appeared to be simple and direct, and its arches with solid keystones were like those of railroad tunnels. His immense, thick walls seemed to offer security against any invasion and yet were uncomplicated and dignified and guaranteed the rights of privacy. Richardson's American version of the earliest medieval architecture was not in fact derivative, and so his American version always had to be modified in its description as Richardson Romanesque.

Just before he died a poll would be conducted in 1885 in which seventy-five architects nominated and then voted for the best ten buildings in America. Five of the top ten were the work of Henry Hobson Richardson, and his Trinity Church in Boston was easily first with 84 percent of all votes. The United States Capitol placed second, and Richard Morris Hunt's design for Alva Vanderbilt's house was third. In various follow-up positions in the top ten were Richardson's State Capitol in Albany, Sever Hall at Harvard, Albany City Hall, and the Town Hall at North Easton, Massachusetts. Not listed in the top ten, but works that would grow in the estimation of critics were the twin houses he designed side by side on Lafayette Square in Washington for his two friends Henry Adams and John Hay, the Cheney Building in Hartford, the wholesale warehouse for Marshall Field and Company in Chicago, the Allegheny County Courthouse and jail in Pittsburgh, and the first gargantuan "summer cottage" in Newport for Watts Sherman, built in 1874-1876.

Richardson was important not only as a designer but as a teacher, and he argued that America should have its own architecture as solid and as grand as its Constitution. His Richardson Romanesque spoke for strength, for simplicity, and it was serious and powerful work. Architects, he argued, expressed in geometric forms a society's sense of itself, and Richardson's material was stone—huge blocks of monumental stone, drilled and blasted out of Quincy quarries, sledded to ships in two-, three-, sometimes four-ton blocks; the same kind of stone heaved up into the monument at Bunker Hill; the same kind of stone consumed by a thousand garden cemeteries; the same kind of stone that spoke of strength, the founding fathers, and repose—like the hymn, "Rock of Ages."

But by the time Richardson died monumental stone was becoming an oddity. Richardson's buildings were among the last in which masonry had to bear the load of the building's walls. His work was transitional because in Pittsburgh the mills were beginning to turn out structural steel. With steel, architects could design a building as a skeleton, then hang the walls like curtains from the building's frame. Moreover, at the time Richardson died architects were being asked to design for a new kind of society, a surging world of new perceptions.

The railroads had connected the great American interior into a single nervous system. With transportation available at the local railhead, the American farmer proceeded to revolutionize agriculture. With barbed wire supplied from the steel mills in the East, the farmer fenced the high plains with a million miles of wire. He brought his cattle in from the range to feed lots, and he grew grain and fed animals on a scale so magnificent that an American population of *any* number could be fed, and much of the world besides.

As fast as Connecticut Yankees could invent machines for the farmer, Mississippi River Valley farms put them to use. McCormick reapers harvested in one day and from one farm tons of food; and one farmer and his wife would fill, in a summer, enough grain elevators to have fed an entire Romanesque kingdom. New strains of grain were developed; refrigerated railroad wagons hauled meats for city packinghouses; and the surplus proteins made incredible concentrations of families possible in gigantic cities. The massive inventions of pre-Civil War America, like the great river steamboats Richardson had admired, began to appear to be mere toys.

The energies available from the revolution in agriculture were spent in creating a nervous system so complex that it would baffle its most expert neurologists. Synaptic inventions multiplied one after the other: the telegraph, stock tickers, typewriters, telephones, electric lights, elevators, phonographs, radios, gasoline engines, on and on—and all these ganglia of information connected by cables as if they were dendrons to the unlimited electric power of the dynamo. It was a machine that could turn at unimaginable velocities and was fueled by organic materials decomposed in the earth's darkest caves. Its power was apparently divisible endlessly and unlimited, theologically, by any magnitude. Unlike the power celebrated by a lusty singing of "Rock of Ages," the melodies emanating from the dynamo were not easily identified. In fact, their hum brought no repose to those who studied their possibilities, but a vague and unnameable terror. If, as Richardson argued, architects were to apply their art to express a society's sense of itself, Richardson Romanesque furnished no example for the new arrangements.

But Richardson did show a group of men how to work together. Among others on the site of his constructions, especially at Trinity Church, John La Farge, Augustus Saint-Gaudens, Charles F. McKim, and Stanford White made friendships that would last throughout their lives. Richardson was their tutor, and Richardson, it was said, would have a thousand imitators but in the design of "titanic gamboling" no successors, except perhaps his chief of drawings, Stanford White.

Augustus Saint-Gaudens remembered meeting Stanford White for the first time when they were both working for Richardson on Boston's Trinity Church. According to Richardson, White was "chief factotum" on the construction. John La Farge was chief of the artists, and he hired Saint-Gaudens, although Saint-Gaudens was a sculptor, to paint the figure of Saint Paul. Saint-Gaudens' painting would be placed just inside Trinity's main entrance, and he would also paint the figure of Saint James on the Boylston Street side. Saint-Gaudens worked on his commissions in a studio in New York—in the deserted rooms above the German Savings Bank on Fourteenth Street. Absorbed in his work, Saint-Gaudens was singing the "Serenade" from Mozart's *Don Giovanni* when White came bounding up the stairs and finished the phrase in a duet with the sculptor. They met laughing with each other.

The first thing White wanted to talk about was not Trinity Church but Mozart. Saint-Gaudens said his "serenade" might have given a false impression. He knew very little about Mozart but sang the "Serenade" from *Don Giovanni* from having heard it ten years before by a howling Frenchman in the Beaux Arts with whom he had shared an atelier. The two young men were instantly friends and began by comparing their ideas on music, art, and architecture. Saint-Gaudens remembered meeting Charles F. McKim, who had also worked for Richardson, somewhat later. Saint-Gaudens explained, "A devouring love of ice-cream brought us together." White and McKim, said redheaded Augustus Saint-Gaudens, "were a couple of redheads who would be thoroughly mixed up in my life."

"Gus" Saint-Gaudens was five years older than Stanny, born March 1, 1848, on Charlemont Street in Dublin, Ireland. His father, Bernard Paul Ernest Saint-Gaudens, was a wandering Frenchman of great charm, a shoemaker with an ebullient style, who finally settled his family in New York and hung up his sign outside the shop downstairs: "French Ladies' Boots and Shoes." The store soon had a distinguished clientele from the society of Washington Square.

Gus inherited his red hair from his mother, Mary McGuiness, from Bally Mahon, County Langford, Ireland. She was from a plasterer's family, and Gus would later explain, when he was America's leading sculptor, that plaster ran in the family. Mary McGuiness Saint-Gaudens raised her three sons—Gus, Andrew, and Louis—in the flat above her husband's shop, and the boys grew up in the streets of the new city as the floods of immigrants arrived. They attended the Chrystie Street School, then the North Moore Street School, and then transferred to the Twentieth Street School in 1860, when Bernard Saint-Gaudens moved his shoestore to Fourth Avenue, almost at the corner of Twenty-fourth Street. He opened at the new address to keep company with his clientele as they relocated on the avenues north of Washington Square.

When Gus reached the age of thirteen, his father explained to him he "had reached the fork in the road. . . . My boy, you must go to work. What would you like to do?"

"I don't care," was his answer, "but I should like it if I could do something which would help me to be an artist."

Bernard Saint-Gaudens apprenticed his son to a fellow Frenchman named Avet, the first stone-cameo cutter in America. To satisfy the prevalent men's fashion of scarfpins with the heads of dogs, horses, and lions cut in amethyst, malachite, or other semiprecious jewels, stones were prepared on a lathe, cut, then delivered to Ball and Black, or to Tiffany. Work on the lathe was both a drudgery and exacting, but Gus Saint-Gaudens learned to cut portraits in cameo. From Master Avet, Saint-Gaudens carried his skill to the shop of Mr. Jules Le-Brethon, a shell cutter, and Gus worked at his stonecutting lathe from seven in the morning until six at night. He would later say that for the rest of his life he could cut a lion's head in cameo "automatically."

After work he studied drawing and modeling in clay at the Cooper Institute until eleven. Eventually he transferred his studies to the National Academy of Design at Twenty-third Street, where he could study under Leutze—the painter of *Washington Crossing the Delaware*. In February, 1867, with money saved from his own labors, supplemented by a contribution from his father and with a subscription raised from the French community in New York, Gus Saint-Gaudens sailed for Paris in steerage aboard *The City of Boston* to study at the Beaux Arts in Paris. He brought with him his stone-cutting lathe as insurance against starvation, and over the next eight years he would frequently need to use it.

By 1875 he was a skilled sculptor, trained in Paris, practiced in Rome, with one or two commissions already sold, convinced that he would eventually win recognition. In later years he would say that "no one ever succeeded in art unless born with an uncontrollable instinct toward it." He was undeniably driven by that instinct himself, because until Saint-Gaudens showed the way, there was little American sculpture to excite the imagination of any young man and none to provide any example. There was nothing but Roman imitations of Greek ideals—George Washington, for example, draped in what seemed to be a toga, as if a Virginia gentleman warrior could be imagined as one of Nero's senators. For their merchant clients, American sculptors turned out real Roman fakes.

After the Civil War, however, it occurred to Americans they had some real heroes of their own. Instead of sandaled noble senators, "classic and beautiful," Americans sensed there might be something heroic in the native combination of shrewdness and idealism in action. Before the Civil War an

American hero like Abraham Lincoln could not be molded into the classical proportions that defined symmetrical beauty. He was a little too long for such artistic rules, and the way his thick ax-swinging wrists stuck out from his coat sleeves would have excluded him from Plato's delicate symposia. After the Civil War, America guessed that if his language differed from Virgil's proportioned verses when Lincoln spun his coondog stories, there might be something about Lincoln that was also divine. And perhaps there were other heroes of the American Republic whose peculiar virtues might be portrayed in a native sculpture. In 1867, at nineteen, Augustus Saint-Gaudens had set off for Europe to study the classic techniques he would need. In 1875 he brought home the disciplined skills of a major artist. American sculpture would begin as soon as Saint-Gaudens could get an opportunity, but he would need commissions for his talent from the elders of Washington Square. While he waited in his Fourteenth Street studio he continued to work at his models and sketches. When he had to, he cut cameos on his lathe to raise cash or gave drawing lessons for small fees to young ladies. He was painting saints on the walls of Richardson's Trinity Church when he met Stanford White.

In addition to the reflected delight the two young men took in each other's company, White and Saint-Gaudens discovered they already shared a mutual client in New York's War Governor, E. D. Morgan. White had been commissioned to design a tomb for the Governor, and Saint-Gaudens had sold the Governor an early work, a statue of *Hiawatha*. For Saint-Gaudens, White went back to his client, suggesting to Governor Morgan that it would be a "bully" idea for Saint-Gaudens to model some "angels" to decorate the Governor's tomb. Governor Morgan thought the cost would be excessive, but White would try to charm him for the extra money.

Meanwhile, they learned that a sum of $12,000 had been appropriated to erect a statue in Madison Square of *Admiral David Glasgow Farragut*, hero of the Battle of Mobile Bay—"Damn the torpedoes. Full speed ahead!" A committee of eleven prominent citizens of Washington Square would choose the sculptor. To assure Saint-Gaudens' selection, Stanford

White used the connections of his prominent father, Richard Grant White, for introductions to each member of the committee. Saint-Gaudens prepared two models, a large drawing, and a bust to display what he proposed, and White and Saint-Gaudens suggested that the base and the setting of the statue, which would be designed by White, be made an integral part of its design—an innovation at the time. The day for the final decision arrived in December, 1876, but the committee seemed to be deadlocked between the proposals of J.Q.A. Ward and Saint-Gaudens. It was Ward who urged the committee: "Give the young man a chance," and the commission was voted five for Ward and six for Saint-Gaudens.

"With that," said Saint-Gaudens, "the tide turned wholly in my favor." Within weeks Saint-Gaudens had another major commission—a statue of *Captain Robert Richard Randall* for Sailors' Snug Harbor on Staten Island, again in collaboration for its base and pedestal with Stanford White. And then John La Farge and Stanford White were commissioned to remodel the interior of Saint Thomas Church, and Saint-Gaudens was named to execute ten-foot bas-relief angels. Apparently the rector of Saint Thomas feared Saint-Gaudens' angels would be too Catholic, but John La Farge wrote Gus not to worry: "There is no danger. There is no such thing as the Protestant in art. . . . Just omit any aureoles around their heads." When they were completed, Saint-Gaudens' angels would be hailed as masterpieces.

To work on the Saint Thomas angels, on the *Randall* statue, and on the *Farragut,* Saint-Gaudens returned to Paris, where he could live cheaply, rent the big studio he needed at 49 Rue Notre Dame des Champs, and find trained assistants in molding and casting. Stanford White wrote Saint-Gaudens from New York early in 1878: "I shouldn't wonder that Morgan would go the nine thousand for the tomb. . . . By the way, how long will you take to do the work; I mean finished stone? I told Morgan eighteen months to two years. How's that, me boy?" White's sales presentations had finally eased the necessary money out of Morgan.

By the spring of 1878 White had saved enough money from his apprenticeship under Richardson to take a leave of absence. He planned to tour Europe, to sketch and study for a year, or "until my money runs out." Saint-Gaudens and his wife "Gussie" offered their apartment in the Rue Herschel to White as "headquarters" for his year of study. While White lived in the Saint-Gaudens apartment, he could work on the *Farragut* and the *Randall* pedestals with Gus in the studio. On June 21, 1878, White wrote from New York: "Dear St.-Gaudens: It is like you to offer me a bunk. . . . I have had to put off my passage, and I now sail on the French steamer *Periere,* on Wednesday, July 3rd. Who do you think is coming with me? Even McKim. I am tickled to death. He is coming over for but a six weeks' trip, but it is still perfectly jolly. We will land and take the express train for Paris, and so will arrive there (I suppose) about the 15th or 16th. SW."

The summer of 1878 would be a mixture of work, study, holiday, excursions, celebrations, exuberances, and enthusiasms, largely instigated by the youngest of the three redheads: White was twenty-four, Saint-Gaudens thirty, and Charles F. McKim thirty-one. Although they should have been—by any common standard—mature men by then, their own accounts of their summer together made them appear as if they were still playful puppies. They were to collaborate for the rest of their lives, and they were at the threshold of their fame. Perhaps they sensed it.

The apartment and studio of "Gus and Gussie" Saint-Gaudens were informal headquarters not only for White and McKim but for other Americans in Paris. In 1877 Saint-Gaudens was one of the founders of the Society of American Artists as a "party of reform" against the National Academy of Art. The reformers met in "The Studio," at 103 East Fifteenth Street, the home of Miss Helena de Kaye and her husband, Richard Watson Gilder. Their membership included artists, writers, sculptors, and poets—Stanford White, John La Farge, Mme. Modjeska, Walt Whitman. Richard Watson Gilder was editor of *Scribner's Monthly* and then *The Century*. When the party of artistic reform met in New York it met at the Gilders'.

When the reformers passed through Paris their headquarters was at the Saint-Gaudens' apartment and studio. For a while Richard Watson Gilder stood as a model for *Admiral Farragut's* legs. Around the Saint-Gaudens dinner table there were both French and American artists, sculptors, and writers, and their arguments about literature and art sometimes went late into the night. The French might be represented by Bastien-Lepage, and the Americans by D. Maitland Armstrong, Kenyon Cox, Carroll Beckwith, and John Singer Sargent. Mr. Samuel Clemens—Mark Twain—came to dinner frequently, smoking his bad black cigars and telling his incredible stories. Saint-Gaudens and Samuel Clemens stood as witnesses for a French artist's marriage in the municipal court of Montmartre.

Late in the summer of 1878 McKim and White burst into Saint-Gaudens' studio from some crazy excursion, dancing and singing. They told Gus they had declared a holiday, and the moment had arrived to make a walking tour of Southern France. No doubt about it, the time to leave was right away.

But Gus put them off because he was absorbed by his work on *Farragut,* who stood in plaster eight feet four inches high in the center of the studio. While White and McKim argued for a holiday, described the cathedrals they might visit, and sang what they claimed were songs of courtly love, Saint-Gaudens' attention could not be diverted from his statue. He ignored them, opening a bottle of wine, pouring a glass for himself, studying his work as if he did not hear a word they were saying. He took his glass to a chair off to one side and asked his friends to tell him honestly what they thought of the hero of Mobile Bay.

They interrupted their songs and analyzed *Farragut* for him. The head was good. The whole effect was intensely human—he certainly appeared to be an admiral with his feet planted four-square on his quarterdeck. It was without question a vital characterization of the admiral's stubborn qualities. But, Stanny said, "Saint-Gaudens, you have given *Farragut* your own legs!"

Saint-Gaudens had listened carefully to their opinions. He restudied his plaster once again—was Stanny right? He put down his glass of wine, took a ladder over to the statue, set the ladder up, carefully removed the admiral's head from his neck, put the head on a bench, then climbed the ladder again, and tipped *Admiral Farragut* over. Plaster shattered across the studio floor in a thousand pieces.

"Come on," said Saint-Gaudens as he headed down his studio stairs. "I'll go to Hades with you fellows now!"

They left Paris the next afternoon, Friday, August 2, 1878, with their knapsacks on their backs, in their hiking boots, and with Saint-Gaudens' tin coffeepot tied to his belt. On their first night they walked no farther than Fontainebleau, then began to cover ground by rail. Stanford White sketched, did watercolors, and wrote home descriptions of their tour. They examined castles, châteaux, chapels, churches, cathedrals, aqueducts, bridges, Roman amphitheaters. They studied and sketched flèches, towers, buttresses. They copied roses, portals, porches, and glass. They penciled the folds of a virgin's skirt. They calculated stresses and strains. They climbed up a stone saint to measure his height from the floor and used a plumb bob to check his balance—to verify that he had stood for centuries with his weight on his heels. They were trained men, and they understood that form was an expression of energy—in fact, as the thirteenth century through which they were traveling had insisted again and again, form *was* energy: an outward sign of the inner organization of matter, every form its own sacrament.

They traveled through the cathedral at Beaune to Lyons, where they boarded a river steamer and swept down the Rhône to Avignon. They got gloriously drunk on the steamer in the hot afternoon *midi* sun and sat up in the shelter of the steamer's bow, singing at the top of their lungs. They were still foolish enough to sing for the sake of the songs. Since they were still young, they could enjoy themselves, for they had not yet consented to any despairs. Since they considered themselves artists, they enjoyed with a positive greed the novelties through which they were passing, and they thought it was their business to study the excitement of illusions, the play of light, the adoration of color for its own romance.

Just as their own New York was the gathering place for incredible energies, the land through which they were traveling also had once been the focus of marvelous illusions. In the thirteenth century it was the countryside of the Virgin, whose church spires could be sighted all along their way, a landscape in which passion had once been understood to be something absolutely real: a concentration of forces whose potentials were immensely more powerful than any Massachusetts power looms, or Mississippi steamboats, or transcontinental railroad engines. The Virgin had exercised curved forces of her own, none of them mechanical conversions, nor any of them Newtonian rationalisms, but real nonetheless—something similar to the twentieth century's geometry of radium.

In the thirteenth century, and in the land through which the three young American redheads were touring, the Virgin's authority had been absolute, but by essence, illogical, unreasonable, feminine; a power beyond any sensible law, beyond the mass of ignorance and petty absurdities of discovered truths; an authority something like compassion without limit—an emotion as clear and strong as love, yet just as unstable, and in which sex was so real that its thrusts—once validated by experience—were obviously equal to the power produced from any corporation's coalpit.

It was an authority in which the mastery of love, the supremacy of thought, the magic of poetry, the delights of costume and make-believe, the honor of charm, and the complexities of grace were all asserted against simple-minded powers of masculine prowess. It was an illusion to which twentieth-century New York might have consented and an authority to which Augustus Saint-Gaudens, Stanford White, and Charles F. McKim might have devoted their art. But when their steamer arrived in Avignon they were Americans first of all, and they went off searching for some place that would serve them ice-cream.

In their travels they had seen nothing but examples of taste. If any of the forces of the Virgin were present, they apparently had missed them. Perhaps, in fact, the Virgin had long since abandoned the world, leaving behind nothing but the empty altars of a deserted faith. Perhaps Saint-Gaudens, White, and McKim had seen all there remained to see—lovely churches, exquisitely decorated, curiosities for tourists.

They went on to visit Arles, Tarascon, and Nîmes, where

they went to the Roman amphitheater, sat on the top row of seats, and imagined themselves ancient Romans. White ran down the stairs into the arena and struck a pose for McKim and Saint-Gaudens, "and commenced declaiming." He then fought off "five or six gladiators," stabbing them with an imaginary short Roman sword, until a guard appeared and chased all three of them back into the streets. From Nîmes they went by train through the mountains to Le Puy. White said he thought the scenery was "quite like that of the Catskills," and he thought the post roads "as good as those in Central Park." They continued on to Tours, into the valley of the Loire, through the châteaux country, angling back to Paris through Blois and Orleans. Stanford White would stay on with Saint-Gaudens in Paris for nearly a year more before his money ran out—until September, 1879, making excursions all over Europe from Gus's "headquarters." By September, 1878, Charles McKim had used more than the six weeks he had intended to spend, and he had to part from his friends in Europe to resume the practice of architecture in New York.

Charles Follen McKim was born August 24, 1847, in Chester County, Pennsylvania, the son of Miller McKim and Sarah Allibone Speakman. His mother's family were Quakers, and although his father was not quite a Quaker, Miller McKim was a leader, a celebrity, of the Abolitionist wing of the Quaker witness.

Miller McKim had started as a Presbyterian pastor but was one of the sixty delegates to the convention called in Philadelphia in 1833 to form the American Anti-Slavery Society. The convention determined slavery to be a sin, and as a moral imperative it called for immediate emancipation. Its demand for justice was not the official position of the Presbyterian Church. Influenced by William Lloyd Garrison and Lucretia Mott, Miller McKim gave up his Presbyterianism, resigned his pastorate, and joined the Anti-Slavery Society as the publisher of the *Pennsylvania Freedman.* He met Sarah Allibone Speakman at the Society's work, and together they devoted their lives to the ending of slavery.

It was a life of considerable excitement, because Abolition was generally an unpopular cause. They were jeered, libeled, and stoned. The issue was real, and their labor unending. They wrote, published, spoke, traveled, and raised money—raising funds was always a problem, and Miller McKim became, in effect, the secretary general of the antislavery cause because he was good at raising the money needed.

They ran an underground railroad. They supported John Brown's "colonization" in "Bloody Kansas," and when Brown was hung in Charles Town they went with his widow to fetch him. It was the McKims who buried John Brown's body at North Elba, New York. While John Brown's body lay a-mouldering in the grave, Miller McKim and his wife Sarah saw the cause for which they had labored certified as victorious by the Civil War.

In addition to her household's cause, Sarah McKim raised an adopted daughter, Annie; her own daughter, Lucy; and a son, Charles Follen McKim. When she gave birth to her son in 1847, her husband was away on a speaking tour—raising money from sympathetic church audiences in Scotland and England. Typically, she named her son Charles Follen McKim to honor Harvard's first professor of German, Charles Follen—a professor whose outspoken and unpopular antislavery views had caused the courageous trustees of Harvard University to suspend the chair of his professorship. The household of Sarah and Miller McKim, the family and associates who surrounded Charles McKim as he grew up, were poor, brilliant, and virtuous—examples of the nation's evangelical aristocracy.

The traditions of this unique aristocracy were centered in Boston. Its membership included living remnants of the Transcendentalist saints, such as Ralph Waldo Emerson and Nathaniel Hawthorne, mixed with a few newcomers established at the *Atlantic Monthly* who said they were "realists," such as Rebecca Harding Davis and William Dean Howells. In 1865 Miller McKim raised the money to found a new magazine, *The Nation,* whose headquarters would be New York instead of Boston. It would be the means to continue the success of the *Pennsylvania Freedman.* It would apply the techniques learned in the politics of Abolition to the postwar struggle for "good government." To their horror the evangelical aristocracy had discovered that the Thirteenth and Fourteenth Amendments to the Constitution, for which they had labored a lifetime, had freed the Negro but also were providing a license for greedy men to plunder a continent.

To raise money for *The Nation,* Miller McKim sought the help of Henry Villard, not yet a railroad president steeped in fraud but still a journalist of rectitude; Villard was a friend of the late President Lincoln, the secretary of the honored American Social Science Association, and the husband of the daughter of Boston's William Lloyd Garrison, who could be described as Abolition's commanding general. The son of William Lloyd Garrison was listed as managing editor of *The Nation*—Wendell Phillips Garrison had married Lucy McKim and shared a house in Orange, New Jersey, with Miller and Sarah McKim.

The Nation could almost be described as a family affair. The editorial board was headed by Edwin Lawrence Godkin—then a thirty-four-year-old Irish immigrant—who would later edit the New York *Evening Post* when Henry Villard bought it. Listed as contributing editors were the leading men of Boston and Harvard, old Abolitionists and evangelical aristocrats every one: Henry Wadsworth Longfellow, Charles Eliot Norton, John Greenleaf Whittier, James Russell Lowell. Representing the best of New York against the corruption of money were: Frederick Law Olmsted and Richard Grant White.

Young Charles Follen McKim, heir to these Bostonian ideals, was educated at Quaker schools, then in Philadelphia's public high schools, where he was tutored in the classics, in Xenophon and Cicero, and prepared, of course, for Harvard. When he arrived in Boston in 1866 rooms had been secured for him on Kirkland Street in the home of a Mrs. Rotch, an antislavery connection of the McKims. He enrolled at Harvard to study engineering under the kindly eye and sympathetic attention of James Russell Lowell. Despite these securities, Charles McKim was soon unhappy with Harvard and Boston and began to lobby his parents for an education at L'Ecole des Beaux Arts in Paris.

It was a notion that disconcerted his Quaker family circle. A letter from his mother brimmed with love and good sense:

"I say nothing, as I am bewildered as to what is best. One thing, I have no unity with thy feeling troubled and unhappy. I can't see the necessity of worrying about the matter. Do the best thee can each day and the way will open up all right, I trow."

By the end of his first year at Harvard, "Charlie the Charmer" was a star of Harvard's baseball team, playing right field and scoring crucial runs in the championship game against Boston's Lowell Club; a social success, but miserable that he could not get to Paris. For his son, Miller McKim wrote to Henry Villard for advice on the cost of living in Europe—Villard guessed it could be done on seven hundred dollars a year—and in September, 1867, Charles McKim finally had his way and sailed for France. "As for wine," his father wrote, "I would put no obligation on your conscience. Do in regard to that matter whatever thee think is right."

He loved Paris. He roomed in a pension with a Harvard friend, Robert S. Peabody of Boston, and he worked in a fever at the drawing competitions of the Beaux Arts from an atelier in the Rue du Four Saint Germain. He practiced until he could draw equally accurately with either his left or right hand. He studied the exact geometrics of classic design. And he began to sort out his own ideas.

The French loved him: *"Mackeem, l'Américain"* was an example of their own vitality, vivid talk. He was quick to perceive and to understand, to *comprendre à demi mot,* brimming with laughter and jokes. When ice formed on the lakes in the Bois de Boulogne "Mackeem" was the center of attention for admiring throngs as he skated, cutting perfect figure eights, taking off in long sweeps on the outside edges of his skates, then returning to take a pretty girl on his arm to waltz. In the spring "Mackeem" would persuade a group of Americans to play catch in the Luxembourg Gardens, and Parisians would line up three deep to watch him hit pop flies to incredible heights. He talked a group of his fellow Beaux Arts students into attending a gymnasium, and to their astonishment he taught them to become experts at the flying trapeze. In the summers he toured the architectural wonders of England, France, Germany, and Italy. It was the classical proportions of Rome which forever fixed his meticulous eye.

When the Franco-Prussian War of 1870 sent Americans scurrying back from Europe, McKim returned to New York and set out with his drawings in a portfolio under his arm to apply for work. He called at the offices of Gambrill and Richardson, 6 Hanover Street, where his Beaux Arts-trained pencil was examined by the gargantuan Henry Hobson Richardson. "My d-d-dear f-fellow," Richardson stuttered, "I haven't a thing in my office for my one and only d-d-d-draftsman to do. However, we are in c-c-competition for the B-B-Brattle Square Church in B-B-Boston, and if we win, I will take you on."

Richardson won the competition and in May, 1870, McKim was engaged "in charge of drawings" at a salary of eight dollars a week. He was twenty-two years old, and supremely happy. He worked on the Brattle Square Church, on the State Hospital Building in Buffalo, and the State Capitol drawings for Albany. By 1872 Richardson's office was in the running for the award of Trinity Church in Boston, and when they won the contest Richardson moved his main office to Boston. Charles McKim stayed in New York, where he was beginning to pick up commissions of his own for houses in Orange, New Jersey, and Saint James, Long Island. He had his first business card printed: "Charles McKim, Architect, with Gambrill & Richardson, 6 Hanover Street, New York." The job of "in charge of drawings" for Richardson in Boston was turned over to another young redhead, who could "draw like a house afire," Stanford White.

McKim's New York commissions continued to grow, and he soon had more than he could handle alone. At that moment another former student of L'Ecole des Beaux Arts walked into the two small rooms McKim had taken at 57 Broadway and offered to help out. William Rutherford Mead was twenty-six, a graduate of Amherst College, and his brother was Larkin Mead, the famous sculptor of *Lincoln* for the memorial in Springfield, Illinois. He too could be considered a member of the Boston aristocracy. His sister, Elinor, also an artist, had married the *Atlantic*'s editor, William Dean Howells, in Venice in 1862.

Mead was quiet, had a bent for engineering, liked to study the practical building problems of design. The two young men took an immediate liking to each other, found their talents were complementary, and without any formal partnership arrangement, worked together at an increasing schedule of constructions. Before 1872 had ended another Beaux Arts student, William B. Bigelow, joined them and "McKIM, MEAD & BIGELOW" was painted on the door at 57 Broadway.

William Bigelow had a very pretty sister, Annie, who was quick and bright and loved parties. On October 1, 1874, in Newport, Rhode Island, Charles Follen McKim married Miss Anne Bigelow, daughter of Mr. and Mrs. John William Bigelow of New York and Newport society. In 1875 a daughter, Margaret S. McKim, was born in the McKim's Newport cottage, but by 1876 Charles McKim was separated from his wife and living as a bachelor again on West Forty-fifth Street, in Manhattan.

When they were finally divorced in the Rhode Island courts, and when Anne Bigelow McKim returned to her family, she took her daughter Margaret McKim with her. Charles McKim would not even see his daughter again for twenty years. In the atmosphere of the divorce's dark accusations and vengeful enmities, William B. Bigelow withdrew from his partnership of the architectural firm at 57 Broadway.

By the summer of 1878, at thirty years of age, Charles Follen McKim had accumulated a baggage train of griefs. The father he had loved, Miller McKim, had died in 1874. His sister, Lucy McKim Garrison, had died in 1877. His mother, Sarah, ran the household in Orange, New Jersey, but she was aging fearfully. The failure of his marriage haunted him, and the gougings and justifications of divorce depressed him. His partner Mead suggested he take a holiday—revisit the Paris he loved. Mead said he could manage to keep the work flowing at the office. By July, Stanford White, McKim's ebullient associate from Richardson's Boston office, had taken Charles McKim's case in hand and had dragged him aboard ship to visit Saint-Gaudens in Paris "and do a little touring."

When Stanford White had finished treating Charles McKim's case in the fall of 1878, when White, McKim, and Saint-Gaudens had returned from their steamer trip down the Rhône and their excursions up the Loire through the châteaux, Charles McKim could resume his work in New York a restored man. A year after McKim returned to New York, Stanford White had exhausted his funds and was forced to abandon his excursions. White wrote his mother from Paris: "Good thunder, to think my wanderings are over, and that I shall again settle down into a respectable member of society, and no longer sleep in one bed one night and another the next, a slave of guide books and railroad indicators, and the prey of hotel-keepers, porters, beggars, pretty girls and the host of spiders that lay in wait for the unwary traveller . . ."

White landed in New York in September, 1879, was offered his old place in Boston by Henry Hobson Richardson, but instead paid a call on the Broadway office of his friend Charles F. McKim. The sign on the door was soon repainted once more to read: "McKIM, MEAD & WHITE, ARCHITECTS."

CHAPTER ELEVEN

ILLUSION OF MARRIAGE:
"Fat is Fatal"

FROM ITS INCEPTION, at the first source-springs of its combination, the partnership of McKim, Mead and White was a roaring success. The extent of their success was somewhat a surprise to the partners—both because it came so swiftly and was soon so permanent; and it was unique—explainable only as a great river is described by the variety of its contributing streams.

The training of the partners in Beaux Arts design and under Richardson was timely. They fell heir to Richardson's reputation. The talent of each individual partner was fortuitously complemented by the others, and they combined their talents in an extraordinary collaboration. They were superb organizers, not only of their own work but of the plans their city and their country imagined for themselves. The offices of the partners served as a headquarters—part school, part salon, part zany circus—for other architects, for sculptors, artists, editors, critics, opera stars, indeed anyone who happened to drop by. Yet the most important contributory to their success was that by the end of the nineteenth century, the city desperately wanted someone to tell it what to do with its accumulating riches. Charles F. McKim, heir to Boston's evangelical aristocracy, and Stanford White, heir of Washington Square, had inherited a social standing that many of their clients lacked. The partnership of McKim, Mead and White could often baptize by design a client's social acceptance, or at least they might imply they were conferring grace by decorating in good taste. Most of their clients had nothing but money.

McKim, Mead and White designed fifty-seven clubs. Charles F. McKim and Stanford White were also the founders, or directors, or trustees of so many associations they were often accused, and only half in jest, of creating memberships in order to secure the commission to design the clubhouse. The significance of their joining any group, however, was not in the commissions they won but in their domination of the social landscape. They were architects first, of course; they were also promoters and arbiters of style.

Partner William Rutherford Mead was the firm's engineer, and in the office his partners fondly called him "Dummy." He was always unruffled, unhurried; a quiet Yankee who saw to it that construction schedules were met, that draftsmen were assigned where they were needed, that every design had been calculated for its costs. Dummy Mead said he gave very little of his own time to design because he said all his time was needed "to keep his partners from making damn fools of themselves."

They called Charles F. McKim "Charles the Charmer." He was their resident classicist, a deliberate perfectionist, demanding plans be redrawn again and again by his draftsmen, who never seemed to complain when McKim required a scheme to be done over. Every building for which he was responsible had to be his best, and in addition, when completed, each building must be "an architectural event" good enough for all history. McKim loved New York for its energy and Paris for its gaiety, but it was the style of ancient Rome which he consciously imitated formal duty, ceremony, arranged for the display of civic duty.

Saint-Gaudens would caricature the three partners by showing Mead struggling with two kites, labeled "McKim" and "White," pulling in opposite directions. Everyone had to agree the wildest kite was Stanny, and when Saint-Gaudens caricatured White he drew in only the bushy moustache and straight red hair standing out from White's head as if it were a halo of energy. White was headstrong and impatient, always working at top speed; impulsive, prolific, and sometimes careless. He would sketch designs that the engineers would insist could not be constructed. He was as much a painter using stone for his materials as he was an architect of forms. Although he had begun as an apostle of Richardson Romanesque, he soon applied Richardson's sense of titanic gamboling in whatever eclectic style happened to suit his fancy. He said he had been converted to the elegance of Italianate Renaissance design, but he also delivered plans in Roman Imperial, Classic Greek, Colonial Grandeur, Federal Elegant, and New England Congregational Simple. He did plain summer cottages in shingle, and he did fairytale castles in marble.

Teamwork was essential to the success of their partnership but would lead to some confusion. Many buildings that the partners had never had anything to do with—buildings that perhaps a former draftsman of theirs had created—were believed to have been designed by the firm. Other buildings were attributed to White that perhaps had been sketched by White, designed by McKim, and the plans drawn by a draftsman under the supervision of Mead. The Century Club, for example, was sketched by White, designed by chief draftsman Joseph Wells, and then its details improved by Mead and by White and by McKim. White drew up the plans of the Villard houses around their central courtyard in Richardson Romanesque. Wells threw out White's Romanesque and redrew the plan in Renaissance style. Using Wells's drawings, which White said he liked better than his own, White headed the crew, which included among others John La Farge and Augustus Saint-Gaudens, in decorating in Italianate detail the Villard houses.

To further confuse art historians, Stanford White sketched continually—on the backs of menus, on envelopes, on scraps of paper—solutions to any design problem brought to his attention. He did magazine covers in an afternoon and drawings for a Pullman car overnight. To a young girl he saw about to start for Central Park with her ice skates, he said, "I will design a skating bag for you." He collected picture frames for artists by the wagonload. For Sarah Bernhardt, he hired a hall for a benefit performance, and sketched scenery for her over dinner. For Richard Watson Gilder, he drew a fireplace for a summer cottage on Cape Cod, using a carpenter's pencil on the back of a shingle. His energies seemed to be inexhaustible, profligate, and many of his ideas were scattered as if they were litter all over the city. He was inventor, promoter, firebrand, enthusiastic. "You haven't seen it?" he would demand about anything new. "Why, it's the finest thing of its kind! It's bully! It's wonderful . . . gorgeous!"

White's enthusiasms, and his generosity, made friends for him among competitors, professors of architecture, painters, editors, directors of railroad corporations, along Fifth Avenue in the drawing rooms of pretty women, on Broadway among the men-about-town. Yet it was his partner and friend Charles McKim who introduced White in 1880 to the Smith family of Saint James and to the daughters of Judge J. Lawrence Smith. According to Prescott Hall Butler, who had married one of the Smith girls, "it was after a protracted siege" that Stanford White advertised his engagement in 1883 to Miss Bessie Springs Smith.

Stanford White and Bessie Springs Smith were married February 7, 1884, at the Church of the Heavenly Rest, Bishop Littlejohn, Protestant Episcopal, officiating; assisted by the Reverend James Bloomfield Wetherill, husband of the bride's sister Kate. The bride and groom left for a six-month honeymoon in Europe.

When they stopped in Constantinople, White became so enthusiastic about a tiled mosque that he purchased the whole building, had it disassembled, and sent the mosaics by ship to New York. Unfortunately, the ship was wrecked off Bermuda, and the tiles went down among the coral reefs. He wrote his mother in April, 1884: "We have escaped the whirlpool of Paris and we are now flying along between Munich and Vienna. . . . I had to work pretty hard getting the tapestries."

By July the Whites were in Saint Moritz, and White claimed it was freezing at seven thousand feet. "The swell rig is fur-lined caps and overcoats." He climbed a ten-thousand-foot glacier, skinned his shins coming down, picked pink flowers from the meadows for Bessie, sent edelweiss in a letter to his mother. By the end of August, 1884, they were getting ready to sail home for New York. He wrote a postscript to his mother. "I have forgotten the most important news. . . . I cannot get the idea out of Bessie's head that she means to present you with a grandchild before the year is out."

In January, 1885, a son was born. Alexina Black Mease and Richard Grant White could smile and play with a grandson for a little while. Then in February, Richard Grant White said he felt tired and that he would have to give up playing in his Thursday night Quartette concerts. He would just listen for a while. His friends played Beethoven and Mozart for him for the last time. He continued to weaken, and then in April he died, just short of sixty-four.

To the grief of his father's death, Stanford White soon had to add another shock. His son fell sick, could not be saved, and died. Stanford and Bessie White buried their first child in the Smith family plot behind the clapboard church in the village of Saint James, Long Island. The stone read, "Richard Grant White II . . . died August 9, 1885, aged seven months and seventeen days."

Bessie was staggered by her loss. Although Stanny invented a grand trip through the South in 1886 as a diversion, his wife seemed to have suffered some permanent wound. When they first married, they had rented and then bought in Saint James a hill site on Crane Neck, overlooking Long Island Sound. Their property, Box Hill, adjoined the properties of two of Bessie's sisters and their husbands: Cornelia Smith—Mrs. Prescott Hall Butler; and Ella Smith—Mrs. Devereaux Emmet. Stanny had immediately gone to work remodeling, expanding, redecorating their house into a gay, rambling, joyous haven.

They also had a home at the corner of Lexington Avenue and Twenty-first Street, on Gramercy Park. Stanny had redecorated the Gramercy Park house in a riot of imaginative details: "Always live better than your clients," he would say. He used his Gramercy Park house to charm, buffalo, wheedle, and convince clients of what they surely always thought their plans should have included. The Gramercy Park house included a music room with nine harps stationed on a platform across one end of the room. Stanny would explain to a baffled client that he did not play the harp, he just liked them. Weren't they a "bully" sight?

Bessie Smith White did not always accompany Stanny on his rounds, soliciting commissions from the prominent for grand designs. On September 26, 1887, a second son, Lawrence Grant White, was born, and Bessie spent more and more of her time at the Whites' "summer" home in Saint James. She liked the quiet of the country. She gradually abandoned her husband's social whirl in the city to the necessities of "his professional interests."

She always accompanied Stanny when he made his tours of Europe, or almost always. Although such things can never be entirely clear, according to one historian of manners Bessie began to gain weight, and Stanny despaired. He was said to have spoken to her about it, but in the placid countryside of Saint James and in the company of her son and her sisters, she continued to expand. For a while Stanny was said to have sent her a dozen roses every day and enclosed a card that read, "Fat is Fatal."

CHAPTER TWELVE

THE ARCH AND THE GARDEN

ALTHOUGH STANFORD WHITE's family in Saint James loved his company and always were delighted by his arrival, the city demanded an increasing proportion of his concentration. "He was," said a loyal city friend, "the chief of all our little entertainments," and by the end of the nineteenth century White's sense of play, his bositerous gamboling, his training in the arts, and his delight in beauty were precisely what New York yearned to worship.

Having abandoned the simple witness once represented by church spires, having deserted every measure of value except money, and beginning to suspect that money might be an unreliable standard, the city was experimenting with "Beauty" as the new transcendental faith. It was a confession with several advantages, especially to the newly rich and ambitious: Beauty depended upon display for its appreciation, and the theater of money's advantages easily won the heart of money's possessors. Even more significant, however, was that the meaning of Beauty was open to interpretation like that of a sentiment such as "Patriotism," and all appreciations of Beauty would have to be accepted as equal. Admission to the city's leading congregations, therefore, could be assured to anyone willing to swear allegiance to Beauty, spend freely, and take a few lessons in Art—which architects, painters, and sculptors gladly offered to supply.

The City Beautiful was soon to be a fond hope similar in its understanding to what the old texts had described as The Promised Land, and it was not long before anyone who doubted the deliverance promised by Art risked the fury of the faithful. Nevertheless, Art worshiped for Art's sake inevitably led to strange practices.

When Art's energies were expressed in permanent form—chiseled from marble, painted on canvas, consecrated in stone, its believers had to adore the materials used instead of what the materials might represent. It would come to pass that the faithful would worship empty buildings, preserve as holy relic batches of paint dumped on canvas, and invoke all the powers of litany to celebrate a rock striated by an unknown glacier. Since artistic works that celebrated the material would in themselves be mute—even more enigmatic than graven images—powerful committees would have to be formed to make the frowning interpretations, and sophistication would eventually be considered the first virtue of Culture's theology. Yet when Stanford White served as one of the early bishops of Art's congregation it was believed that Beauty conferred Grace in simple ways and with much gaiety.

In the beginning, all the city yearned for was some decoration, much in the same way a restless woman might want to display an emerald necklace—as an emblem of her success and a promise to herself of her constancy. From Stanford White, the city would learn the delights of style. He would teach her how to add luster to her appearance. He invented banquets and arranged balls to divert her, choosing and arranging the flowers dedicated to her amusement, and the menu to satisfy her taste. He built houses for her, then decorated them, choosing even her intimate interior colors.

When a client wrote for advice on the decoration of her bedroom, he replied, "Any color as long as it is red." In imitation of his example, the occupation of "interior decorator" sprung up to supply carved mantles, Oriental rugs, Aubusson tapestries, Louis XV chairs, and Regency mirrors. He toured Europe constantly, buying up the best art he could obtain and was reproached for robbing the Old World to decorate the New. He answered that dominant nations had always plundered the art of their predecessors, and in his wake the major art dealers began to move their headquarters from London and Paris to Fifth Avenue.

To honor his city's old faiths, he created magnificent Byzan tine-jewel churches—so polished, ornate, and lavish, said one critic "that a clever Empress might have built it." When the richness of his churches was criticized as incompatible with the imperatives of the old Presbyterian faith White answered that he constructed "a modern church, and in a style natural to and belonging to the religion which it represents and the country in which it is built."

For his city's heroes, White promoted statues and monuments placed advantageously in her public parks. His collaboration on the statue of *Admiral David Glasgow Farragut,* Union hero of the Battle of Mobile Bay, with Augustus Saint-Gaudens was typical. White helped Saint-Gaudens win the commission, worked to raise the money, designed for Saint-Gaudens the base and pedestal, selected the marbles to be used and haggled with the contractors over their prices, required his father Richard Grant White to edit the inscription, chose the site in Madison Square, and placed Saint-Gaudens' work so that reflections from the windows of the Fifth Avenue Hotel would not blaze the admiral's stance. When the man who had said "Damn the torpedoes, full speed ahead," was finally cast and ready to be unveiled on May 25, 1881, Stanford White helped to arrange the ceremony.

Farragut stood opposite Delmonico's and the Hotel Brunswick, at the point where the aristocratic part of Fifth Avenue began, and where the Money Kings would see him every day. "There is a swing to unveilings," said Saint-Gaudens, "and the moment when the veil drops from the monument certainly makes up for the many woes that go toward creating the work."

The rope to unveil *Farragut* was pulled by John H. Knowles, the sailor who had lashed the admiral to the mast in the Battle of Mobile Bay. A battery of artillery set up in Madison Square Park fired salutes, and as the smell of cordite drifted away on a spring afternoon, a company of sailors presented arms. Then Mr. Joseph Choate gave the oration.

The *Admiral Farragut* that was revealed, all agreed, was a major work; the combination of man and pedestal were praised. In *Scribner's,* editor Richard Watson Gilder wrote that *Farragut* was "a sign of the increase of the art spirit in

America." Art critic D. Maitland Armstrong said he was surprised to see how "the rabble about the statue spoke of it, and how they seemed touched by it. It is a revelation to them, and what is more, I feel they are ready and longing for better art. It cheers one to think . . ."

Working with Saint-Gaudens, White cheered America's artistic impression of itself by unveiling a series of works, all of them declared masterpieces, and each one defining permanently some landmark of the national imagination: in 1881 *Captain Randall,* privateer and freebooter, benefactor of Sailors' Snug Harbor, was dedicated on Staten Island; in 1887, in Springfield, Massachusetts, *The Puritan* was revealed—stalwart, determined, righteous, stubborn; in 1895, the monument to *James A. Garfield* portrayed the kind of man Ohio sent on to the presidency; in 1897, in a niche beside the Cooper Institute of Science and Arts, *Peter Cooper* took his place as an example of New York's admired citizen; in 1905, in Philadelphia, *The Pilgrim* was recalled as archetype of American adventure; and in the same year, a memorial was dedicated next to Trinity Church, Boston, with a statue of *Phillips Brooks,* the century's greatest preacher. The *Standing Lincoln* by Saint-Gaudens and White, unveiled in Chicago in 1887, and their *Seated Lincoln,* not entirely finished until 1930 were both definitive portraits.

But their collaboration on the *Adams Memorial* in Rock Creek Cemetery, Washington, D.C., completed in 1891, seemed to disturb the national conscience. Although every critic would agree the *Adams Memorial* was the finest example of sculpture in America and a masterpiece that rivaled in its excellence the greatest works in history, it had a quality that puzzled its visitors and perhaps raised questions that were uncomfortable.

Henry Adams had commissioned his friends Saint-Gaudens and White to prepare a memorial to his wife Marion Hooper Adams, who had committed suicide on December 6, 1885. Henry Adams was the line descendant of the first name in American history: great-grandson of John Adams, author of the Constitutions of Massachusetts, New York, and the United States of America, Vice-President under Washington, then

President himself; grandson of John Quincy Adams, Vice-President, President, congressman, last of the New England Federalists; son of Charles Francis Adams, United States Minister to London when British intervention would have ruined the Union cause.

Distinguished not only by his illustrious name, Henry Adams was his century's leading historian, its most admired philosopher, a teacher, and an active editor in the issues of nineteenth-century American politics. His wife's death, he said, shattered his life, and he wanted in her memory something that would be a representation of "Nirvana . . . a peaceful acceptance of death and whatever lay in the future."

Adams wrote to Richard Watson Gilder about the figure Saint-Gaudens fashioned. "The whole meaning and feeling of the figure is in its universality and anonymity. My own name for it is 'The Peace of God' . . . a real artist would be very careful to give it no name that the public could turn into a limitation of its nature."

The figure of the *Adams Memorial* could have been a woman, but Saint-Gaudens deliberately used both men and women as models so the result would not represent either sex. Saint-Gaudens' figure was seated upon a block of stone, with its back against a polished stone monolith, topped by a classic frieze. White's background, said Saint-Gaudens, "was very fine, sober and strong." And White's landscaping and surrounding trees would eventually make the enclosure an almost secret grove.

The seated figure was draped in a great cloak, which might ward off the chills of eternal frosts and which fell in long simple folds from the head, over parted knees, to the feet. The cloak veiled the face, hid it behind a hood, half-concealing a narrow chin, a strong nose, and eyes forever cast down. The figure's lips were silent, never likely to speak again. A visitor asked Saint-Gaudens if his figure represented happiness. "No," said Gus, "it is beyond pain, and beyond joy."

Henry Adams said he would stop there often to see what the figure had to tell him that was new, "but, in all that it had to say, he never once thought of questioning what it meant." Adams said he was fascinated by the responses of those who came to stand before his wife's *Memorial*: it became a tourist attraction, and there were a variety of explanations from both visitors and guides on the meaning of "Nirvana." The majority lacked all conviction, Adams noted, but the clergy were an exception. They were full of passionate intensity and spoke out to their companions against the expression they saw in the figure of their own despair. "Like others," Adams recorded, "the priest saw only what he brought. . . . The American layman had lost sight of ideals; the American priest had lost sight of faith." Seated before his wife's *Memorial,* Adams would admit that he too drifted in the dead waters at the turn of the century, "where not a breath stirred . . . or fretted the mental torpor of self-content."

With his brother, Charles Francis Adams, Jr., Henry Adams had studied the power of the new riches. He saw "a class of men who will wield within the State a power created by the State, but too great for its control." He predicted that as the new corporations subjected the State to their own control, they would combine "the natural powers of the individual with the factitious powers of the corporation"; and that the result would be the introduction of dictators to both corporate and national life. "The individual," the Adams brothers had forecast, "will hereafter be engrafted on the corporation,—democracy running its course, and resulting in imperialism."

Adams was not only dismayed by the advent of Caesars to his country's institutions but could cite energies "whose style of education were violently coercive"; forces like the railway system, "which already approached the carnage of war; or automobiles and firearms universally distributed," which, he predicted, would make "an earthquake almost a nervous relaxation." He was gloomy about what he understood, guessing that mankind had begun to worship the illusion of power, a devotion that would lead to universal war and an acceleration of "vertiginous violence . . . an immense volume of force . . . detached from the unknown universe of energy."

When Henry Adams sailed up New York's lower bay from Europe in 1904 he found the approaches to the city's skyline more striking than ever, but he noted that the city had become unlike anything man had ever known—some quantum leap had occurred in the social landscape. What he saw roaring up Broadway was "the two-thousand-year failure of Christianity . . . a city frantic in its effort to explain something which defied meaning." Something had exploded, said Adams, "and thrown great masses of stone and steam against the sky. The city had the air and movement of hysteria, and the citizens were crying, in every accent of anger and alarm, that the new forces must at any cost be brought under control."

The uncontrolled and alarming forces described by Henry Adams, combined with the city's terror at having abandoned all hope of any Nirvana, and added to the city's refusal to give up the endless repetition of its illusions, all created a demand for Stanford White's talents. Against chaos, the city presumed White might summon up the powers of Art, and both Fifth Avenue and Broadway imagined White's presence as pervasive. As critic John Jay Chapman explained, "He swam on a wave of prestige that lifted him into view like a Titan. . . . Not a day passed without hearing something new about him. His flaming red hair could be seen a mile; and every night at the opera he would come in late, not purposely advertising himself, but intuitively knowing that every millionaire in town would see him, and that the galleries would whisper, and even the supers on the stage would mutter: *There's Stanford White.*"

White's clients consulted his opinion and demanded his talent for more than architecture. Real estate millionaire Robert Goelet wanted a yachting prize to be executed by Tiffany: "I wonder whether that famous cup you designed for me is finished?" Vanderbilt heiress Consuelo, Duchess of Manchester, wrote, "Don't forget about the monument I want put up in Woodlawn." The editors of the *Century* Magazine wanted cover designs. "Will it be possible for you to give us the necessary designs before your departure, at a price somewhere in the neighborhood of $500?" Harper Brothers, book publishers, wanted a cover drawn for a deluxe edition of *She Stoops To Conquer.* For a collection of Eugene Field's poems and for an edition of Izaak Walton's *Compleat Angler,* White designed covers and title pages. For Eleonora Duse, actress, White supplied a jeweled Byzantine cross and chain to wear as part of her costume.

In addition, White was expected to manage the affairs of the leading clubs. He organized benefits, arranged shows for artists, and if the artists lacked the proper frames for their portraits, White could be counted upon to get the frames from the warehouse—even if the trip to the warehouse caused him to be late for the opera. Moreover, he supervised the membership lists. For example, in 1904 he was writing to Saint-Gaudens: "You long-nosed farmer you! What do you mean by backing out of the Brook Club? It's not your 'mun' we want, but your name and yourself. That is, we want you as a nest egg and an attraction for a dozen men we want in."

Above all, the demand for his drawings constantly increased: the Hotel Imperial, Broadway and 31st Street; a country palace for Pierre Lorillard, heir to a snuff fortune, in Tuxedo Park; an entire block of flats between 138th and 139th streets in Harlem for contractor David H. King, Jr; the Maryland Society's *Battle Monument* in Prospect Park, Brooklyn; and residences for Mrs. E. M. Patterson in Chicago; Mrs. K. A. Wetherill in Saint James, Long Island; Mrs. Eliot F. Shepard in Scarborough, New York; Charles T. Barney at 67 Park; Stuyvesant Fish at Madison and 78th Street; Henry W. Poor at 1 Lexington Avenue; Thomas Page Nelson in Washington, D.C.; and for various Whitneys on Fifth Avenue and Long Island.

Besides residences, there was an unending stream of commercial commissions: a powerhouse and workers' houses for the Cataract Construction Company, Niagara Falls; the Cosmopolitan Building, in Irvington, New York; the Herald Building on Herald Square—a recreation of the palace of the Doges in Venice; the Havana Tobacco Company Store; the Knickerbocker Trust Company; and the Gorham Building on Fifth Avenue; the powerhouses of the Interborough Transit Company on Twelfth Avenue, and the restaurant and ballroom for Louis Sherry on Fifth Avenue.

In a period of twenty-five years the partnership of McKim, Mead and White designed and built over a thousand works.

Stanford White had to be credited with the redesign and re-building of the campus of the University of Virginia and for the uptown campus of New York University. Charles McKim had to be credited with the designs of the Columbia University campus. Most of the work at West Point was generally credited to White; most of the work at Harvard was credited to McKim.

In addition, Boston Symphony Hall, the Boston Public Library, Pennsylvania Station, the General Post Office on Eighth Avenue, and J. P. Morgan's Library at Madison and Thirty-seventh were generally credited to McKim; but in every design they undertook, the partners were constant consultants and contributors to each other. An English critic would summarize the firm's work: "Future generations, I am confident, will come to look at the great, if rather impersonal architecture which came from the McKim, Mead and White office . . . as we do now at the work of the great Italian giants . . . the finest aspirations of a great people at a great epoch."

The partnership was constantly engaged in public works. McKim founded the American Academy of Rome to train American artists, sculptors, and architects. White organized dinners and auxiliary women's committees and raised money to support the school. When the Senate Committee on the District of Columbia needed a plan to restore the Capitol of the United States of America, they turned to McKim for the plans. By 1901 the offices of McKim, Mead and White had drawn up the plans for the Great Mall, located the War College and designed it, drawn the plans and provided for the landscaping of the Memorial Bridge, the Reflecting Pool, and the Lincoln Memorial.

When President Theodore Roosevelt decided to restore, redecorate, and furnish the White House, it was McKim, Mead and White who were given the commission. By 1902 they had spent $475,445 to refurbish the nation's Executive Mansion—adding grace notes to its "classic revival" style, creating a State Dining Room, providing portrait galleries, hanging tapestries, installing elevators, and fixing the fireplaces so that they would draw.

The White House, the plans for the Memorial Bridge and

the Mall, the founding of the Academy of Rome, and McKim's constant insistence on classic style for both public and university buildings combined to make the influence of McKim, Mead and White permanent; imitation of their work would abound. Although the influence of the partnership in the design of the Chicago World's Fair of 1893 was not as obvious, it was perhaps more significant than their permanent works. The Chicago World's Fair came and went in two years, but its example fixed American public style for at least the next half-century.

In the spring of 1890 President Benjamin Harrison signed an Act of Congress providing for "The World's Columbian Exposition of Arts, Industries, Manufactures, and the products of the Soil, Mine and Sea." Although the Fair would be held in Chicago and a Chicago architect, "Uncle Dan" Burnham was appointed chairman of the Fair Committee, the first thing Uncle Dan did was to call a "planning committee" meeting in the offices of McKim, Mead and White in New York. At the turn of the century the boast of Uncle Dan's city was that "Chicago didn't have no culture yet, but you could bet that when Chicago got some, they'd sure make it hum." To get Chicago humming, McKim, Mead and White would gather the architects, artists, landscape designers, and sculptors "to work for a common effect."

Charles McKim defined their common purpose as "the uniform use of classical motives to control the style." Under McKim's leadership, the artists of New York would transform sandy dunes at the edge of Lake Michigan into a "classic White City," so orderly that "it would appear the vision of an enchanter rather than the work of men."

The Fair would be called "The White City" because its materials would be those of ancient Mediterranean construction—white marble, and if not exactly marble, then Wisconsin hardwoods painted to look like marble. There would be fountains and reflecting pools and malls. Inside the halls there would be exhibits of American ingenuity—McCormick reapers, and Bell telephones, and Edison electric contrivances, and steam-operated punch presses, and there would be dynamos—the products of hard work and invention. Inside the halls of the exhibition a Connecticut Yankee might wander endlessly, taking notes on what a little tinkering might do to improve the progress of manufactures. Outside the halls of the exhibition a Roman senator might wander along the facades, satisfied that classical proportions were permanent additions to history. More than six million dollars were spent on the Chicago Fair, and forty-four nations, together with twenty-eight colonies and provinces, erected pavilions. Six thousand workers labored to build, according to Daniel Burnham, "what the Romans would have wished to create."

When the Chicago Fair opened in 1893, it was a smashing success. Huge crowds milled through the exhibits, marveling at the wonders of American technology. The curious could also entertain themselves by riding on George Ferris' giant wheel or be scandalized by watching Little Egypt perform her bellydances. As proud of Chicago's creation as its visitors, Daniel Burnham told a doubting apprentice architect, Frank Lloyd Wright, "The American people have seen the classics on a grand scale for the first time. I can see all America constructed along the lines of the Fair, in noble, dignified classic style."

Despite Burnham's preaching, young Frank Lloyd Wright was appalled, and Wright's teacher—Louis Sullivan—was even more distressed. Sullivan had designed the Fair's Transportation Building, to house examples of steam engines, in a style that seemed something like Classic but that later would be recognized as Modern. Sullivan described the "Classic" vision in Chicago as "unhappy, irrational, heedless, pessimistic, unlovely, distracted and decadent structures." He prophesied, "The damage wrought by the World's Fair will last for a half century, if not longer. It has penetrated deep into the constitution of the American mind, effecting there lesions significant of dementia."

Unlike Wright or Sullivan, Henry Adams rather liked the classical fantasy created by his friends Burnham, McKim, La Farge, Saint-Gaudens, and White. Adams was no more disturbed by the fashion in Chicago's architecture than he would have been angered by the style of ladies' hats. He wandered

Evelyn Nesbit arrived in New York in 1900 at sweet sixteen. She posed as "Dawn" and as "Innocence."
(CULVER PICTURES, INC.)

When Evelyn first met Stanford White in 1901, he was nearly fifty and the city's leading citizen.
(CULVER PICTURES, INC.)

In *Floradora* the men sang on bended knee to the beauties in the sextette: "Tell me, pretty maiden, are there any more at home like you?"
(THE BETTMANN ARCHIVE, INC.)

Bessie Springs White began to spend more of her time at home in Saint James, Long Island.
(CULVER PICTURES, INC.)

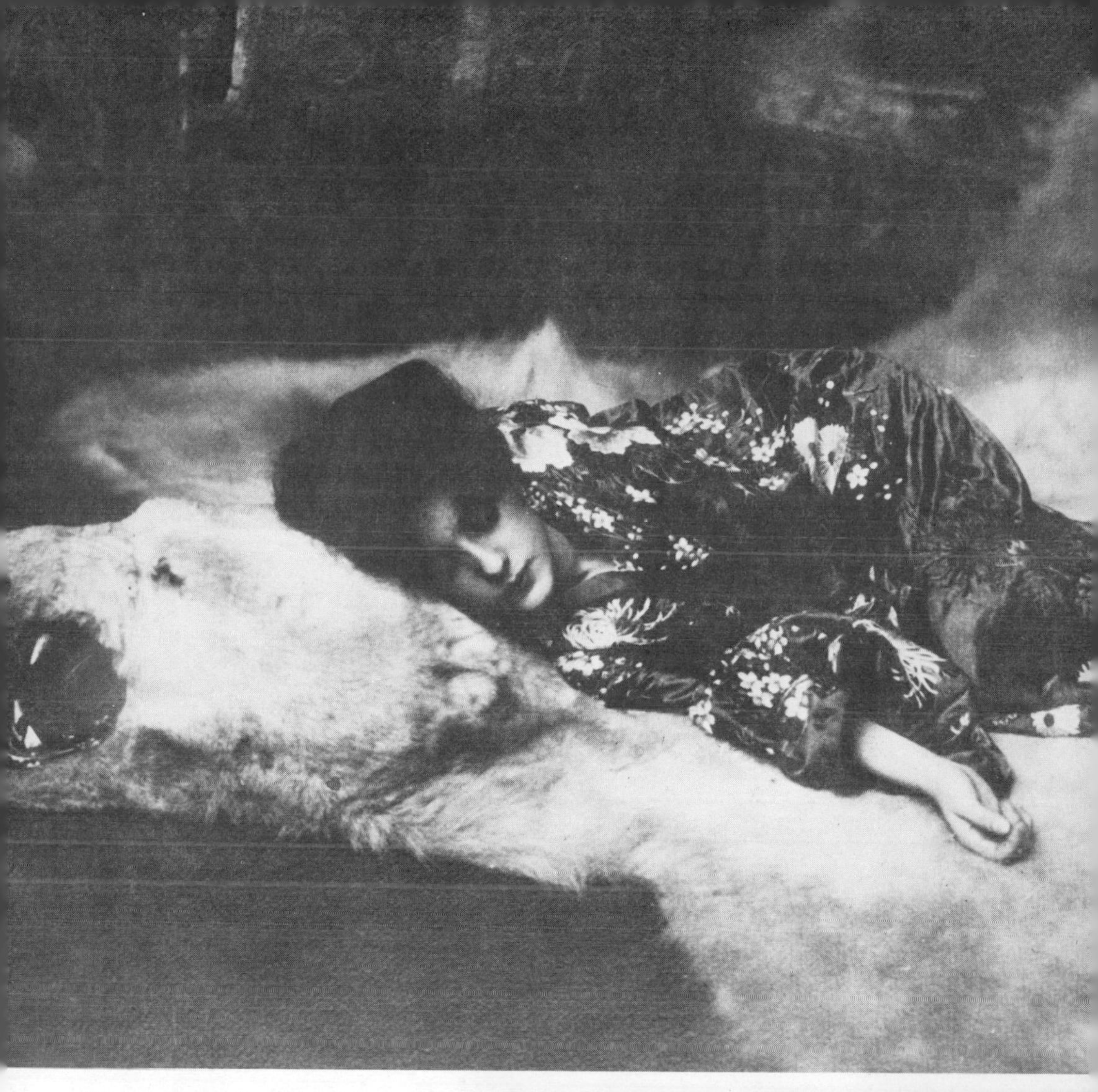

Evelyn posed in one of Stanny's fabulous kimonos on a white polar-bear skin. She was still only seventeen, but a "tired butterfly."
(CULVER PICTURES, INC.)

McKim, Mead, and White were not only architects, but arbiters of taste and the authorities of style.
(CULVER PICTURES, INC.)

MDCCCXCIII PALACE OF MECHANIC ARTS
AMERICAM

The World's Fair at Chicago in 1893 set a standard for the nation. Inside the Palace of Mechanic Arts, dynamos hummed; outside, a senator from Nero's Rome or Washington, D.C., would feel at home.
(CULVER PICTURES, INC.)

"Boss" Tweed invented machine politics: He said he needed men who understood addition, subtraction, and silence.
(THE BETTMANN ARCHIVE, INC.)

Henry Villard gave up rectitude and the honors associated with the abolitionist aristocracy to plunge into bonds.
(THE BETTMANN ARCHIVE, INC.)

In 1880, when McKim, Mead, and White went to work, the landmarks on the horizon were church spires. Fifth Avenue, looking south from Forty-second Street, was lined with brownstones. The Egyptian Reservoir, in the right foreground, was opened in 1853–the year White was born.
(THE BETTMANN ARCHIVE, INC.)

The marble arch in Washington Square Park would become a permanent landmark of the city's imagination; but the first arch designed by Stanford White spanned lower Fifth Avenue, was built of wood, and featured President Washington atop its lintel.
(THE BETTMANN ARCHIVE, INC.)

White and Augustus Saint-Gaudens collaborated on the city's memorials. General Sherman's horse followed Victory toward the Plaza Hotel day and night. Gussie Saint-Gaudens forgave her husband for his brief affair with Victory's model.
(THE BETTMANN ARCHIVE, INC.)

Designed by White and Joseph Wells, decorated by Saint-Gaudens and John La Farge, the palace on Madison Avenue would be occupied by the Whitelaw Reids, the United Nations, Random House, and cardinals of the Church, but they would always be called the Villard Houses.
(WIDE WORLD PHOTOS, INC.)

When it was completed in 1893, White's Garden stood at the corner of a fashionable park. The Jerome family mansion, on the right, was across the street from the landmark tower. Diana swung on ball bearings—a weathervane—300 feet above the street. No matter where it was later located, it would always be called Madison Square Garden.
(THE BETTMANN ARCHIVE, INC.)

White and Saint-Gaudens decided the first Diana was too tall. At their own expense they recast her thirteen feet high.
(THE BETTMANN ARCHIVE, INC.)

Harry Kendall Thaw was heir to $40 million in Pennsy bonds and was described as a "Pittsburgh Idler."
(CULVER PICTURES, INC.)

Alice Cornelia Thaw, Countess of Yarmouth, was sold to an English lord for $1 million, cash in advance.
(CULVER PICTURES, INC.)

When Evelyn Nesbit Thaw took the stand, C. Allan Gilbert sketched her for *The New York Evening World*. Within a week thousands of copies of her costume appeared on the streets.
(THE NEW YORK PUBLIC LIBRARY/ ANNE MOONEY)

The New York Evening World reprinted the sketch they had printed in 1895 of Susie Johnson coming up out of the pie in Jimmy Breese's studio.
(THE NEW YORK PUBLIC LIBRARY/ANNE MOONEY)

Mother Thaw, sketched by Gilbert at the first trial, paid for all the trials to follow. She promised to pay Evelyn for her testimony.
(THE NEW YORK PUBLIC LIBRARY/ANNE MOONEY)

William Travers Jerome, an incorruptible district attorney, was never able to shake Evelyn's story.
(THE NEW YORK PUBLIC LIBRARY/ANNE MOONEY)

After Thaw's escape from Matteawan it took Jerome nearly a year to get him back into the Tombs, where the chaplain greeted Harry like an old friend.
(CULVER PICTURES, INC.)

When Mother Thaw wouldn't pay, Evelyn took to the road. She danced down the vaudeville trail with Jack Clifford, introducing the new ragtime dances—the one-step, the two-step, and the fox-trot.
(CULVER PICTURES, INC.)

By 1928 Harry K. Thaw, arriving on the *Ile de France,* looked as if he were a distinguished old gentleman, but he was still getting arrested.
(CULVER PICTURES, INC.)

along with Chicago's exuberant crowds and enjoyed immensely their vulgarity. Yet he was puzzled; he wondered how the Beaux Arts had been induced to spend two summers in Chicago—a city best known as a mining camp on Lake Michigan built four stories high, with a railroad terminal, and hogyards.

Behind the facades of imperial majesty, Adams studied the exhibits, and he began to consider "the economics of force." From examples of Yankee ingenuity, he prophesied that the twentieth century would be absorbed by the unlimited forces represented by the dynamo. At Chicago, Henry Adams began to wonder "whether the American people knew where they were driving."

In fact, the Fair provided a demonstration that the American people knew perfectly well where they were headed. Architect Daniel Burnham would be largely correct. Not only did the nation's Capitol adopt the Classic as the permanent expression of architectural style, not only did Washington, D.C., line McKim's Mall with one Roman temple after another, but after 1893 almost every public building in the land seemed to have been transplanted directly from the history of the Caesars.

The American imperial fantasy was an odd but accepted combination. The national political tradition required of the ambitious they pretend to have been born in a log cabin. If no rough-hewn cabin was available, those who sought office could substitute a white frame house with a front porch on an elm-shaded street. Once having gained power, however, the American fantasy required of its governors they occupy Classic buildings built of white marble on a scale so grand that even Nero would have been envious. From behind these magnificent facades, America would develop the power delivered by legions of dynamos.

The Roman architecture of Chicago's Fair and imperial Washington was foreshadowed in 1889 by Stanford White's design of an Arch as a memorial to George Washington in New York. White's first Arch was a temporary structure built of wood, then painted to look like marble. It was erected to coincide with a three-day celebration at the end of April, 1889, of Washington's inauguration as the nation's first President.

The Washington Centennial festivities included rowing President Benjamin Harrison across the Hudson in a barge from Elizabethtown, New Jersey, to the Battery. President Harrison landed at the foot of Wall Street, just as Washington had done, and then led a parade up Broadway to Washington Square. Red, white, and blue bunting decorated the route, and Stanford White had arranged for flags, banners, and streamers. Cannons were stationed in Washington Square Park, and upon the arrival of President Harrison the guns fired their salutes. John Greenleaf Whittier had composed an ode, which the mayor read, and Mr. Chauncey Depew made the address. Stanford White's Arch was then "unveiled."

It stood on slender columns spanning the lower part of Fifth Avenue. A statue of *Washington* was centered atop its lintel, his hand cocked on his right hip. He faced south into the park with his swallowtailed coat seen from behind from the vantage of upper Fifth Avenue. After President Harrison had gone back to the duties of his presidency the merchants of Fifth Avenue could not restrain their pride in the Arch. "A careful research of the records justifies the belief that this is the only arch in the world erected by private subscription to mark a historical event." The city's editors took up the merchants' clamor for civic decoration and urged "the noble arch in Washington Square be made permanent."

A committee was duly organized to raise the money. Within a month the accounts of the committee showed $40,000 already subscribed. Then fundraising paused because the members' charity was needed to help thousands of victims of the Johnstown, Pennsylvania, flood. By May, 1890, however, the Arch fund had resumed its activities and showed "$80,000 in hand."

A foundation could be laid and a ceremony conducted for the laying of cornerstones, which were now set back into the park—no longer spanning Fifth Avenue itself but instead laid out across the curved path that William Marcy Tweed had cut across the old parade grounds to enhance the value of his property on Washington Square South. The cornerstone ceremony opened with a prayer by Bishop Henry Codman Potter, Protestant Episcopal, a chorus of two hundred voices sang hymns, and construction could begin.

The day for the dedication did not finally arrive until May 4, 1895, but once again Bishop Potter was on hand to open the proceedings with a prayer. New York's Governor Levi P. Morton reviewed the troops as they marched under the completed Arch. It no longer stood on slender columns but on solid bases, each with four black obsidian Corinthian columns. It was no longer a temporary Arch of wood, but built with white marble. On the south side a frieze showed the American eagle and Washington's initials modeled in its center. Curiously, George Washington did not appear at all on the Arch in 1895. Statues of him would not be added for twenty years, and then in niches at the Arch's base.

In the program for the dedication ceremonies in 1895 Stanford White wrote the description of his own Arch: "In style this monument is distinctly classical, and by this is meant Roman. When brought in close comparison, however, with the triumphal arches of Rome and the Roman Empire many differences are to be noted—that of the size of the opening being the most striking. No arch of antiquity containing but one opening has a span as great as that at New York."

White's program notes compared his Arch to the greatest triumphal arches of the Roman Empire—at Salonika, at Alcántara, at Aosta—not one of them had a span as wide as the Arch of Fifth Avenue! The Arch on Washington Square could be imagined as greater than all the arches through which Roman emperors had paraded their legions—conquerors followed by their long baggage trains of spoils, their strings of manacled slaves shuffling behind polished chariots; and the dazzled mob cheering, stamping its feet, shouting—Hail Galba! Hail Otto! Hail Vitellius! Hail Vespasian! Hail! Hail! Hail! Hail!

To some historians the scenes recalled by a triumphal arch seemed a peculiar way to memorialize the virtues of George Washington: Virginia gentleman farmer, aristocrat of Old Whig tendencies, surveyor of the Northwest wilderness, who believed certain truths to be self-evident, fought his king for the sake of life, liberty, and the pursuit of happiness, then served two modest terms as President, but immediately retired to his Potomac River farm.

Washington was a hero precisely because he consistently declined the opportunities of Caesar. Although Stanford White's Arch on Washington Square had very little connection to the father of his country, except perhaps the initials "G.W." on the frieze, it was nevertheless a magnificent structure, and it became one of New York's permanent delights. By the time the Arch was dedicated the four-story-high brick facades of the old houses along Washington Square North were scraps of evidence that a pious merchant aristocracy had once held sway over the city's fortunes. Running north from their old village green and from the focus of their Arch, Fifth Avenue had thrust up a jagged-tooth skyline—apartment buildings, stores, banks, insurance companies, office towers, each rising as high as their elevators and mortgages would take them, six stories, ten stories, fifteen, twenty stories, and even higher. The result of their soaring growth was to convert Fifth Avenue into a canyon, and to cast its side streets into constant shadow. As the shadows lengthened along Fifth Avenue's vista, Washington's Arch was illuminated by the sunlight of its park. By comparison to the stone and steel heaved up along the canyon's walls, the Arch appeared to grow smaller until it almost seemed to be dainty—a charming, bright, little anachronism, with a span greater than any arch in the Roman Empire, but a delightful monument to Stanford White's imagination.

White would bequeath to New York another landmark altogether different: a permanent palace of pleasures, always called Madison Square Garden no matter where, or how often, it moved. White was promoter, successor to P. T. Barnum, ringmaster, host, impresario, master of ceremonies, fundraiser, shareholder, noteholder, bond floater, and vice-president of the first Madison Square Garden Corporation. His was not the first hippodrome at the Madison Square location, but when the city needed a permanent *circus maximus* Stanford White provided it and, of course, designed and built it, too.

In the 1860's the entire block bounded by Madison and

Fourth Avenues between Twenty-sixth and Twenty-seventh streets was occupied by the railroad sheds of the New York Central and Harlem Railroad and was called the Union Depot. When Madison Square became the city's fashionable location after the Civil War, Commodore Vanderbilt abandoned the Union Depot to move uptown to Forty-second Street and Park. The tracks of the old depot were torn up and the shed leased to a group of promoters who renamed the arena they created "The Great Roman Hippodrome." They went broke selling tickets for various circuses and could only make money by promoting fights.

But fights were supposed to be illegal, and by 1873 Phineas T. Barnum had acquired the lease to the train shed, renamed it "Barnum's Hippodrome," and said that it would be the permanent home of Barnum's Circus. In 1875 Barnum let his lease expire, and Patrick Carsfield Gilmore took over the old train sheds to present band concerts. Gilmore's Marching Band lost just as much money as Barnum's Circus, and despite the money Gilmore could make promoting "scientific exhibitions" between two "professors" in the "illustrated art of pugilism," Gilmore abandoned his hopes in 1878.

Commodore Vanderbilt's son, William H. Vanderbilt, announced that the Central's men would operate the entertainments in the shed themselves. Vanderbilt's lieutenants paid their counterparts at Tammany Hall handsomely to allow the fights, and in 1882 John L. Sullivan demonstrated in a "scientific exhibition" how to knock an English "professor" by the name of "Tug" Collins unconscious. For his abilities at giving "illustrated lectures," Sullivan was awarded a diamond-studded belt, declared "Heavyweight Champion of the World," and accepted a share of the purse. On the night Sullivan kayoed Collins, William H. Vanderbilt sat ringside with a party of his friends, dressed in evening clothes and black silk opera hat, banging his silver-headed walking cane on the floor, cheering himself hoarse for the champion. Unfortunately, Tammany explained to Mr. Vanderbilt that the price for continuing exhibitions of the illegal fights would be going up. In turn, Mr. Vanderbilt estimated that the cost of the fights would be too high, and that without the fights the

Central's arena would be a hopeless money-loser, and therefore the Central would raze their sheds and find some other practical use for their property.

Vanderbilt's conclusions were heard with general dismay, particularly by the directors of the National Horse Show, an institution of peculiar influence in New York's new topography of money. During the 1880's the city had acquired the habit of making an extraordinary display every November. A pageant of chariots, equipages, four-in-hands, hunters, jumpers, trotters, and pacers would appear in an arena and then be judged for excellence. The Horse Show became an opportunity for those who said they were leaders in society to reassure themselves that training was, of course, important, but in the end, breeding was what counted. Moreover, by a mysterious common consent, The Opening of the Horse Show became the date that replaced Epiphany as the opening of the social season, and an invitation to join the Horse Show Association was a summons from the kingdom of the most high, a bid frantically attractive to those poor souls who might be suffering from the possession of more money than social standing.

The roster of the Horse Show Association members was to some an unfathomable list, but it was used as the nucleus for the concoction of the first *Social Register* by Mr. Louis Keller. He printed a directory of the socially acceptable on a good rag paper, using a handsome serifed type, and bound his list in a plain black cover with red lettering, in what everyone supposed must be a limited number of copies. It was soon called "the blue book," even though there was nothing "blue" about it, and often referred to as "the stud book."

The Social Register listed the home address and correct spelling of each of the anointed, and it included the names of eligible sons and marriageable daughters, and even listed the summer "domiciles" at Newport, or Oyster Bay, or Saratoga, or wherever social business needed to be conducted. In all seasons it was considered a useful little book to have near at hand, because it contained the roster for successful parties. After the influence of the neighborhood churches waned, the city yearned to reconstitute itself into something resembling the old parishes and needed a parish list that would reflect whose pews were paid up. *The Social Register* was a substitute for the old lists of the sextons, and by circumstance, membership in its pages was considered to be identical to membership in the National Horse Show Association.

When William H. Vanderbilt announced the razing of his sheds on Madison Square, the directors of the National Horse Show Association, and hence the leading arbiters of the city's social standing, were determined men. They formed themselves into a corporation, subscribed from among themselves a fund of capital, and bid $400,000 for the New York Central's block on Madison Square, which Vanderbilt accepted. In the summer of 1887 the directors of the new Madison Square Garden Corporation announced they would issue $1,500,000 in common stock; that as soon as the stock was subscribed the old depot shed would be torn down and a new arena built in its stead "offering a more appropriate background for the annual equestrian extravaganza."

The financing was quickly subscribed, not because the new Madison Square Garden was expected to be profitable but because an investment in the Garden was understood to be a guarantee of social acceptance. The directors of the new Garden were headed by Mr. J. Pierpont Morgan, chairman, Mr. Stanford White, vice-chairman. Although J. P. Morgan was clearly responsible for the Garden's financial reputation, Stanford White was understood to be in charge of everything else. Morgan owned 3,000 shares of the Garden's stock and was its largest shareholder; White owned 1,100 shares in his own account and another 150 shares in the account of McKim, Mead and White. What the newspapers described as "The Horse Show Men" began the work of tearing down Commodore Vanderbilt's old train sheds on August 7, 1889, and announced there would be no Horse Show in 1889 but that the new Garden would be ready for the 1890 show.

After a competition for the best design, oddly enough the award was made to McKim, Mead and White, and by June, 1890, Stanford White's incredible "Palace of Pleasures" was almost complete—perhaps as much as $2,000,000 over its original budget of $1,575,000. The new Madison Square Garden occupied the entire block, 465 feet long and 200 feet wide, with side walls rising 65 feet. Its main amphitheater could seat 8,000 for the Horse Show, and as many as 17,000 for the fights. In addition, the southwest corner housed the largest restaurant in town, the northwest corner included a 1,200-seat theater, there was another street-level theater, an arcade of shops along the Madison Avenue side, an open-air theater on the Garden's roof for light comedy in the summertime, and rising above all a Tower on the Twenty-sixth Street side, topped by a nude statue of *Diana* by Saint-Gaudens, 300 feet above the sidewalk.

The exterior of the building was described as "Middle Spanish Renaissance," and White said that his Madison Square Garden Tower was modeled after the Giralda Tower in Seville. If the sources of White's inspiration seemed to be Spanish Renaissance, his completed construction was unquestionably original—a riot of loggias, niches, girandoles, cartouches, carved flora and fauna, columned belvederes, shielded colonnades, and ornate flourishes. The Garden's roof was topped by eight huge domed cupolas, which some observers said reminded them of Saint Paul's in London and others insisted were Byzantine, perhaps Moorish in their effect.

The grand entrance on the Madison Avenue side reminded some critics of the Paris Opéra because White used lavender marble. He insisted upon bright yellow brick and white Pompeian terra-cotta for the Garden's exterior walls. The inner walls of the arena had to be soft red, and White insisted upon just the perfect red to complement the lacework of girders above the main arena painted in a complementary yellow.

White would explain to those who would listen that he was concerned not only with the design and form of the building itself but how it would look, how it would feel, when the cigarette smoke curled up into the yellow spotlights—how the color would *sound* when the band struck up, how the arena would *smell* when the scents of powder and perfume and the acrid odors of excitement were mixed. He strung thousands of Edison electric light bulbs in long pearly necklaces inside the arena and through the colonnades, and he festooned the Tower with lights and then played spotlights up its sides.

Starting at the Garden's roof, White's Tower was thirty-eight feet square at its base and contained a central elevator shaft surrounded by a spiral staircase. The elevator rose through five floors of apartment studios, each with narrow Moorish slits for windows. The Tower of the Giralda in Seville was adorned at its top by a sculpture of *Faith;* White's Tower was topped by *Diana,* an arrow pulled across her drawn bow, modeled by Saint-Gaudens from hammered sheet copper and so perfectly balanced on ball bearings that she swung with the wind as a weather vane, although she weighed more than a ton. The first *Diana* was some eighteen feet high, but White and Saint-Gaudens decided she was too big and they took her down, and at their own expense put up another *Diana,* better proportioned at thirteen feet.

The formal opening night of White's Madison Square Garden was delayed until June 16, 1890. By then society had left town for its ritual promenades at Saratoga, Newport, and the Hamptons. To require society to return for a single evening's entertainment, to demand of them that they appear and dress as if they were attending the opening night of the Horse Show itself, would be a tour de force for the social leadership of Morgan and White.

But society came, some seventeen thousand altogether, ushered to their seats and boxes by men in costumes designed by White, terra-cotta coats and flame-colored waistcoats with big silver buttons and white satin scarfs and white gloves. On opening night they could see each other, and a ballet billed as *Choosing a National Flower,* followed by a concert conducted by Eduard Strauss and his Viennese orchestra. For opening night, Strauss dedicated a new composition to Thomas Edison titled "Phonograph Polka."

The New York *Tribune* reported that Maestro Strauss was —"a veritable prince charming. Old dowagers, ancient bucks, fresh blades, young brides, dewy buds, belles and sprigging beaus followed the lithesome wave of his baton as though spell-bound."

The New York Times concluded the evening was "one of

the most brilliant ever witnessed." And everyone agreed they had a new landmark equal to the Statue of Liberty, the Brooklyn Bridge, and Central Park.

Within four months of its grand opening the Madison Square Garden Corporation was in financial trouble. The building had cost too much. The authorized capital stock had to be increased to $2,000,000 and J. P. Morgan began to guarantee a series of loans to the company. In November the National Horse Show was a brilliant success, but the tickets sold for the Horse Show could not pay the Garden's expenses twelve months a year.

Despite its financial difficulties, White's enthusiasm for what he believed was his creation never faltered. For the Horse Show, he installed Turkish rugs in the boxes, and wicker chairs. For the Westminster Kennel Club Show, he built special dog runs in the basement. He acted as impresario for flower and food shows. He introduced six-day bicycle races—the first races were on machines with a front wheel six feet in diameter and a tiny wheel in the rear. He brought Barnum's Circus every spring and sat in his private box day after day with as many children as he could gather.

By 1900 the Garden had a $2,000,000 mortgage, backed by the House of Morgan. It cost about $20,000 a month to operate, and fixed costs—repairs, taxes, and insurance—came to about $16,000 a month. Rentals seldom exceeded $1,500 a night, which would have made a total of about $45,000 per month if the Garden could be rented every evening, but there were long gaps in its bookings, and its mortgage bonds were constantly in danger.

White hired Gilmore's band to march again. One summer White converted the main arena into a miniature Venice; the happy ticket-holder could glide through "canals" in a miniature gondola, listen to slushy violins, and then dine on a "tropical island." Another White invention was an "Actor's Fair"; he organized the reconstruction of the Globe Theatre of London, of Shakespeare's house in Stratford-on-Avon, Goethe's home in Weimar, Dickens' Old Curiosity Shop—and the stroller could pass by his favorite drama.

He created a toy town, a children's fair for the Christmas

holidays, reproducing old Nuremberg complete with Albrecht Dürer's house, the castle, a marketplace with over one hundred toy shops, performing dogs, marionettes and a Punch and Judy show. He organized "Expositions of Manufacture and Invention." He flooded the main arena again and created "The Caribbean": Each night, miniature warships refought the Battle of Santiago, and the Spanish navy went down in smoke as the band struck up, and Old Glory was unfurled, waving in victory in the Garden's spotlights.

Almost every one of White's delights seemed to be successful. Shakespearean actor Richard Mansfield filled the Garden's theater for years, Paderewski was a triumph in the Garden's concert hall, Adelina Patti sang "for the last time" on several occasions and always filled the main arena; but the only events that made money were the fights. Licensing the fights, or at least allowing them under the subterfuge of "exhibitions," was Tammany Hall's business.

In 1896 a law was maneuvered through the committees of the New York State Senate in Albany that declared boxing legal if the fight was conducted in a building "leased by an established athletic club for at least one year." The Garden Corporation, and its National Horse Show directors, created a lease-back contract, and a group was promptly formed called the Twentieth-Century Athletic Club, which in turn promoted fights several times a week.

For fights, the Garden drew crowds of eight to ten thousand fans. The gate ran as high as $25,000 for each "exhibition," and the income was split fifty-fifty between the fight promoters and "the house." Yet it was never entirely clear whether Tammany would take its cut from the house or from the promoter, or from both, nor could the directors of the Horse Show ever be entirely sure how much Tammany might require in each instance "to improve the conditions of the sport"; consequently the Garden's mortgage payments were constantly threatened.

The forces of Reform were an even more dangerous risk to J. P. Morgan's Madison Square Garden bonds than Tammany's greed. By the turn of the century Reform was on the march again, righteous of the iniquities of the city, angry about "demon rum," the plight of the poor, the corruption of the police, the ubiquity of sin, and especially "the fights." In a fit of virtue, upstate Republican assemblymen repealed the 1896 enabling act that had allowed boxing "exhibitions." Then Mr. William Travers Jerome ran for election on a Reform ticket as a "fighting District Attorney," promising to "enforce every law on the books." To their despair, Jerome's opponents were forced to conclude that the new District Attorney was incorruptible.

On the night of August 30, 1900, fight fans paid the Garden $56,350 to see "Gentleman Jim" Corbett give a lesson in the manly arts of self-defense to a "Professor" McCoy. During the course of their exhibition Corbett knocked McCoy out—accidentally, of course. As McCoy was sponged back into consciousness, the Garden audience rose as a man to sing "Auld Lang Syne." With professional boxing illegal once again, Stanford White's Madison Square Garden would be in deep financial difficulties.

White's Garden would be torn down in 1925, its bonds in default, to make room for an insurance-company skyscraper. Yet White's legacy would continue. The succeeding Madison Square Garden would be at Fiftieth Street and Eighth Avenue, and when that pleasure palace was razed another was built at Seventh Avenue and Thirty-third Street—a Garden nowhere near Madison Square, and constructed over the demolished ruins of McKim's Pennsylvania Station.

All the Gardens would follow an established pattern: All would serve as arenas for Barnum's Circus; all would serve as sites for raucous Democratic Party Conventions; all would make money from "the fights," and if fight money could not be earned all would turn to the city's treasury to make good their promoters' bonds.

All the Gardens demonstrated permanently the lessons taught by the testimony of Boss Tweed and the example etched by Henry Villard: that two ingredients were necessary to success in the city—some combination of fraud and violence. To his credit, Stanford White seemed to be too absorbed with the necessities of the beaux arts to notice the new imperatives. William Dean Howells, novelist of realism, would recall standing with White on the deck of a Staten Island ferry when a stoker from a nearby tug fell overboard. They watched together in horror as the man was sucked under the tug's stern, then caught up and mangled by its screw. According to Howells, White was dismayed: "The poor devil!" And then, involuntarily, as the victim's blood spread into the tug's wash, "My God! What a color!"

CHAPTER THIRTEEN

ILLUSIONS OF GAIETY:
Girls out of Pies

BY THE TURN of the century newspapers served as both oracle and chorus to the city's fates, encouraging some heroes and warning others, and their editors obviously considered the activities of Stanford White as "good copy." To satisfy the demands of circulation for "color," editors gathered evidence to substantiate allegations that White was one of the lucky few with an inside track to the city's delights.

Editors could show that White was pervasive as a Master Builder in defining the city's style. They could certify White as a leader of Fifth Avenue's society. They could report White as a celebrity of Broadway's entertainments. And they could guess, usually correctly, that when millionaires set each other up to banquets in private rooms where everything was soft and velvet, Stanford White would probably be found among those at the feast.

When Stephen Crane was still a newspaperman he was standing one night with the fight crowd on the floor of the main arena at Madison Square Garden. He looked up to catch a glimpse of Stanford White and his guests behind the red velvet curtains of a private box. Crane estimated there would be a party in White's Tower when the main bout was over, and wondered what secret rites must be performed to be included among the anointed.

Whether White actually gave a party that night or whether there were in fact any secret rites was immaterial: that "Stanford White was there" became in itself a certification of an evening's significance. After the theater White would be reported to have had supper at Rector's, or at Delmonico's, or at Sherry's, or to have stopped to gamble at Canfield's Casino. As a result, for that night the theater he had attended and the restaurant he enjoyed were news.

There may have been some element of truth in all the reports. Some observers described him as being always in a hurry, "dashing about, a big man, his body bent forward, taking very short steps, trotting along, intent and busy." Other reporters agreed that he was a big man but described his stride as long and loping and pictured him as erect as "Vercingetorix, bright red hair and the whitest skin, strong as a prizefighter, but gentle. . . . Red hair is, of course, supposed to mean violence, but White never lost his temper. He was sensitive and tender, with a tenderness that ordinary mortals sometimes find it hard to believe in."

Whether Stanford White was an ordinary mortal might be disputed, but all accounts agreed on his generosity—his donation of designs for monuments, his open-handed loans to artists, his care for the unfortunate, and all reports made clear that his energy seemed to provide an almost inexhaustible reservoir which served him in both work and play. That he loved to play was never questioned—he adored beautiful girls and extravagant parties, and there were many parties. White played host constantly for his friends, and his parties were often spectacular, leading the newspapers to confuse the details of one gathering with another or to combine the details of many into one report. Even years afterward the newspaper accounts of one of White's parties, according to Evelyn Nesbit, "would bring a cold sweat to Stanny's brow."

Besides Evelyn Nesbit's version of one scandalous evening, there would be biographical defenses by White's contemporaries, fictionalized reactions in novels, and newspaper reports in *Town Topics,* the New York *World,* and the New York *American.* Every version agreed the party was a "stag affair." In fact, The New York *American* listed the names of twenty-eight prominent men who were alleged to have attended. Evelyn Nesbit said the party described by the *American* was given at Jimmy Breese's "Studio" at 5 West Sixteenth Street, and that "somebody must have talked."

When the details began to leak out, according to Evelyn,

"Stanny managed to keep the stories out of the newspapers for a while, but despite all his efforts, the *World* published the story." According to the *World,* the story came to light when an outraged mother discovered a twenty-dollar gold piece in her sixteen-year-old daughter's shoes after the girl returned home from a "theatrical evening." Although the girl's story might have been concocted in part by newspaper editors, or in other versions the details created by inspired imagination, the scandal would be equally as instructive of White's style as his permanent landmark, the Arch on Washington Square, or his moveable landmark, Madison Square Garden. White's parties were fables of the city's new morality.

Suppose, for example, that an invitation were to be delivered to an ambitious artist who hoped to join the inner circles of the city's celebrity. Soon enough he would find himself, on the evening the bid had specified and at the hour appointed, pushing the bell of a brownstone just west of Fifth Avenue. When the door opened he would be greeted by a black butler. He would give up his coat to the butler in the vestibule and then mount the stairs to the second floor, where his host would greet him, soothing the initiate's obvious uncertainty by saying, "Don't worry, there'll be lots of fun."

The host would move away to greet other guests of greater importance, but as the butler's wife passed champagne cocktails the initiate would recognize a half-dozen friends. They would be men like himself who had attended the Beaux Arts in Paris and returned to New York, just as he had, to search for clients who would pay for "beauty." They would be men he had always found it a treat to engage in talk, and he would soon feel almost at home and considerably more at ease. Then he would find himself talking to other men he had long wanted the opportunity to meet—men who commanded the fortunes of great railroads, or who managed trust accounts at famous banks, or who sat simultaneously on the boards of museums and universities.

The initiate would notice how the room had been emptied of furniture, except that the floor was covered by a yellow rug of fabulous weave. There were tapestries equally as expensive hung on the walls, and the doors and windows had been closed off by heavy drapes. Between the tapestries on the walls there were framed photographs of lovely models—pretty girls posing in the latest fashions or perhaps actresses in their stage costumes—recognizable because they were faces that had appeared in the newspaper supplements. There were also photographs of nudes—perhaps they were the same women—which the newspapers had certainly never printed.

Along the walls candles had been set in sconces, and their light added warmth to the predominant reds and yellows of the tapestries and rugs. In fact, red and yellow had been used throughout the room as a motif—not so much as a decoration, but as an emotion, as if the host had painted a background for the scene he would present, imagining in advance the effects of the yellow candlelight on the red punch bowl on the sideboard, on the rising cigarette smoke, on the flush beginning to appear in the faces of the men as they waited.

When it appeared as if all the invited had arrived the black butler and his wife entered bringing small tables; each table already set for two men, with its silver and china and wineglasses arranged, and its napkin folded like a tricornered hat, and a bowl of flowers. When the tables had been arranged around the sides of the room, beneath the sconces, the master of ceremonies said to the butler, "Now, Sam, get out of here and don't show your face until tomorrow noon." As Sam and his wife disappeared the host directed his guests to place cards at each table, saying, finally, "Gentlemen, be seated. Our comedy is about to begin."

As each man took his place he discovered his card had seated him with another man in such a way that their paired association would not only make some exchange of views natural, but would also, perhaps, mark some beginning for them—an exchange of some common purposes, even a contract each would recognize as mutually advantageous. Almost as soon as they had settled and shaken down their napkins swinging doors at the back of the house parted, and a file of beautiful girls entered. A hurrah went up from every man present, and some banged their tables with the butts of their knives.

The file of girls came bearing plates of *saucisson chaud,*

each plate already sliced and arranged for its designee. The girls were young, and naked except for a scarf clasped at the shoulders, wound under their breasts, and then down across their thighs. Their hair hung loose over their shoulders, and their feet were wound into sandals. Not one of them could have been more than twenty, and two dozen of them made a dazzling scene—as if they were a processional from some ancient frieze. They set down the first course and filed out again in perfect order, every one of them as solemn and serious and exact as priestesses would be in a temple. The men applauded their disappearance, too.

A blond girl appeared and poured the white wine, and a brunette—who could have hardly been older than fifteen—poured the red. As each course followed—hors d'oeuvres replaced by fish, then a meat making a harmonious contrast—the menu served as an example of the host's well-known discrimination in food: exquisite gluttony combined with rare wines. Tongues and heads both began to run loose. Each course was cleared away by the procession of women and replaced in its turn, but always in unison—a file that appeared and disappeared in marching order through the swinging doors.

The room soon hung heavy with acrid smells—the combination of wines, too much food, a fog of cigarette smoke, the sweat of the men mingled with the streaming sweat of the girls that mixed with their powders and perfumes. As the atmosphere in the room grew denser its laughter exploded here and there more frequently, first in one corner and then another. There was an increasing frequency of raucous joking, and the girls of the procession also began to abandon their disciplined solemnity, smiling at first, giggling more often, forming pairs and quartets at the tables they served, embarrassed ensembles of flirtation and familiarity, of advance and retreat.

When the meat course had been cleared away and every glass refilled all the girls disappeared in their file through the swinging doors. At first there seemed to be a delay of some kind. The men grew restless but were quiet, although some attempted to continue their banter with each other. Every eye stole glances at the swinging doors.

Then a faint tingling of bells could be heard, and the procession reappeared once again in Indian file; but they were no longer wearing their sashes, no longer wearing anything at all except sleighbells attached to their ankles and castanets on their fingers. Every man was silent.

To the rhythm of their castanets, clacked in a practiced unison, they began to dance—a delirious dance in which the invitations they seemed to present were being made absolutely in unison, every girl presenting herself to every man without any particular distinction, stamping their feet and snapping their fingers precisely together. Not one of the girls smiled, nor did any of them choose with her eyes any selection for her attention. They ended their dance by prancing once around the room as if they were galloping, their heads tossing from side to side, shaking their hair across their shoulders as if they were flicking their manes, their eyes fixed irrevocably on the ceiling. When they had disappeared beyond the doors there was silence for a moment, and then unable to speak to each other, the men cheered and slapped their thighs, and thumped their tables, and raised their glasses in toasts to each other and their host.

There was another lull. Talk at the tables made half-hearted attempts to begin again. Someone was heard to say that it had begun to snow outside; he had peeked out behind the drawn curtains next to his table and could see the snow falling. No one seemed to care what he had seen.

Then a whistle sounded and through the swinging doors a file of Roman slave girls reappeared, their bodies streaked with sweat, bearing a huge trestle, six girls on each side of it. Upon the trestle was what appeared to be a monstrous pie, the crust a meringue of ermine white and the base surrounded by banks of red and blue flowers.

The girls placed their burden in the center of the room, on the rosette in the extraordinary yellow rug. They had changed their costume once again, and now they wore dainty liberty caps in red, white, and blue, gauzy veils clasped at their waists, but their breasts were bare. One third of the veils were white, a third were blue, and a third were red.

They began to circle the pie and to sing to it, their voices now heavy with wine and passion and incipient catarrh:

> "Sing a song of sixpence,
> pockets full of rye,
> Four-and-twenty blackbirds
> Baked into a pie,
> When the pie was opened . . ."

And at the cue, the top of the pie rose up, and birds—doves, canaries, and nightingales—began to fly everywhere in the room. Some arched past the smoking sconces in terror. Others perched trembling above the valances of the curtains. All were piteously piping, flapping their wings in waves of excitement, hoping for some shelter in what must have been a blinding landscape.

As the birds scattered a shining blond child rose from the center of the pie, making graceful weaving motions with her arms, as if she had been instructed to play the part of a swan. Her breasts were tiny, tender, still rose-colored. Her hips had barely matured, just begun to swell past the land's end of puberty. The master of ceremonies stood up from his table and went over to lift his pink darling to the floor. He cradled her in his arms as if she too were a frightened bird. His tender smile seemed to reassure her, and as he disappeared behind the arras that led to the stairway and the rooms upstairs his guests could see that she had turned her childlike face into his chest and closed her eyes. A lusty cheer went up from the guests the host had abandoned to their own pleasures.

Of course, when the New York *World* displayed a caricature of "The Girl in the Pie" on their front pages, she was depicted as clothed or at least draped in enough gauzy materials so that no reader could take offense at the newspaper's "immorality." According to the *Sunday American*, "Susie Johnson was the model in the pie. Two days after the party she disappeared from her home. The Gerry Society searched for her, but without result. After a few months of a model's life, and many cruel experiences, Susie became disgusted with it.

She was afraid to return home and went for help to Mrs. G. S. Perhaca, 210 Grand Avenue, Brooklyn, the wife of an artist who had treated her kindly. She later married, but her husband threw her off because he heard of the 'Pie Dinner.' She is buried in Potter's Field."

CHAPTER FOURTEEN

MONEY'S BRIDE

IN OCTOBER, 1903, when Evelyn returned to New York from Paris, she hoped she might recreate the glories of her affair with Stanford White, but her pregnancy and her tour of Europe with Harry Thaw, she had to admit, had been long interruptions. Her hopes rose when Stanny was obviously delighted at her reappearance, but she seemed to be unable to claim his exclusive attention. She knew she was competing with Edna McClure and perhaps others as well. She tried out stratagems of jealousy, but she had to admit that "nothing seemed to make Stanny jealous." She appealed to Stanny's fatherly weaknesses, and bit by bit fed to him the stories of Harry Thaw's degeneracies, but Stanny's response, though certainly protective, was no longer passionate. He arranged for her to fill out the affidavit against Thaw and to sign it in the offices of Howe and Hummel, and he promised her that Harry Thaw wouldn't bother her anymore. But what she wanted had nothing to do with law or even protection. When Stanny failed to ask her to his annual Christmas Eve party at the Tower she accepted Harry Thaw's invitation for a celebration at Rector's.

Despite his lawyer's advice to stay away from Evelyn, Harry conducted a methodical, determined campaign throughout November and December, 1903—notes, telegrams, and flowers every day. His notes were full of supplications to "his angels, her tumtums, her tweetums, her boofuls." He sent ambassadors with the notes and with gifts and sent missionaries to plead his cause.

Mazie Follette appeared as one of Harry's messengers, and

Evelyn thought Mazie was more honest than some of the others. "I need a warm coat," Mazie admitted, "and Thaw will buy me one if I get you to go out to lunch with him."

Evelyn agreed to help Mazie get her coat. Within the week, Evelyn and Harry Thaw and Mazie rode a carriage through Central Park, then had lunch, and after lunch went to Lord & Taylor. While Mazie tried on coats and Evelyn waited in a chair, Harry got down on his knees before Evelyn and began kissing her hands: "If her angel forgive, if her angel come to dinner. Please, please, angel, please!"

The Lord & Taylor sales staff hovered near the scene, snickering to each other and sending word to still others until almost every clerk in the store had passed through the coat department on one pretext or another just to get an eyeful of Harry Thaw on his knees. As Mazie Follette tried on one coat after another, Evelyn recalculated her position: her innocence had given her power over White, but Stanny's passions had apparently cooled; to fascinate Thaw she might have to call upon other powers in her possession, but Harry's manias could have their uses. She relented and agreed to have dinner with him.

She began to see him regularly again. By January, 1904, Harry told her he had hired detectives to follow Stanford White and had employed others to protect Evelyn and himself from Stanford White and the notorious Monk Eastman gang. They were desperadoes from Hell's Kitchen, said Harry, hired by White to do him in. Evelyn said nothing to dissuade Harry from his fantasies.

In February, Harry called upon Anthony Comstock, president of the Society for the Suppression of Vice, with information about "three dens White maintained." Harry specified one of the dens was the Tower studio in Madison Square Garden, which he admitted to having seen once during a party and which he told Comstock would be "impossible to reform." Harry also specified the upper floor of 22 West Twenty-fourth Street, which Evelyn had described to him. Harry told Comstock that at Twenty-fourth Street "workmen outside had heard girls scream. . . . Their custom is to drug the victim, usually an American girl, innocent and about fifteen years of age." Harry also described an apartment at East Twenty-second Street, "which contains works of art . . . and probably a vast collection of obscenity." Harry Thaw provided Anthony Comstock with exact figures; he calculated that White had "ravished three hundred and seventy-eight girls."

Mr. Anthony Comstock accepted Harry Thaw's testimony about ruined girls and, with a certain amount of pride, promised Thaw he would look into the matter "directly."

In June, 1904, Evelyn and Harry sailed again for Genoa, and then Paris, on the *Kaiser Wilhelm der Grosse*. By then Harry carried a revolver at all times—on the advice of his detectives, he told Evelyn, for protection "against the Monk Eastman gang."

Evelyn tolerated Harry's little oddities because in Paris, she said, "Our manner of living would have ruined an Indian potentate: Dinners. Suppers. Theaters. New hats and gowns for every occasion. At the races Harry bet heavily and generally lost."

They went to Monte Carlo and stayed at the Hermitage Hotel. Their rooms were directly under Caruso's suite, and every morning Evelyn could hear Caruso practice by the hour. After five weeks on the Riviera—Harry gambled every night, and continued to lose what Evelyn considered to be "marvelous" sums—they returned to Paris. At a party in Paris, Evelyn heard that Francis Belmont—Fannie Donnelly of the *Floradora* Sextette, the same Fannie who had stood up Harry and his friends for supper at Sherry's—was engaged to marry Lord Ashburton in London. Evelyn noted that "Fannie was rising in the world," that a *Floradora* girl would soon be Lady Ashburton, and Evelyn reviewed her own possibilities.

Harry announced they would take another motor trip. They drove through Switzerland, through the Midi, into the Côte d'Or. If at times Evelyn suffered through scenes of Harry's perversions, she had learned how to make Harry beg. She would make him get down on his knees to apologize and kiss her hand as if she were his queen. He would have to plead with her. She would make him kiss her foot, and she would never grant him absolution until he had humiliated himself sufficiently. Sometimes even if he crawled, she would toss her head and refuse him. She knew too she could always drive him to distraction by referring to Stanford White.

They had a compact between them that she would always refer to White as "that beast." But at her convenience Evelyn would forget to call him "a beast." Harry would fly into a paroxysm of rage, and the web of Evelyn's net would be secured by one more knot. Evelyn learned how to get him started on his obsession with hardly more than a flick of an eyelid, and Harry would soon be raving about Stanford White, "wholesale ravisher of pure American virgins." When they motored into the village of Domrémy in France, they visited the shrine of Joan of Arc. Evelyn said something to the effect that all artists admired Saint Joan, with the result that Harry returned to write a notation in the visitors' book: "Joan of Arc would not have been a virgin long if Stanford White had been around." They drove out of Domrémy with Harry raving about White.

They left Europe to return for the "winter season" in New York, arriving not long after the National Horse Show. When they disembarked in New York they took a carriage to the Cumberland Hotel, where newspaper reporters followed them to check on their registration, and there were front-page stories the next day in which Harry Thaw denied he had married Evelyn Nesbit.

Early in 1905 Evelyn again had an attack of "appendicitis," and checked into the private sanatorium of Dr. Clement Cleveland on East Thirty-third Street, where her appendix could be removed for the second time. Dr. Cleveland advised Evelyn would need six weeks to recuperate from the operation, and Harry had a telephone installed at her bedside, sent flowers every day, and had roast partridge and champagne dinners delivered by Oscar's waiters from the Waldorf. Harry would visit every day for a week or so and then disappear for several days. There were days when Evelyn's telephone never rang.

When Evelyn left the hospital she chose a small apartment for herself just off Madison Avenue on Thirty-eighth Street. From the security of her apartment she could intensify the campaign she was waging against Harry Thaw. She could receive him there with every sign of delight at his arrival. She could refuse to see him, on a whim, and let his fevered imagination describe for him where she had spent her evening. Within a month Harry announced, "My mother is coming to town especially to see you. She knows all about you."

Evelyn received Mrs. Thaw over teacups, and after an exchange of the required pleasantries between the two women they settled down to business. Mrs. Thaw said, "My son is very much in love with you, Evelyn, and I wish you would marry him." Mrs. Thaw brushed aside Evelyn's indications of Harry's sometimes odd behavior, admitting that Harry had always been a cause for anxiety, but she expressed renewed hopes for Harry now that he had found a woman he loved. Nothing would please her more, said Mrs. William Thaw, than to see her son happy and settled down to a quiet, normal life in Pittsburgh.

Just as one sovereign would accept the representations of another, Mother Thaw and Evelyn concluded their tea by shaking hands and promising how much they would enjoy seeing each other again. Evelyn returned to Pittsburgh, the city of her birth, on April 5, 1905. On the same afternoon she stepped off the train she was joined in holy matrimony to Mr. Harry Kendall Thaw in the Rectory of Dr. McEwan, pastor of the Third Presbyterian Church. Most of the newspaper reports noted that a *Floradora* showgirl had married into a fortune estimated at forty million dollars. One of the newspaper stories reported that the bride wore black: a tailored black suit, with a powder-blue shirtwaist, white collar, and black tie, under a black velvet tailored coat. Two small black ostrich plumes adorned her black hat and black illusion veil.

After the wedding ceremony a formal dinner was held at Lyndhurst, the Thaw family estate in Pittsburgh's exclusive East End. Exactly six people were present: the bride and groom; Mrs. William Thaw and her son Josiah Thaw; the bride's mother, the former Mrs. Elizabeth F. Nesbit recently remarried to Charles J. Holman of Pittsburgh; and Mr. Holman, the bride's stepfather. Other members of the Thaw family were said to be unable to attend.

After the family dinner at Lyndhurst the bride and groom left immediately for their honeymoon. Because the marriage of Mr. and Mrs. Harry K. Thaw of Pittsburgh was front-page news, their train was besieged by reporters clamoring for a statement at every stop—all the way to Chicago. West of Chicago the honeymooners were bothered less and less.

They toured the Grand Canyon, descending the Bright Angel Trail to the Colorado River bank; they spent several quiet weeks in Pasadena, California, drove up into Yosemite Park, rode donkeys to Lookout Point, and climbed to the top of Yosemite Falls. A week later they were driving along a California dirt road in an old-fashioned wagon when the horses reared, and the wagon driver reined them to a stop.

Directly in the path of the wagon a large rattlesnake lay coiled and rattling. No one in the wagon moved at first, except Evelyn, who stepped down and began searching along the side of the road for a stone. Harry asked her what she planned to do, and she replied that snakes did not frighten her at all—she was looking for a stone big enough to kill it.

Harry followed her, and when they had found a large enough stone, Harry used his brass-tipped umbrella to spear the snake into the ground, and Evelyn crushed the writhing head with her rock.

When Harry would recall the adventures of their honeymoon he would say, "There were five rattles, so it was not so small either." Evelyn would remember that on their honeymoon Harry had insisted on staying at a seedy, old-fashioned hotel in Chicago because it was called "The Virginia." Anything about virgins, she explained, set off Harry's mania. They had stayed at The Virginia because Harry said it would "annoy your friend Mr. White, who is so different."

They returned from their honeymoon to take up residence at Lyndhurst with Mother Thaw. If Evelyn was not a happy bride, no one heard her complain. Mother Thaw set aside a wing on the second floor of the house for Evelyn and Harry. Evelyn's and Harry's bedrooms were separated by a long corridor, a bathroom, and a small dressing room in which Evelyn set up an aquarium for angelfish.

Evelyn described the interior of Lyndhurst as a house that had never had an interior decorator. Hideous brass beds stood in the bedrooms. The drawing room was filled with overstuffed, gilded furniture and an ugly black piano that no one knew how to play. There were a few good paintings on the walls—two Corots and several Isabeys, foisted on the Thaws by some clever dealer. They were complemented by some cloisonné vases picked up by Mrs. William Thaw at the Chicago World's Fair. The dining room was gloomy, paneled in dark wood and fitted with chairs of no particular period, and even the crystal chandelier that hung in the center of the ceiling over the long mahogany table could not relieve the room's shadowed emptiness.

There were always more servants than guests. Mother Thaw's other children seemed to return to Lyndhurst only when circumstances made it absolutely necessary. Harry's older sister, Margaret, had married George Carnegie, nephew of Andrew Carnegie, and the couple lived in New York or in their house in Roslyn, Long Island. Harry's younger brother Joseph was also married and his wife Mary was expecting a baby, but they used the baby as their excuse to stay away. Alice Thaw seemed to be having difficulties with His Grace the Earl of Yarmouth in London, and there was already talk of divorce. Edward Thaw, another of Harry's brothers particularly irked Mother Thaw by his absence, but he stayed in Paris.

Evelyn was lonely, but she played out the part of the dutiful wife and even set about redecorating their suite. She found cabinets of Moorish design in the attic, brought them downstairs, had them repaired and cleaned. She appropriated a mahogany boudoir table that had been Alice Thaw's and added it to her suite's collection. She was determined to do something about the brass beds, but waited for the proper opportunity. She made friends with the dogs, particularly an old Pomeranian named Fenris. Fortunately Harry's cousin Mary Copley, a girl of her own age, had been sent back from Kansas when her father, Mother Thaw's brother, was confined to an insane asylum. Mary Copley had a sweet, sad face and a quiet grace and she provided virtually the only companionship Evelyn could find. Besides, Evelyn felt sorry for Mary Copley because as Mother Thaw's "poor relation" she was at the mercy of all Mother Thaw's whims and caprices.

The household servants always addressed Mother Thaw as "Mrs. Thaw," and Evelyn as "Mrs. Harry." Mother Thaw's dinners soon had Evelyn in an agony of boredom. Harry always sat at one end of the long mahogany table and Mother Thaw at the other. Mother Thaw would place her guest of honor at her right, and Evelyn at her left. In order to entertain Mrs. Thaw, all spouted Presbyterianism "ad nauseam," Evelyn said.

To relieve her boredom, Evelyn required Harry to take her to every play and concert that came to Pittsburgh. One evening when Mr. and Mrs. Andrew Mellon were the favored guests at still another Presbyterian dinner and there was another one of those long lulls in the conversation, Evelyn started to say something to Mr. Mellon about that afternoon's concert by the violinist Jan Kubelik.

"What's he," Mrs. Thaw asked, "a pie-anist?"

Mrs. Mellon delicately turned the subject toward music in general, and "Pan" fluttered through her sentence.

"Who's Pan?" Mrs. Thaw wanted to know. "Another pie anist?"

From his distant end of the table, Harry explained to his mother that Pan was the pagan god often seen playing the flute.

"Well," Mother Thaw concluded, "what would a poor Christian woman know about pagan gods?"

Because she used her money to do Presbyterian good works, an endless procession of Presbyterian ministers, missionaries, charity workers, committee chairmen, schoolmasters, and their wives, paraded to the doors of Lyndhurst. One evening in the summer of 1905 a big Irish setter padded up to Dr. McEwan, pastor of the Third Presbyterian Church in which Evelyn and Harry had been married, a church built from the proceeds of William Thaw's Pennsy stock. Dr. McEwan was sitting in a wicker chair on the veranda, enjoying an after-dinner cigar.

The Irish setter arrived and licked the hand of the minister. In return, by way of introduction, Dr. McEwan gave the dog a healthy kick, and the dog ran off howling in pain.

Evelyn was furious and jumped to her feet, the dog's howls undoing in an instant months of Evelyn's practiced restraint. She screamed at the minister, "How dare you do such a damnable thing!"

Mother Thaw rose up from her wicker chair in answer. "Child," she imposed, "do you realize that you are speaking to the cloth?"

Evelyn refused to apologize and ran to her room.

The incident was dropped, and as summer passed Evelyn began to believe she could discern a few good qualities in her mother-in-law. In the fall of 1905, after about six months of marriage, Harry began to disappear on "business trips" to New York. When he was away Mother Thaw and Evelyn had no one but each other for company. "In spite of her religious fanaticism, her narrow-minded prejudices and her lack of education," Evelyn said, "Mother Thaw had some nice qualities."

Besides, Evelyn had to calculate the realities of her situation. Harry was quoted in the newspapers saying something about his income, and Mother Thaw instantly upbraided him: "How dare you say, *my money, my income*—when you know you are utterly dependent upon me for every cent you spend?"

Yet it was not only the money. There might be certain circumstances in which Evelyn would need Mother Thaw as a protector or at least an ally. In the fall of 1905 Evelyn had a nightmare—something about a shapeless form menacing her with a long writhing snake whip. She woke up screaming, which brought Harry running down the hallway from his room, and then a moment later Mother Thaw appeared in her nightgown and nightcap. Glaring at Harry, she demanded, "Did you strike her?"

Evelyn quickly explained that Harry had not whipped her, that she had been having a nightmare, and that everything would be all right. But she was grateful for Mother Thaw's quick appearance.

Mother Thaw turned to Harry, her voice low and deliberate. "If you ever lay a hand on her, I'll cut you off without a penny." Then she turned and stalked out. Evelyn needed no more than a glance at Harry's face to realize she only needed to bide her time.

At the beginning of their marriage Harry had given Evelyn the impression that he enjoyed his conversion to the role of sedate married man, but summer had not passed before he was biting his nails again, staring off into space, and seething with an uncontrollable restlessness. Evelyn suggested they take a trip up to New York.

Once in the city, Harry would allow her to see only two of her friends—Mrs. J. J. Caine and May Mackenzie. Harry's explanation was that "Mrs. Caine is a decent married woman, and May Mackenzie is a virgin."

If Harry was right, May Mackenzie had been the only chorus girl with Weber and Fields to have been a virgin. She was an old confidante of Evelyn's and had given up the chorus line to write a sensational gossip column in the New York *Morning Telegraph,* which she signed "Marion the Maid." She was petite, perky, and full of fun, lived in a furnished apartment in a brownstone walkup. When Harry had proposed it was May who had advised Evelyn it was the best thing she could do—the Thaw money would guarantee her security for life. "And," May had said, mimicking a society dowager putting a lorgnette to her eyes, "when you visit New York to do a little shopping, will you condescend to visit a mere chorus girl?"

In addition to May Mackenzie, Evelyn had Harry's permission to visit Mrs. J. J. Caine, who was a great favorite of his. Before he had married Evelyn he had sent her to Mrs. Caine's apartment one evening because he was convinced that the Monk Eastman gang, desperadoes from Hell's Kitchen, would attempt to attack them that very night. He instructed Mrs. Caine not only to protect Evelyn against the possibility of their viciousness but to collect all of Evelyn's jewels into a chamois bag, which he provided, and sleep with them under her pillow. Although no attack occurred, Harry took it as testimony to Mrs. Caine's reliability that the next morning she returned all of Evelyn's jewels intact. It was to Mrs. Caine that Harry went when he needed an emissary to Evelyn's mother—offering Mrs. Holman $100,000 if she would give her consent to Evelyn's marriage. After they were married Harry would often take Mrs. Caine along with them as "chaperone," and Mrs. Caine never complained of her opportunities to have a night on the town, see the latest shows, and dine at Sherry's or Delmonico's.

One night Harry, Evelyn, and Mrs. Caine were having dinner at the Saint Regis. They had hardly started their soup before Stanford White appeared with his wife and took the corner table facing them. Evelyn could see Harry's mood change instantly—his lips stretched into a thin, hard line as he glared at White, but White appeared not to notice them.

Mrs. Caine bent over and whispered in Evelyn's ear, "What's the matter with Harry, Evelyn? He has a revolver on his lap under his napkin."

Evelyn felt a chill of terror, but she recovered quickly. She caught Harry's eye and then said to him in an even tone, "If you don't put that gun away, I'll leave the table."

His shoulders hunched as if he meant to spring, but she repeated her warning, put her napkin down, and started to rise. He suddenly relaxed and broke into a smile. "It's all right, angels, don't her worry," and he slipped the gun back into his pocket.

But Evelyn was still furious, and said things had gone too far. She pushed her soup away and explained to Mrs. Caine they had to leave, immediately. Poor Mrs. Caine could not get any explanation from anyone, but Harry followed them out, making apologies all the way home. They dismissed Mrs. Caine, dropping her at her apartment, returned to their hotel, had dinner sent up to their suite, and ate it in silence. Perhaps the next time they were in New York they might have a gayer time, but they took the train for Pittsburgh the next day.

At Lyndhurst neither Evelyn nor Mother Thaw ever knew when Harry might explode into fits of rage. In the spring of 1906 Evelyn's maid Nellie decided to give their suite a thorough spring cleaning. In the process she discovered more than a dozen whips under a ledge of one of the cabinets Evelyn had brought from the attic. Nellie gave the whips to Mrs.

Harry without understanding their significance. Harry happened to be there, and his face turned chalk-white when he saw them. Evelyn told Nellie that she would take care of the whips.

An hour later Nellie returned to Evelyn's bedroom to help Evelyn dress for the evening's dinner with Mrs. Thaw. Nellie's eyes were red with weeping.

"What's the matter, Nellie?"

"Nothing, madam, nothing."

Evelyn drew it out of her. "It's because of them whips I found. Mr. Thaw talked something terrible to me."

Evelyn reassured Nellie she would protect her from any of Mr. Thaw's threats, that Mr. Thaw sometimes got excited over silly things.

But when Harry quarreled with Bedford, his valet, Evelyn could do nothing. Once, in the middle of a shouting match between Harry and his valet, Harry picked up an iron Bedford had been using to press his master's clothes and threw it. Fortunately, Bedford was practiced at ducking. The iron missed his head, went sailing through the window, shattered the glass, and landed out on the lawn.

There happened to be a gardener working on the shrubbery directly beneath the window, and the iron had narrowly missed him. He took his complaint to Mrs. Thaw, who smoothed it over, and the incident was soon forgotten, or ignored, just as all the others were. No one in the household ever mentioned Harry's outbursts. What happened was that Mother Thaw would lecture him in private, and Harry would become "as meek as a kitten for days." Then he would begin to brood and bite his nails again.

In June, 1906, Mother Thaw announced that she would go to Europe to visit her daughter Alice. For some reason she had chosen to travel by cattle boat, which she said she preferred. To Evelyn's great relief, Harry balked at the idea, and said they would follow Mother Thaw on one of the German liners, perhaps the *Amerika,* which Harry said he liked because they could have their meals served in their suite.

They left Pittsburgh for a summer in Europe, stopping first for two weeks in New York, staying at the Hotel Lorraine,

Forty-ninth Street and Fifth Avenue. Harry and Evelyn had a suite of rooms several floors above Mother Thaw's. Harry spent his afternoons gambling at the Whist Club, and after Mother Thaw sailed on her cattle boat, Harry and Evelyn began a round of dinners with Harry's friends, Thomas McCaleb and Truxton Beale. Harry made a great fuss over Beale, because Harry said Beale had shot a man in California over a woman and had been acquitted in the trial because "the unwritten law" and public opinion had been on Beale's side.

By June, 1906, Evelyn realized that wherever she went—shopping, or to meet May Mackenzie for tea while Harry was playing whist—Harry had her followed by detectives. She had tried to argue with him about it, but he said it was for her own protection—against the Monk Eastman gang, and other dangers. It was impossible to argue with him.

On Monday morning, June 25, Evelyn woke up with a sore throat. Harry insisted she see a doctor before they sailed for Europe. He made an appointment for her to have the throat swabbed by a specialist. As she was coming out of the doctor's office she ran into Stanford White. They hugged each other, as old friends would, and Stanny wanted to know if she was well, if she was happy. He told her how beautiful she looked, just as he had always done. They parted after only a moment, but because of Harry's detectives she thought she'd better tell Harry her own version first.

Evelyn was waiting for him when he got back from the Whist Club. He said he'd won that afternoon—not much, but he'd won just the same. Before they started dressing for dinner, she brought the subject up. "According to my promise, I must tell you that I passed the beast on the street today."

Harry's face darkened. He started biting at a nail. "Did he speak to you?"

She said he hadn't.

"What did he do?"

"He just looked at me for a moment, and then I ran into the doctor's office."

"You are sure that was all?"

"Yes."

"Your word of honor?"

"Yes."

"That's right," he said, seeming to approve her. "All I ask is that you tell me any time you see him. If you don't tell me, I'll find out anyway. There are plenty of people who will tell me."

He said they would meet Truxton Beale and McCaleb for dinner at Martin's. Then they had tickets for the opening-night of the show *Mamzelle Champagne* at the Roof Garden Theatre of Madison Square Garden. Although Evelyn wondered why Harry would choose a show at Madison Square Garden, she kept her silence.

While Evelyn dressed, Harry told her he might go ahead for a drink, and that she should be ready when he sent the car to pick her up at eight o'clock.

Evelyn agreed, but she wanted to take a long soaking bath first—New York in June was hot and sticky and the city's grime seemed to get into every pore. She would use the soaps she had from Paris—they smelled of violets and the country.

CHAPTER FIFTEEN

ILLUSIONS OF DECENCY:
Mr. and Mrs. Basil March

THE GRIT THAT EVELYN would sponge away in her long bath had become a standard component of the city's atmosphere. In 1906 much of it would be coal dust, but there would be other tailings as well, all of them the inevitable by-products of the city's consumption of power.

Most citizens would have argued that a little grime was a small price to pay for the powers the city had provided. For example, as the city had transformed itself from a ship captain's village to a cosmopolis during the nineteenth century the most important progress that could be cited was that the life span of the average man had been increased to forty-nine years—an increase in life's tenure by something like a decade. Surely the postponement of death was a considerable advance.

Besides progress in medicine, there were all the other incredible discoveries of science, most of which had practical—and convenient—application. Some of these inventions were obvious, such as the airplane, automobile, radio, telescope, microscope, motion pictures, electric light; but each obvious improvement was connected to a stream of other inventions just as necessary, delivered from the sciences of chemistry, physics, metallurgy, tool design, mining, shipping, and still others. All the inventions combined to make life easier, quicker, happier, faster. All consumed increasing quantities of power—resulting, unfortunately, in a slightly sulfuric odor through the city's streets.

Nevertheless, despite the carping of a few utopian critics, the progress of the nineteenth century actually did improve life for the average middle-class family; not only did they live longer, they lived better. To the credit of the families who prospered under the new conditions, they recognized the landscape they inhabited as a social force just as powerful as the Nature their forebears had met and conquered. They understood that, like Nature, the cityscape was likely to contain energies not always benign. Against the menaces that the city might contain for the family, the middle class created defenses, especially for the sake of their children, and adopted, as part of their manners, the protective feathers of gentility.

The typical middle-class family honored money, just as the city did, but they were realists and did not believe they would make a fortune quickly and abundantly as the rich managed to do by some incredible stroke of good luck. Instead, they eyed most boosters' schemes with distrust. When they had money to invest, they did so cautiously, saying with earnest moral purpose that they were "saving." They believed in modern business success, and they could see examples of it everywhere they looked, but they would participate in its advantages by working hard, doing their duty, and hoping for a raise—something like another $2,000 a year.

They never supposed they were selfish, nor did they guess they were sentimental. They were devoted to their children and always discussed every issue in "reasonable" but moderate tones. They believed firmly in progress and in the future, and if they had to renounce its pleasures for themselves, they did so because they knew with absolute certainty that their children had to be prepared for the future's even more expansive possibilities.

Above all they were patient, and because the promises of the future could not always be made good in the immediate present, family life was absorbed by the most delicate adjustments—negotiations between their hopes and their abilities. For example, as the city grew and the price of a house passed over the horizon of the possible, they adapted to the apartment. They agreed to accept less space than they believed was their due. The kitchen lacked the view that the matron of the house had once dreamed she would have; the children could not each have a room of their own to develop their distinct personalities; the man's office was smaller than the dignity of his position warranted. Yet they would explain to anyone who asked that the city's crowded streets were the best display of its excitement.

Most average middle-class families took pride in what they considered "a rather decent education." He believed a good education was more necessary to his occupation than to hers, but both husband and wife would admit they had traveled a bit, had seen something of the world. In fact they often had developed tastes that they could not indulge because their budget set limits to what they considered important to their experience. Nevertheless, behind the locked doors of their apartments they had created a life of "inner elegance"—something more than just "the proprieties," because it was informed by almost daily discussions right at home of the world's major events and issues, which they had gathered from reading books, magazines, and the better newspapers.

If at times the practical, matter-of-fact, safe, commonplace lives they worked out for the sake of the children began to bore them, they could play the romantic. Just down the street were the best restaurants in the world, they would say, tastes imported from every place they had promised themselves, or their children, they would visit someday. Besides, New York provided perfectly marvelous libraries and universities, great museums, the most delightful ballet, symphony, and opera, and Broadway's theater was the best in the world, as everyone knew, and they went as often as they could.

They would insist that life in the city was gay. They were optimistic, and at their best, noble. They were wistfully aware there were others who had some positive experience of bliss, or some ecstasy, some glorious adventure to recall, and that they had somehow diminished their own lives. From time to time, just as the city's weather might often change suddenly, a damp, melancholy gale seemed to blow against the locked doors of their apartments.

The novelist William Dean Howells drew a realistic portrait of a middle-class New York couple, Mr. and Mrs. Basil March, as they searched for an apartment. "Yes, gay is the word," Mrs. March admitted to her husband. "But frantic. I can't get used to it. They forget death, Basil; they forget death in New York."

CHAPTER SIXTEEN

"I COULD LOVE A THOUSAND GIRLS"

THERE WAS NEVER ANYTHING frantic about the Hotel Lorraine at Forty-ninth and Fifth, where Mr. and Mrs. Harry K. Thaw of Pittsburgh were registered. The Lorraine was a family-style residence, considered to be a bit old-fashioned and sedate. The tub in which Evelyn spent an hour soaking away the grime of a hot June day was not a new one made of porcelain but an old sheet-iron tub, standing on a raised platform with feet like lion's paws. Yet the Lorraine was an oasis: while Evelyn was soaking herself in perfumed suds—between six and seven P.M.—the city acted out, according to the New York *World,* "the busiest hour on earth."

Newspaper editors took a curious pride in estimating the city's frenzy. They proved with statistics a condition of perpetual stress approximately as follows: The critical mass of density at the nerve center, on the island of Manhattan, about 16¾ square miles of land, was inhabited by about 2,223,000 souls; or, 10,720 acres with 207 people per acre. Actually, many of the acres had much higher densities because 468,492 souls were packed into 14,872 tenements.

Significantly, it was a mass of high velocity, assaulted by noises of amazing variety—sirens, screeching trains, clatter and clamor, unexplained screams—and subjected to sensations of sight and touch and smell too diverse to be assimilated. It was a mass whose perceptions were beyond the boundaries of its experience, and the newspapers could recite the events likely to happen between the hours of six P.M. and seven P.M. on Monday, June 25, 1906, with absolute certainty, but without anything but random understanding: "150,000 people crossed the Brooklyn Bridge; 1,900,684 cubic feet of gas was consumed; 52,000 telephone calls were made; 123,000 rode the subway; 39,746 letters were mailed; 486 immigrants arrived; 175 ferryboats departed; 14 cubic feet of water per person consumed; 18 people arrested; 8 people married; 18 children born; 12 people died; STREETCAR STRIKES AUTO; PRESIDENT SAYS HARD-BOILED EGGS HIS BREAKFAST."

Every June the newspapers would report the departure of the city's rich to their summer resorts—palaces in Newport, lakeside cabins in the Adirondacks, houses in the Berkshires, cottages behind the ocean dunes at Montauk. In June, 1906, newspaper editors passed on the parting message of the Episcopal Bishop of New York: "SUMMER VACATIONS NECESSARY TO HARD-WORKING PREACHERS." The editors also repeated Bishop Potter's advice that while preachers and wives were away, the men who remained behind to work in the city "should be good."

Of course, the poor never escaped, not even when heat, humidity, and the fumes of the city's spent energies made summer evenings almost unbearable. The poor would take to the rooftops where there might be traces remaining from the harbor's sea breeze, and midway between the melted pitch in the streets and the sky overhead there was usually an odd gaiety. To the roofs of a tenement someone might haul a block of ice up the fire escape, and an entire community of families would share beer from a tub until the moon rose. Many tenement families dragged their mattresses to the roof not only because it was a cooler place to sleep, but because it was an escape from the overwhelming odors of the stairwells. For youth, the rooftops sometimes had advantages over stoops in pursuing courtships. For the old, rooftops made congregation natural, and rooftop conversations seemed to ramble easily, curving along gentler paths at night. For the children, the settlement houses and public schools stayed open until ten o'clock so that hopscotch could be chalked out even when the asphalt on the street had turned to ooze, and rope could be skipped until bedtime.

Like the poor, the middle class were also required to remain in the city in the summer, even when it could reasonably be described as an inferno. The middle class took to rooftops not only because they would be cooler, but because roof-garden restaurants and roof-garden theaters advertised to the middle class "evenings of gaiety and romance." Mr. Oscar Hammerstein promised his Paradise Gardens would feature "foreign novelties to appease a sensation-loving public." Mr. Joe Hart presented his revue on a roof renamed The Wisteria Grove. Mr. George M. Cohan presented his new revue, called *The Governor's Son,* on the roof of the New Amsterdam Theatre.

The hotels—the Waldorf, the Hoffman House, the Astor, the Saint Regis—all had rooftop restaurants, sometimes with small reviews, but all with terraces decked with flowers and strung with Japanese lanterns, and tables lit with candles set in hurricane lamps. As a matter of fact, roof gardens were appealing settings precisely because they were such marvelous contrasts to the vicious daily life on the streets below them. They were like visions of paradise—a mysterious ride by elevator halfway to the sky, sometimes the moon overhead, sometimes dew settling on the tiny tables, the theater in midair—a lot of musical nonsense with pretty girls, and everywhere the summer girls in their summer laces, laughing at the opportunity presented to them by wives minding children somewhere else. The Roof Garden Theatre and Restaurant at Madison Square Garden, designed and managed by Stanford White, was one of the city's most popular entertainments.

June 25, 1906, was not one of the city's outrageously hot days. The temperature had climbed to just over eighty at 4:30 P.M., but a sea breeze had relieved the density of the air, and after the sun set at 7:30 P.M. it would not be unbearable. Since Evelyn was still closeted in her tub, Harry Thaw walked out of the Hotel Lorraine and four blocks down Fifth Avenue to Sherry's at Forty-fifth Street to have a drink. He was wearing his summer straw hat and an overcoat.

At Sherry's he stood alone at the long mahogany bar—it was too early for any crowd. The hat-check girl made several attempts to take his coat—a long, black, flowing garment worn over his dinner jacket, but Harry Thaw insisted he wanted to keep it on. He ordered a whiskey, drank it down, ordered two more. To pay the tab, which was about a half-dollar, he pulled a hundred-dollar bill from his wallet and laid it on the bar. The bartender asked if he had some smaller denomination, and when Harry Thaw said he did not, the bartender said it would take just a moment or two to make change.

From Sherry's, Harry Thaw walked the four blocks back to the Lorraine to get Evelyn. He instructed the chauffeur to follow in the touring car. One or two cabbies waiting along Fifth Avenue's curb recognized him. They touched the peaks of their caps and sailed good evenings in his direction—he was known to be a good tipper. If the overcoat in June caught their attention, they pretended not to notice.

At the Lorraine, Evelyn was waiting for him. She wore a white summer dress, covered with English eyelet embroidery, a black picture hat—they were very much in vogue—pulled down over her right eye. She had chosen the small pearl necklace and the pearl pendant earrings Harry had bought for her in Paris. They took the car to Martin's at Twenty-sixth Street between Broadway and Fifth, arriving a little after eight. Thomas McCaleb and Truxton Beale were waiting in the bar, and Mr. Harry Thaw's party of four was ushered directly to their table in the main dining room.

The building that housed the Café Martin had once been the site of Delmonico's, but when Delmonico's abandoned it to move to Forty-fourth Street, Francis Node, manager of Martin's, had redone the building completely. He fitted out the Broadway side as a French café, with marble-top tables along a balcony, so that in summer patrons could linger over coffee or an aperitif, scan the traffic along Broadway, or read a newspaper as if they were in Paris.

Entering Martin's from the Broadway side, as the Thaw party did, the foyer and the stairway to the café were passed unseen and the main dining room, which was inside, was entered directly. The balcony café could be reached by passing through the Broadway foyer—a useful arrangement if the lady was not the gentleman's wife—or by walking in from the Fifth Avenue side, then crossing through the main restaurant and being seen by everyone.

The main dining room was brilliantly lit by huge chandeliers from an oak-paneled ceiling. It was decorated in gold and white, with French doors and windows eighteen feet high, and hung with heavy white linen curtains tied back in gold. The waiters wore the traditional full white aprons, and the sommelier his golden key and chain. At Martin's, New Yorkers could dine well, and see and be seen. Harry Thaw thought it was "first class."

The Thaw party's table was near the aisle along one side of the great room. Harry Thaw, as host, sat with his back to the room, with a view of no more than two couples he did not know at banquettes against the wall. Truxton Beale sat on his left, Thomas McCaleb on his right, and Evelyn sat opposite Harry, where she could watch the room and the parade of diners who were making their way through the main dining room to the café on the balcony.

McCaleb had been secretary of some company in San Francisco and now allowed as how he would be a literary man and do some writing. In any case, he was full of talk and amusing. He was twenty-six, with reddish hair brushed straight back. Beale was also in his midtwenties, and more taciturn, an old friend of Harry's from Pittsburgh. Of the three men around Evelyn, Harry looked the youngest. He could have passed as an undergraduate, hardly more than eighteen. His round, boyish face, his quick nervous gestures, and his empty smile all contributed to the impression he gave of immaturity. Though he was six feet, there seemed to be none of a man's bulk to him. His eyes were still set as smoothly as a baby's, and when they went vacant their stare could be attributed to innocence, or perhaps the conceit of youth. He was thirty-five.

During dinner they chattered, or at least McCaleb and Beale and Evelyn did. According to the newspapers, the President's daughter, Alice Roosevelt, and her new husband, Nicholas Longworth, were on their honeymoon. They had been received on the Kaiser's yacht. At the table they talked about that and about money—the rate on call money had risen to 1½ percent, and steak had gone to the unbelievable price of twenty cents a pound. Harry Thaw ordered a second bottle of champagne, and the dinner began to turn quite gay.

The show they would attend at the Roof Garden at Madison Square was a premiere—*Mamzelle Champagne.* It had a book by Edgar Allan Wolf and music by Cassius Freeborn. Evelyn explained how much she wanted to see it because it was Freeborn's first musical and he would conduct himself. He couldn't be more than five feet tall and would need a conductor's podium a foot higher than anyone else's just to see over the footlights.

In the midst of Evelyn's chatter Harry noted something had happened. He interrupted her to ask what was wrong. She said it was nothing. Harry insisted. She asked McCaleb for a piece of paper and a pencil, wrote a note, folded the paper, and passed it across the table. The note read: "That B is here." Harry turned to look, but Stanford White had already passed through Martin's main dining room and gone out to the café on the balcony over Broadway. Although Thaw had missed seeing White, it was probable that White had seen Evelyn but had given her no more than an imperceptible nod.

Out on the balcony White would have dinner with his eighteen-year-old son, Lawrence Grant White, and a Harvard classmate, LeRoy King. They would be sophomores in the fall and had come down from Cambridge to start their summer vacations. After dinner White would leave them at the New Amsterdam, where they would see Cohan's new revue, *The Governor's Son*. He would take his electric hansom to Madison Square Garden for the opening of *Mamzelle Champagne*. He told them he would be home a bit late because he was working on the details of Dr. Parkhurst's new church. He'd be sketching in what he called his "snuggery"—his studio in the Garden's Tower.

After White had passed through Martin's, and Harry had read Evelyn's note, any further conversation at the Thaw table seemed to be impossible. Evelyn could see that Harry had begun to stare and that he was biting at a fingernail. She feared he would begin one of his incredible scenes. She asked him for the time, because she did not want to miss the opening. When he immediately signaled for the check, she believed they might get out of Martin's safely.

They walked the three blocks to the Garden, and again Harry directed the chauffeur to follow them. Harry had checked his overcoat in Martin's, but he had put it back on again. Evelyn thought it was odd to wear an overcoat on a hot June night, but she guessed Harry was in no mood to discuss the subject. They took the elevator to the roof and found their table far from the stage along the south or Madison Avenue side. Harry took off his straw hat when they sat down but still wore his coat. Evelyn saw him glance up at the shadows of Stanny's Tower, looming above the potted palms and Japanese lanterns of the Roof Garden.

Within a minute after they had sat down Harry wandered off. He had spotted James Clinch Smith, Stanford White's brother-in-law, sitting at a table near the back on the Twenty-sixth Street side. Smith had an empty seat at his table, and Thaw asked if Smith would mind if he joined him for a while. He told Smith he had only been able to get three seats for the show and "was forced to stroll." Smith said he didn't mind at all.

Thaw offered Smith a cigar and asked if he was speculating on Wall Street. They began an easy conversation. Thaw said if he had any money to invest, he'd put it all into steel or copper stocks. He asked if Smith was going abroad, and Smith said he was, next week on the *Deutschland.* Thaw said he didn't like the *Deutschland* because "she breaks down too much. I'm going abroad pretty soon, but I think I'll go on the *Amerika.*"

Smith liked the *Deutschland* because he knew the captain, and the captain was very nice to his wife.

"Where's your wife?"

"She's in Paris."

"Are you very much married?"

Smith asked him what he meant by that.

"Well," Thaw said, "are you above meeting a very nice girl? She isn't here on the roof, but I can give you a note to her. She's a buxom brunette, not good-looking but very nice."

From the advantage of his fifty years and with the dignity of his gray hair, Mr. James Clinch Smith thanked young Mr. Harry Thaw politely but said he didn't care to meet any girls, then turned his attention to the stage, clearly ending their conversation.

Harry Thaw attempted to renew the association, remarking

that the show, as it began to unfold, seemed rather slow for a summer revue. Smith agreed, somewhat curtly, but kept his attention on the stage. After a few minutes Harry Thaw excused himself, gesturing toward the Madison Avenue aisle, explaining that he was going that way. Smith only nodded because he thought Thaw to be an odd duck—wearing an overcoat on such a warm night.

The show they had halfheartedly been watching was struggling toward its curtain. It was indeed a slow production for a summer review. Viola de Costa, as Mamzelle Champagne, had popped out of a papier-mâché bottle of champagne to applause—but only because she was a very pretty girl. Maude Fulton had put over the song "Can I Fascinate You?" and won a round of applause because she was Maude Fulton—the song really wasn't much. Harry Short had played the part of Fuller Spice, an American theater manager at Maxim's in Paris, and when he sang "I Could Love a Thousand Girls," twenty girls in the chorus pranced about, but the applause was very thin, and the buzz of conversation at the tables continued to rise.

During Harry Short's number, "I Could Love a Thousand Girls," Stanford White could be seen making his way along the aisles to the table always reserved for him near the stage. He was alone, which was unusual, but he was recognized, as he always was: a big man, perhaps six feet two, in his early fifties, the flaming red hair and the thick moustache bristling as if charged with electricity. "There's Stanford White . . ."

His passage to his table was typical of him, half-ramble, half-stride, nodding to friends on the way, a personal word to a group along his path, a wave to another table too far to reach, a star of Broadway brighter than any of those performing on the stage in *Mamzelle Champagne,* a show he had backed. Almost immediately after he had taken his seat Harry K. Stevens, the Garden's caterer, came over to join him. As the two men talked White's hands, his head, his shoulders, his eyes—every part of him—were always in motion. The corona of energy around him was a distraction from the business on the stage. When he laughed at something Harry Stevens had said he threw his head back and his teeth flashed. As Harry Stevens got up to leave, White's hand came down like a lion's paw on Stevens' forearm—an easy gesture, intimate, something warmer than a politician's trick. Then with the touch done, White turned his gaze to the stage, his chin resting temporarily in his hand, apparently enthusiastic for the silly spectacle of the show's closing number.

The ladies of the chorus were in their finale—the "fencing girls" routine. They wore tights that showed their figures well and came marching up to the footlights with épées drawn. "I challenge you," they sang. "I challenge you to a duel, a du-u-el." Stanford White beamed backed at them; he wanted them to know they were just "Bully!" "Marvelous!"

By then Harry Thaw had worked his way along the aisle to within three feet of White's table. From beneath his black overcoat he pulled out a revolver, held it at arm's length, and as White felt his presence and turned toward him, Thaw aimed for the eyes, then fired three shots.

Stanford White half rose, as if he were going to stand up, then pitched forward across his table, taking the edge of the tablecloth with him. Silver scattered, and a wineglass crashed.

The music stopped, and the chorus stood transfixed, their swords poised. There was complete silence for a moment, then someone near the back of the audience laughed: surely it must have been part of the show. The eerie laugh was followed by a woman's scream—a long, piercing, thrilling, wail—and the chorus girls began to join her, which was the signal the crowd needed. It began to gather momentum for the exits. In the panic that followed, Harry Thaw stood over his victim, holding the smoking revolver high in the air so that all might see it, and then calmly emptied its chambers, the unexpended bullets falling beside the body of his victim. The significance of the empty revolver was lost on the mob; they had no thought but to rush for the streets.

Lionel Laurence, the stage manager, kept his wits and ordered the chorus to, "Dance! Sing! Keep it up!" Five-foot conductor Cassius Freeborn ordered his orchestra to play again, and they dutifully turned their books to "I Could Love a Thousand Girls." By the time they had completed no more than two bars, Laurence had got the house lights up. The orchestra faded again, and Laurence waved a straggling chorus offstage. From the footlights he shouted, "It's all right. It's all right. Ladies and gentlemen, a most serious accident has occurred, but it's all right. Please keep still. Please leave the house as quietly as possible."

The mob finally began to quiet, but more than a dozen women had fainted in the crush near the exits, and there were small groups giving attention to each one. A Dr. Techner volunteered his assistance from the audience and pronounced White dead. A waiter pulled a tablecloth over the powder-blackened face, but blood seeped through the cloth immediately, and it seemed the best thing to do was to add another tablecloth on top of the first.

During the panic Harry Thaw had not moved away from White's body. Then, with the revolver still in his hand, he had walked to the elevator where Fireman Paul Brudi of Engine Company 60, who had been detailed to the show, saw him coming. Brudi grabbed the pistol from Thaw's hand. It was still hot. Thaw did not resist, and together they stepped through the open elevator doors. "He deserved it," Thaw said to Brudi. "He deserved it, and I can prove it."

A man and woman followed them into the elevator; then recognizing Thaw, the woman began to cry. Thaw turned to the elevator operator, who seemed frozen, and said: "We've got to go down anyhow. Suppose you take me down now, so as not to annoy these people."

Before the elevator man, Walter Paxton, could close his doors, Officer Debes of the Tenderloin District Command entered, touched Thaw on the shoulder, and announced, "You're under arrest."

"All right," was all that Thaw said.

Then Evelyn appeared. She had fought her way through the panic that had swirled toward the stairwells, elbowing her way upstream against a pushing, angry mob. She too walked into the elevator, threw her arms around Harry's neck. "Oh Harry," she said, "why did you do it?"

He hugged her, and they all heard him say: "It's all right dear. It's all right. I have probably saved your life." He then turned to the couple standing with them, opened up his wallet, and handed a ten-dollar bill to the man. "I wish you would call up Mr. Andrew Carnegie at number ten ninety-three Fifth Avenue and tell him I'm in trouble. I am Harry Thaw of Pittsburgh."

Officer Debes signaled to Paxton to take the elevator down. Once they were at street level on Madison Avenue, Evelyn turned toward the Thaws' touring car. Debes described Thaw giving her a wave "as calm as Sunday," and then he walked his prisoner to the police station. Debes held the door open for him, then brought him up to the railing.

Sergeant McCarthy began the procedures. "What is your name?"

Thaw was leaning against the railing nonchalantly. "John Smith."

"What is your occupation?"

"Student."

"Where do you live?"

"Number eighteen Lafayette Square, Washington."

"Do you know the man you shot?"

The prisoner looked at Sergeant McCarthy a moment, then at the floor, and finally at the wall. "Well," he answered, after some deliberation, "well, I can't say."

ACT III

FAITH

"This was not life, and yet it was not death;
If thou has wit to think how I might fare
Bereft of both, let fancy aid thy faith."

—DANTE, *The Divine Comedy,* "Hell,"
Canto XXXIV, lines 25-27

CHAPTER SEVENTEEN

REQUIEM IN PACE

AFTER THE GEORGE M. COHAN REVUE at the New Amsterdam, Lawrence White had a drink with his classmate LeRoy King, then walked home to his family's townhouse on Gramercy Park at East Twenty-first Street. Near midnight he received the news of his father's death from Madison Square Garden by telephone. Without waiting for details, he went to the Garden, got his father's electric hansom, and started driving for his home in Saint James, Long Island. He crossed the Brooklyn Bridge, went north to the Jericho Road, then east to Smithtown and to North Country Road. It was about 2 A.M. when he finally arrived.

He roused his mother and told her his father had been shot. She seemed to take the news calmly. She did not ask for details, but Larry would not have known many of them. His mother lay on her bed, just staring. At seven the next morning Lawrence drove her to the city, and other members of the family took the 6:44 A.M. train from Saint James, following them to the house on Gramercy Park. By the time they arrived, there were crowds of newspaper reporters waiting. They demanded to see the woman "Harry Thaw had made a widow."

There were already extra editions on the street supplying details of the murder—it was a sensation, pushing every other kind of news off the front pages. From the city the story was being sent out over the wires to the front pages of every other city in the world—a moral drama described under shrill headlines, groaning paragraphs, hoarse quotes, and intimating delicious details in tongues mixed and mingled. Daily circulation was up everywhere.

There were the standard obituaries of Stanford White, New York's leading architect, and column after column listing his major works. There were background stories that featured White as a "leading clubman," a society leader, and an arbiter of taste. There were pages of pictures of White, of Harry K. Thaw, Pittsburgh millionaire, and of Mrs. Thaw in an endless variety of poses, dug up from her career as Evelyn Nesbit, artist's model.

From his cell at the Tombs prison, Harry Thaw happily gave interviews, explaining that he had shot White because the famous architect had ruined young girls, and stories soon appeared that suggested that perhaps Stanford White was "a satyr." Reporters sought out White's friends for their comments, asking for confirmation or denial that White "had kept harems."

"Strange to say," the New York *World* reported, "the men who constituted Stanford White's intimate friends did not rally to the defense of his memory yesterday." Harry Thaw's allegations "were almost corroborated by the silence of the well-known men-about-town." Reporters sought out Peter Cooper Hewitt, who maintained a studio on a floor below White's in Madison Square Tower, but Hewitt "declined persistently to discuss his friend's relations with Mrs. Thaw, and disappeared to the seclusion of his club."

The newspapers reported that James Lawrence Breese had "dropped out of sight," and was not even to be found at his clubs; that White's friends seemed to have scattered in all directions; that Tommy Clarke and Henry Poore could not be found; that the author Duffield Osborne, when found, was silent. All efforts to induce him to defend the dead man against Thaw's charges were "unavailing."

Late on Tuesday afternoon the reporters caught Charles McKim on the steps of the Gramercy Park house. They duly reported to their editors that in answer to their questions, Mr. White's partner said, "There is no statement to make. In obedience to Mrs. White's wishes there will be no information coming from us." They noted that Mr. McKim ignored all questions related to Mrs. Evelyn Nesbit Thaw.

The New York *World* was, however, able to describe Stanford White's body lying in state in his house on Gramercy Park "almost at the foot of the *Venus Genetrix,* a statue found in the Tiber, which Mr. White purchased and placed in the great drawing room of his Gramercy Park home. Living, he placed chaste Diana atop his great work—Madison Square Garden; dead, he was stretched in the shadow of Venus; she who brought him to the shadow of death."

On Tuesday afternoon Mrs. White announced through Charles McKim that funeral services would be held Thursday at Saint Bartholomew's at Madison and Forty-fourth Street, and the Reverend Leighton I. Parks would officiate. There would be ten pallbearers, whose names would be announced.

On Wednesday the family announced that the plans had been changed. There would be no pallbearers, and services would be held at the Episcopal church in Saint James, Long Island, where Mrs. White's family maintained pews. The newspapers duly noted again that White's friends had disappeared: "They had gone to ground."

At 8 A.M. Thursday newspapermen still maintained their siege of the Gramercy Park house, and in addition a small crowd of the city's curious milled and gawked. A hearse and two carriages drew up to the door. But both crowd and reporters were disappointed as the carriages followed the hearse, because they were filled with Mrs. White's relations, none of whom were certified celebrities: Mr. James Clinch Smith, brother of Mrs. White; Charles S. Butler, nephew of Mrs. White; Mr. and Mrs. Connolly, cousins of Mrs. White; Mr. and Mrs. Barrett Lefferts, a daughter of Mrs. Kate Wetherill, another sister of Mrs. White. The newspapers could only report that two more sisters of Mrs. White—Mrs. Devereaux Emmet and Mrs. Prescott Hall Butler—had remained with the dead architect's mother, who was seventy-five years old and had been told that her son was shot by an anarchist.

The hearse and its two carriages were driven to the East Thirty-fourth Street ferry, then passed to the Long Island side, where a special train was waiting. The casket was placed aboard the train in a combination baggage-smoker, banked by floral tributes, and the car occupied by members of the family. Some two hundred friends of White and his family filled three day coaches, and when steam was up, the train departed Long Island City, at about 9:15 A.M. Mrs. Stanford White was not aboard because her son Lawrence had driven her from the city by auto to avoid reporters.

At the family's request, the train was run slowly, not arriving at the Saint James Station until 10:30 A.M. About fifty people from the village met it. Undertaker Darlin and six assistants lifted the casket from the train to a hearse, and a funeral cortege started for the church, a distance of no more than three-quarters of a mile. At the corner of Lake Avenue and North Country Road, Lawrence White, driving Mrs. White, wheeled the electric hansom into the line at the head of the procession. Behind them the road was crowded with every kind of conveyance—hackneys and carriages and autos driven up from the summer colonies in Southampton, or Westbury, or Wheatley Hills.

Three big elms marked the entrance to the plain white-plank church. Except for seven small stained-glass windows, it looked like the chapel version of a New England Congregational church but it had an Episcopal sign—the gold cross above the latticed belfry tower, symbol of the combination of Puritan and Tory strains. The single tower rose above a steeply pitched roof, and the plain walls were set upon foundations of red federal brick. It was the church of the Smith family of Smithtown—a simple, plain determined faith, the same faith the White family of Connecticut and New York had once served.

Inside, more than two hundred fifty friends were crowded into straight-backed rows, six pressed into pews designed for five. Flowers hung everywhere—wreaths of roses, orchids, sweet peas, and calla lilies. They were set against the simple altar and hung along the plain painted walls and were even suspended from the organ loft at the rear. From the loft a choir of fourteen voices from Saint Bartholomew's led the hymns. The Reverend Park, assisted by the Reverend Holden, archdeacon of Saint James, read the services of the dead. There was no sermon or eulogy.

Then the undertaker's six men did their part as pallbearers, hoisting the casket to their shoulders, and the procession formed for the graveside. The march led from the church down a vista shaded on both sides by rows of yew trees. The grave site was visible in the sun ahead; the choir sang in a measured cadence, and when their song paused, summer birds could be heard twittering in the shade.

At the graveside a rough pine box stood ready to receive the casket. At Mrs. White's request there was no pile of earth visible beside the six-foot trench. The gravediggers had carried it away, concealing the earth behind the privet at the graveyard's edge. They had placed evergreen boughs over the discolored soil beside the pit. When the procession had assembled beside the grave, the coffin was let down into its place, "Dust to Dust, Ashes to Ashes" was said, and a few handfuls of dirt were tossed to complete the ceremony. The choir led the mourners away, singing "Abide with Me."

Mrs. White and her son, Lawrence, lingered a while, as did James Breese and Charles McKim. They stood near the head of the open grave, beside a stripling Scotch pine that had been planted there. Then they too turned back toward the church. Three gravediggers appeared and bent to their spades. Stanford White was fifty-two.

CHAPTER EIGHTEEN

HOLY WRIT, DATELINE NEW YORK

THE FUNERAL HELD THURSDAY, June 28, 1906, in rural Saint James, Long Island, drew a rather large crowd, but few of those present were celebrities the reporters might recognize, consequently their editors had to print descriptions of a simple and decorous burial. "Those who looked for any sign of emotion at the grave of Stanford White yesterday," said the *World,* "were disappointed."

But as soon as a decent burial was done the city's newsmen could get about their business. One enterprising journalist was able to dig out a quote from an unnamed neighbor of White's to the effect that "the murder of Stanford White is not the tragedy, it is but the culmination of it." The New York *World* had proudly listed its circulation at 537,734 on the day White was shot. Within a week circulation had gained nearly 100,000 copies each day. From Paris, White's friend and intimate James Gordon Bennett, Jr., cabled instructions to his editors at the *Herald* to "give him hell." On July 2, not to be outdone by their competition, the *Evening Journal* began to serialize the story of Susie Johnson, "The Girl in the Pie." Miss Johnson had unfortunately died, but supposedly had told "everything" to an unnamed friend, as if it were a last testament, which was certainly convenient for the *Journal*'s circulation.

From beyond the grave, Susie Johnson gave witness to the *Journal*'s daily readers that she had lived with her father, mother, and sister at 104 Eighth Avenue; that she was offered fifty dollars to be The Girl in the Pie at the Breese dinner;

"and when the banjoists struck up Four-and-Twenty Blackbirds I burst through the crust, opened the cage, and found myself stared at by thirty men."

Her posthumous letters described her evening as "Queen of the Revel"; and for the enlightenment of the faithful she gave the details of her sacrifice. She had been taken in a "stupefied condition" by Stanford White to his studio on Twenty-fourth Street, apartments "that were fitted up with Oriental splendor." She had trusted him, she said, and he had sent her to Europe to be educated for the stage, but she had been in Europe for only three months before he stopped her allowance and she had been forced to take the steamer home. "I begged him not to turn me out penniless on the world, but to all my entreaties he turned a deaf ear. I tried to live an honest life, but it was no use."

Since Susie Johnson was buried in Potter's Field, she was unavailable for further comment by papers competing with the *Evening Journal,* but Mr. Anthony Comstock, president of the Society for the Suppression of Vice, and recognized authority on the city's moral standards, was very much alive and constantly available to interviews by all representatives of the press. Mr. Comstock stood ready, he announced, to present to the grand jury "information damaging to Stanford White and three of his associates." The source of Mr. Comstock's information, he revealed, was Harry Thaw, who had brought "these matters" to Comstock's attention over the past year and a half. He added, "This evidence against White I firmly believe was prompted by the purest motives."

To corroborate Thaw's allegations, Comstock recounted how he had attempted to rent rooms in Madison Square Garden Tower on floors near White's studio but had been refused the opportunity to pursue the investigation. Instead, he had succeeded in posting men to watch the Tower, and his observers had gathered "much incriminating evidence against White and his associates in connection with their midnight revelry." In answer to questions posed about Mr. Comstock's incriminating evidence, he stated he would reveal it at the proper time and to the proper authorities. He stated he had letters in his possession corroborating Thaw's allegations of young girls ruined by White but pointed out that the letters would, of course, have to be anonymous.

When asked if he had talked to any of the victims, Comstock allowed that he had interviewed and obtained statements from them. "But," he admitted, "when it came to preparing a case against White, many difficulties confronted me." He explained that many of the girls were underage, or unfortunately "had been spirited away," before his Society for the Suppression of Vice could bring their cases to the appropriate court.

Besides the testimony of Susie Johnson from beyond the grave, and the ever-present Anthony Comstock, an unnamed friend of White's was quoted: "What if poor White did play around with stage-girls? They were nothing but little butterflies to him. Why make such a fuss because a few of them fell by the wayside? They were gay, brief playthings. That sort of thing is to be expected."

A Miss Katherine Poillon was discovered, who would agree to be quoted by name. She said "the stories of Stanford White and the men around him only state half the truth." In an exclusive interview for an afternoon edition she told "of scenes that took place on board a certain yacht owned by one of White's intimate friends, which baffle description." According to Miss Poillon, when she found herself aboard the yacht and "could bear the affair no longer, I went to the owner and demanded to be put ashore, and finally carried my point." She was quoted saying she would be glad to make public a hundred other such instances and that "the nest of moral lepers who to my knowledge have infested upper Broadway for years cannot be too soon wiped out."

A member of the fencing chorus of *Mamzelle Champagne* appeared in print to disagree with Miss Poillon. "Temptations? Nonsense! Most of the chorus girls considered it a great feather in their cap to be seen with Stanford White or his associates. He paid doctors' bills for chorus girls he never saw; he paid hundreds of dollars for cabs for girls and their friends. Every girl knew what his attentions meant and most of us would have given a year's salary to get those attentions.

"On one occasion he gave a little dinner to a lot of the

girls, each of whom found a $20 gold piece under a box of candy at her plate. There was not a girl there who did not know what delicate hint was hidden in that gold piece, by which they were given to understand that things would become pretty lively before the night was over and that anyone who did not care to contribute her share might leave her $20 gold piece and go. Those who stayed did so because they wanted to stay."

After surveying the reports from members of the chorus of *Mamzelle Champagne,* Miss Poillon, Anthony Comstock, Susie Johnson, and other highly informed sources, the Reverend Charles A. Eaton, pastor of John D. Rockefeller, had a statement to make: "It would be a good thing if there was a little more shooting in cases like this."

Surely what he meant, in all charity, was that the city's ethical sensibilities had changed somewhat by 1906; that the topics discussed as news on Bowling Green when New York was a village—when church spires dominated its horizon—had lost their moral distinctions; that the whirlwinds of the new dispensation reflected a citizenry devoted to anarchy; and the editors who assembled the daily collage should be absolved because they were only reporting what was happening. "History must be the judge," the editors could argue, and they assigned their reporters in battalions to the latest drama.

As the result of the efforts of enterprising reporters, it was revealed that Harry Thaw had hired detectives to shadow White and that White had hired detectives to discover who was following him. Moreover, the allegations made in Mrs. Lederer's suit for divorce, naming Evelyn Nesbit as corespondent, could be reviewed in the evening editions. For editions published both weekday and Sundays there was always Evelyn herself—posing as a fashion model, sketched as "The Eternal Question" by Charles Dana Gibson, pictured as leading New York beauty, artist's model, *Floradora* girl. From the morgue editors could extract vignettes of her affair with John Barymore, rewrite the news she had made in Europe at parties with Harry Thaw, and retell in Sunday Supplement features the story of the "Beauty Who Married Pittsburgh Millions."

Evelyn understood exactly how quickly the metropolitan newsmen would be on her scent. As soon as she left Harry by the elevators at the Garden, she found McCaleb and Beale waiting by the touring car, but it was an open car, and she asked them to get a hansom cab instead. Inside the cab, as they started up Fifth, McCaleb asked her who it was that Harry had shot. When Evelyn told them he had killed Stanford White they both groaned. They asked her where she wanted to be taken, and she finally decided that it would be too risky to return to the Hotel Lorraine. She wanted to be dropped off at May Mackenzie's, at 148 West Forty-ninth Street. McCaleb and Beale left her there.

After May had let her in and brought her a glass of water while Evelyn explained what had happened, they called the landlady, a Mrs. Molloy. May Mackenzie and Evelyn Nesbit had hardly begun to explain the situation to Mrs. Molloy before the doorbell rang. At least a dozen newspapermen were standing on the stoop, shouting questions to Mrs. Molloy, who was peering out the second-story window: Did May Mackenzie live at this address? Did May Mackenzie know where Evelyn Nesbit was? Could they talk to May Mackenzie? Did Mrs. Molloy know what had happened? Mrs. Molloy played her part to the hilt. Nobody in her house knew anything, and she slammed shut the window, which sent them away temporarily. But there were soon others, stragglers who rang the downstairs bell all night. No one in the house could sleep.

In the morning May telephoned George and Margaret Carnegie, and they slipped into May's apartment for a conference. Harry's sister agreed to get Nellie, Evelyn's maid, to bring over a change of clothes and a hat with a veil. They hoped Evelyn would be able to return to her suite at the Hotel Lorraine without being seen. They decided the staff at the Lorraine might be able to give her better protection from the newshounds.

Since Mother Thaw was still on the high seas, George Carnegie would take the situation in hand. He called upon Evelyn at the Lorraine on Wednesday afternoon to give his advice. "Evelyn," he began, "we have all known for a long time that

Harry is crazy. They're all nutty as bedbugs, but don't say I said so or they'd kill me. What the family should do is lock Harry up in the bughouse where he belongs!"

He advised her not to talk to anybody. He had engaged Mother Thaw's lawyers—Black, Olcott, Gruber and Bonynge—and they would be coming to see her.

They appeared at the Lorraine the next day, Thursday, the day Stanny was being buried. Ex-governor Black and Judge Olcott advised her of her rights. If the District Attorney insisted upon subpoenaing her, she was to accept the subpoena, but she did not have to say anything to anyone and indeed should say nothing. Before they left her Judge Olcott promised he would make arrangements for Evelyn to visit Harry in the Tombs.

Later the same day Bedford, Harry's valet, appeared and asked Evelyn to show him where her husband had concealed the locked suitcase—the one with Harry's "paraphernalia." He had been instructed to pick it up, he said, and as she handed it over to him she thought Bedford looked pale. She asked him what was the matter. He said he didn't know but that he felt very ill. When he died a few days later in Presbyterian Hospital, the newspapers reported the story cautiously. The cause of death was given in guarded paragraphs as "acute appendicitis."

As a result of Judge Olcott's efforts, Evelyn made her first visit to the Tombs. She was nearly mobbed. The police had to form a cordon to get her through the crowd, which pressed in from every side to get a look at her. Mounted officers had to be used to clear the way. As Evelyn ran up the steps to the Tombs, she could hear the mob shrieking behind her, "There she is. . . . It's Evelyn. . . . There she is." It was an ugly sound, and it frightened her.

Inside the prison it was quiet. A newspaper reporter confronted her. "Do you intend taking the witness stand in your husband's defense?"

She answered him firmly: "I will do everything in my power to help save his life."

Evelyn Thaw went to the Tombs regularly, and through the mob every time. Once inside and safe, she would be searched by a matron and then led upstairs to a special tier of cells known as Murderers' Row. Harry would be sitting there in his shirtsleeves, a soiled handkerchief around his neck and his straw hat on his head. He said there was a terrible draft in his cell. He knew people who would love to see him dead of pneumonia. He had stuffed newspapers between the bars at the top of the cell "to keep out the drafts."

When Evelyn said she thought it was really very hot and stuffy he cut her short and looked as if he were about to fly into one of his rages. He talked constantly about his lawyers. He said his lawyer Delafield was a "traitor," and was trying to convince his lawyer Judge Olcott that he was insane. He would shout, "They are trying to railroad me into an insane asylum. That's what some of them are going to try to do." He instructed Evelyn not to let them talk his mother into it.

As soon as Mother Thaw arrived back from Europe she took charge of her son's defense. She announced she would spend a million dollars, if necessary, to save Harry's life. She hired a press agent, Ben Atwell, to present Harry to the newspapers in the role he might have to play at a trial—the chivalrous avenger of his wife's honor. Following Atwell's suggestion, Mother Thaw backed a play that opened at the Amphion Theatre on September 24 in which three characters named Harold Daw, Emeline Hudspeth Daw, and Stanford Black acted out scenes similar to those reported in the newspapers. In one scene Stanford Black knocked down an old blind man who begged to know what had happened to his beautiful young daughter. In another scene a pretty girl sprang from a pie. The curtain came down on a declaration from Harry Daw, made from a cell at the Tombs, "No jury on earth will send me to the electric chair, no matter what I have done or what I have been, for killing the man who defamed my wife. That is the unwritten law."

But Black, Olcott, Gruber, and Bonynge would not defend Harry on the grounds of the unwritten law. Just as Harry had predicted, Judge Olcott wanted to avoid the risks of a verdict by trial, and argued for a plea of insanity. Mother

Thaw paid them off. She then called in D. T. Watson, Esquire, an old friend from Pittsburgh, for advice, and Counselor Watson asked to interview Evelyn alone.

Watson sat with Evelyn in her suite at the Lorraine. He asked her if she was willing to take the stand in Harry's defense. He asked her if she understood what that might mean, that on cross-examination the prosecuting attorneys might drag her past into public view.

She answered that Harry's lawyers had told her she might be the only one who could save his life. Watson agreed that might be true, but he wondered if Harry had made any provision for her so that, if anything should happen, she would be taken care of financially. She said she was sure that Mother Thaw would do the right thing.

Mr. Watson was thoughtful. He asked if she thought Harry would always love her.

She said she believed so.

"From what I know of this man and his people," said Mother Thaw's attorney, "you are making a great mistake."

CHAPTER NINETEEN

SPECTACLE OF JUSTICE

THE CASE OF the *People v. Harry K. Thaw* opened on the morning of Wednesday, January 23, 1907. The clerk of the court, a Mr. Penny, sang out the call, "All rise," and the judge strode into the courtroom, heaved his bulk up the two steps to the bench, took his seat, and rearranged his black robes. He was James Fitzgerald, Justice of the Supreme Court of New York, Criminal Branch. As Judge Fitzgerald surveyed his packed courtroom Clerk Penny indicated that all might resume their seats.

The District Attorney, Mr. William Travers Jerome, read the title of the indictment, then took his place at the prosecution's table beside his assistant, Mr. Francis P. Garvan. The clerk of the court called, "Harry K. Thaw to the bar!"

At the rear of the courtroom the door opened, and the defendant entered. On his way to his place at the table for the defense he smiled and nodded greetings to his wife and to his mother in their seats beyond the rail. When he had taken his place among his counselors the clerk of the court resumed his incantations. "Harry K. Thaw, if you intend to challenge a juror, you must do so when the juror appears and before he is sworn."

The next eight days were spent assembling a jury. The number of veniremen who had to be excused was unprecedented. Each prospective juror had to be asked if he had already formed an opinion, if he could give an impartial hearing to the case despite the fact that it had been front-page news for six months. Moreover, each venireman had to be examined on whether he knew the victim, if he could serve until the end of the trial, if he knew the defendant or any members of the defendant's family or any members of the defendant's counsel. Both prosecution and defense took their time and had the right to challenge jurors both for cause or peremptorily. As each juror stepped up into the witness chair for examination Mrs. Harry K. Thaw could be seen signaling to her husband her estimation of the juror's prospective sympathies, and apparently the lawyers of his defense relied upon her instincts for their challenges.

Five lawyers surrounded the defendant at his table, for evidently Mother Thaw had spared no expense: Mr. George Peabody, Esquire—a rotund and genial face; Mr. John B. Gleason, Esquire—elderly, stout, with spectacles that needed adjustment frequently; Mr. Clifford Hartridge, Esquire—an old friend of the Thaw family, legal adviser and counselor, designer of trusts and wills; Mr. Hugh McPike, Esquire—a gentleman from San Francisco's Bar said to be present as assistant to Mr. Delmas; and, Mr. Delphin Michael Delmas himself, a defense attorney of national celebrity.

Delmas was a short, stocky man with a lion's head and heavy pouches under his chin and narrowed eyes. He was a man described as the Napoleon of the Western Bar, a courtroom performer with a reputation for majesty before the jury box, a speaker who used ornate language in biblical cadences and had an enviable record of clients found innocent regardless of the number of witnesses to the crime. Mr. Delmas took no part in the examination of jurors, leaving that to the defendant's lesser counsel, and increasing the court's anticipation of his entrance in the case.

At the end of the first day, only two jurymen had been selected. After Judge Fitzgerald announced that the jury would be sequestered for the length of the trial, certified excuses multiplied geometrically, and the number of veniremen who claimed to have known the dead architect suddenly soared. The selection of twelve good men and true slowed to a snail's pace, and the courtroom longed for entertainment. Charles K. Harris, songwriter and author of the hit "After the Ball" was called and examined and appeared willing to serve but was excused by both prosecution and defense with enthusiasm.

Another prospective juryman was asked the standard question, "Do you know any of the defendant's counsel," looked across at the group assembled around Harry Thaw, and asked if that was all of them. William Travers Jerome, the District Attorney, had the opportunity to quip, "I hope so," and the courtroom was relieved for the first time of its tedium.

When the Thaw trial opened Jerome was one of the city's heroes. Like Teddy Roosevelt, he was a descendant of the Washington Square merchant aristocracy, and he had the President's manners, looks, and attitude. He wore the same pince-nez glasses, he parted his hair in the middle, and he could laugh with others and at himself. He was known as a "good egg." He was an activist and a reformer. He spoke with Teddy's righteousness. "When I say a senator is unfit," he had thundered from the platforms of his campaign, "I mean Depew. When I speak of a self-seeking Boss, I mean Odell!"

Jerome wore bow ties, smoked incessantly, and could swear lavishly. He made less of the "outdoor life" than Teddy, but Jerome was as audacious and fit as the President. Jerome was no pompous moralist, nor an idealist, but a practical politician, known widely as the friend of the common man. For a while in New York the phrase "to go to Jerome" meant to find a defender of the oppressed. Before he won election as District Attorney by swamping Tammany Hall he had been famous as a just judge. "When the law says a year," said a man who had served under him, "Jerome don't give a man eleven months, nor yet thirteen. Jerome, he gives him a year."

Judge Jerome had moved to the Lower East Side, to Rutgers Street, so that he could receive the complaints of common citizens day and night. Jerome found that he was responsible for closing gambling dens, and he would arrive in their rooms with a raiding party before anyone could escape, hold court on the spot, and pass sentence. When he campaigned for District Attorney in 1901 he pointed out that it was the antiprostitution laws, the antigambling laws, the antiliquor laws which were the causes of perjury and corruption, the "blackmailing league between vice and police," the source of bribery, hypocrisy, and fraud in the courts.

District Attorney Jerome worked to break up the alliances

between vice and police and courts. He went after "the men higher up." Until he took the case against Harry K. Thaw there was talk that William Travers Jerome, *beau gent* of Old New York, might consider serving as Governor of New York, and if that went well, might even consider the White House. In the courtroom he was quick and catlike as he moved, making his points as if he were hammering down nails; terse, abrupt, snappish, reaching his conclusions with "the mechanical precision and swiftness of a cash register or patent adding machine."

As the process of choosing jurymen dragged on, the press waited for the confrontation between District Attorney Jerome, popular hero and honest man before the bar, and counselor for the defense, Mr. Delphin Michael Delmas, representative of the western school of silver tongues, suave, courtly, courteous, costumed for his part in frock coat and long hair, "with rings on his fingers and bells on his voice."

While they waited for the drama to open, the press found other items to report. More than a thousand spectators gathered each morning to catch a glimpse of Mrs. Harry K. Thaw, described invariably as "the woman in the case." Because of the milling crowds, the police needed reinforcements to form a cordon for Evelyn to reach the courtroom doors. Inside, extra seats were installed for the unprecedented number of reporters—more than one hundred were provided passes, and despite the additional seats, no one could be admitted from the "general public" because the witnesses of the case, the lawyers, family, and friends of the defendant occupied every space available. Only one "associate of Mr. White" could be identified—his secretary, Mr. Charles Harnett.

"The Thaw trial," said *The New York Times,* "is being reported to the ends of the civilized globe. The eminence of the victim, the wealth of the prisoner, the dramatic circumstance of the crime, and the light it sheds not only on Broadway life, but on the doings of the fast set in every capital have caused special arrangements to be made for the press."

There was a telegraph office set up in the main hall of the Criminal Courts Building. Cables hung from the skylight in the old court's central hall like strange black vines, and through their copper cores, reports went out which differed so considerably that they must have derived from the nuance of each reporter's assignment. *The New York Times,* for example, seemed to take the point of view that it was reporting an historical event, but history's truths varied: one report described how Harry Thaw was in good spirits, laughing and talking with his attendants; another report described him as sallow, with his head sunk low between his shoulders. The defendant was reported to be calm and apparently in control of himself; he was also reported to be unable to control a slight twitching of his thick lips. He was described to have white, hairless hands, to have poor complexion and dry coarse hair streaked with gray, an almost childish droop to his mouth, and unsteady eyes that he could not control. He was also described as having a lovable face, both willful and weak. It could be imagined he had been an easy boy to spoil and that "even without his fortune, Harry Thaw would have been popular with women."

Each day as Harry Thaw's family entered the courtroom from a room behind the jurybox and took their seats among the spectators beyond the rail there were newspaper descriptions of their appearance: the impressive Mrs. William Thaw, empress dowager of Pittsburgh coal and Pennsylvania Railroad bonds, white-haired, dressed and veiled in black, "a widow determined to save her son from the electric chair." She had assembled her family at her side, in seats reserved for them, evidence that the Thaw women were there to support the defendant: Alice, Countess of Yarmouth, wearing a green coat, black hat and veil; Mrs. George Lauder Carnegie, wearing black, a thick brown veil tied around a turban hat; and sitting beside Mother Thaw, the woman for whom every eye strained, her daughter-in-law—Harry Thaw's wife.

For the part she was to play Evelyn had chosen her costume carefully. Before the trial began Mr. Delmas had interviewed her for hours on end so that, he said, he would not be met with any surprises. Among the knowing members of the press, reports circulated that the price of Evelyn's testimony would be one million dollars, but of course such reports were surely exaggerations because any payment of a witness for his or her testimony would be illegal under the laws of the State of New York and of the United States of America. When Mr. Delmas finally seemed satisfied with his rehearsal of Evelyn's testimony he asked how she would dress when the day came for her appearance in the courtroom. Evelyn told him she would wear what she always wore in the daytime —a plain, dark blue, tailored suit; a shirtwaist and a boyish collar. It would be almost the costume of a schoolgirl, and she thought its simplicity would put her best foot forward— her youth and her innocence.

"Quite right," Mr. Delmas had said. "And what hat?"

For Mr. Delmas she tried on nearly every hat she owned before he would settle on a black velvet trimmed with violets. She appeared in the approved costume every day, with the result that even before the selection of the jury could be completed her costume had become the new fashion on the streets of New York. Copies by the thousands suddenly appeared, taken from the newspaper drawings made by the artists engaged to sketch the trial. Every store sold all the violet-trimmed black velvet hats it could stock.

Despite objections from Mr. Delmas and Mother Thaw, Evelyn insisted she must have her friend May Mackenzie by her side, as company and support for the ordeal she faced. Mother Thaw had demanded May Mackenzie move out of Evelyn's suite at the Hotel Lorraine. Mr. Delmas had wanted Evelyn's gaudy friend barred from the courtroom. When Evelyn insisted, Mother Thaw and Mr. Delmas were required to let May Mackenzie stay. While the trial was in progress, the defense had to keep its chief witness satisfied.

In contrast to the row of decorous and somewhat gloomy Thaw women, May Mackenzie dressed to suit her own tastes. On the first day of jury selection she appeared in a resplendent purple suit, with purple gloves, and a rakish hat trailing two long ostrich feathers. The newspapers delighted in her apparent buoyancy and described her as "cheerful, almost chirpy." They noted that in the courtroom and before the eyes of the jury everything seemed cordial enough between Mother Thaw and Mrs. Harry Thaw but that once out of sight of judge and jury May Mackenzie and Evelyn Nesbit

Thaw would have nothing to do with Mother Thaw or the other Thaw women.

Mother Thaw was also appalled by a strategic assignment of reserved courtroom seats by District Attorney Jerome. He had called John Barrymore as a possible witness and assigned Barrymore a seat directly behind Evelyn. Barrymore, who had been starring in *Captain Jinks of the Horse Marines* in Boston, was described as "gnawing nervously at his mustachios."

He was interviewed on the District Attorney's subpoena, and he answered, "I am at an entire loss to know why the District Attorney's office desires my presence at the Thaw trial. I was not present at the tragedy on the Madison Square Roof Garden. I dislike this notoriety exceedingly and only wish that I might be kept entirely out of the Thaw case. I can't see why the District Attorney's office should drag me into it."

Evelyn's family also seemed to avoid making any appearance. Evelyn's version was that her family's absence made her feel bitter and alone. The absence of Mr. and Mrs. Charles J. Holman, however, could be explained. According to some reports, Mother Thaw had consented to Harry's marriage to Evelyn only on condition that Evelyn sever relations with her mother. "Not once," said Evelyn, "did my mother make a statement to the press, or grant an interview."

Actually, Evelyn was not being entirely accurate. On January 2, 1907, Mr. and Mrs. Charles J. Holman of Pittsburgh had announced to the newspapers that they planned to travel to New York and offer to the District Attorney testimony in "vindication of Stanford White's good name." They said they planned to turn over to the proper authorities all letters they had in their possession concerning their daughter, Stanford White, and Harry Thaw. "The letters," Mrs. Holman announced from a Pittsburgh dateline, "would show that Thaw never had any intention of marrying Evelyn, and only did so when he was forced to." She said her daughter was "headstrong, self-willed and beautiful, and that led to all her trouble."

Immediately upon reading Mrs. Holman's announcement,

Mother Thaw's counsel, Mr. Clifford Hartridge, departed for Pittsburgh. Informed sources in the newsrooms estimated that Mr. and Mrs. Charles J. Holman had asked $50,000 for their letters and at first had been refused by Mrs. William Thaw, but that upon examination of their contents Mr. Hartridge had met their price. Upon Mr. Hartridge's return to New York on January 5 he was asked about the letters. He stated that because of Mrs. Holman's "delicate health" she and her husband had changed their minds about offering testimony at the trial.

To District Attorney Jerome it seemed as if any evidence he might gather to defend the dead man's honor escaped his grasp, and all evidence that could be gathered to show the defendant's vices disappeared as quickly. Jerome was, moreover, in a somewhat delicate quandary. He would have been willing to accept a plea of insanity because he had every reason to believe that Harry Thaw was in fact insane. But once a jury was selected and a plea of not guilty entered, it was his duty to demonstrate beyond a shadow of a doubt that Harry Thaw had murdered Stanford White with premeditation, before several hundred witnesses, and in the first degree.

Mr. Delmas, for the defense, was in an equally delicate situation because his client insisted he was sane, despite a considerable amount of evidence to the contrary. Mr. Delmas was going to have to convince his jury that Harry Thaw was a perfectly sane man, except for the few moments when he had shot a man: sane before the event, and sane after the event, but temporarily deranged in the instant when he fired three shots, point-blank into the eyes of the city's leading citizen. To prove his point, Mr. Delmas would need the testimony of Evelyn Nesbit, and she would have to convince a jury of her own innocence.

Juror number twelve was finally accepted by both prosecution and defense on Friday, February 1, 1907. Court was recessed until Monday, and the jurymen and alternates were sequestered once again in the old Broadway Central Hotel across from the courthouse on City Hall Square. The jury included a manufacturer of umbrellas, a dealer in machine parts, the manager of a steamship line, the manager of a piano warehouse, a grain-and-hay salesman, a retired railroad official, a manufacturer of gas machinery, a railroad freight agent, the manager of a woolen mill, an advertising agent, an underwear salesman, and a clerk.

On Monday, February 4, the newspapers hoped for a dramatic confrontation between prosecutor Jerome and defense attorney Delmas. Instead, assistant prosecutor Garvan gave the opening speech to the jury, brief, and to the point. Harry Thaw shot Stanford White, said Mr. Garvan, and it "was a cool, deliberate, malicious, premeditated murder, and we shall ask for a verdict of murder in the first degree." White-haired John B. Gleason did the work for the defense, and Mr. Delmas stayed in the background.

Assistant prosecutor Garvan began the calling of witnesses. Lawrence Grant White, nineteen years old, was called first and described leaving his father after dinner at the Café Martin. Lawrence White said his father seemed to be in excellent spirits, with nothing troublesome on his mind. He was excused when the defense had no questions. Lawrence was followed to the stand by Walter Paxton, engineer at Madison Square Garden, who testified that he witnessed the shooting, that he saw Thaw in the elevator afterward and that he heard Thaw say to his wife, "It's all right, dear, I have probably saved your life."

Others followed Paxton—witness Meyer Cohen, songwriter, saw Thaw shoot White; so did Henry F. Blaese, partner in *Mamzelle Champagne*. Then Fireman Paul Brudi, who first seized Thaw; police officer Anthony L. Debes, who arrested the defendant; and Dr. Timothy Lehand, coroner's physician, who testified on the course of the bullets and identified them as exhibits for the court. The prosecution's final witness was called before lunch: Dr. Marvin Techner described how Harry Thaw had passed his seat at Madison Square Garden, that he heard the three shots, and then saw the defendant move away from White's table, the smoking revolver held high in the air. Dr. Techner identified the defendant at the table from among his lawyers.

After lunch on Monday, John B. Gleason began the defendant's case to the jury in a long, wandering oration, and then court was recessed for the day. On Tuesday morning Gleason called as his first witness Dr. Charles J. Wiley from Pittsburgh, and introduced him as a specialist in mental diseases.

Dr. Wiley recalled seeing Harry Thaw on a streetcar at about nine o'clock one evening in Pittsburgh, and remembered a disagreement between Thaw and the streetcar conductor over whether the blinds should be pulled. From that experience and under the questions of counselor Gleason, Dr. Wiley concluded that the defendant, in his expert judgment, was insane. When Gleason relinquished his witness District Attorney Jerome finally rose to take charge of his case.

Jerome went to work on the witness in a memorable display of courtroom style. "Did Dr. Wiley understand Romberg symptoms? Couldn't Dr. Wiley explain at all what was a Romberg test? What books had Dr. Wiley studied as an expert? Didn't Dr. Wiley notice in Haekatuck's book a description of the Romberg test? Didn't he know anything about it? Had he ever read Dr. Hammond on nervous diseases? Did he know what alienists meant by Argile-Robertson symptoms?"

As Jerome was bringing his cross-examination to a close, he demanded to know of the hapless Dr. Wiley whether Argile-Robertson was a real person or whether he was merely a creation of Jerome's fancy. Dr. Wiley gazed at the ceiling and then said he had seen the name in a textbook. Jerome was after him like a cat. "What textbook?" Dr. Wiley couldn't say. "Can you name any textbook on God's green earth where such a name is used?" Dr. Wiley couldn't. He said he had come to testify as to facts, and Jerome had tried to convert him into an expert. Jerome dismissed Dr. Wiley with a withering question, "Do you think the conversion will last?"

Although Jerome had a field day with the Thaw defense by "expert alienists," showing them one by one to be frauds, Mr. Gleason stumbled on, calling Dr. Charles Francis Bingamon, family physician during Harry Thaw's childhood, and Dr. John T. Deemar of Kittanning, Pennsylvania, who had also treated Thaw for childhood illnesses. At the end of the day the other lawyers of Harry Thaw's defense asked John

B. Gleason to step down and to let Delphin Michael Delmas conduct the case.

The next morning Mr. Delmas took the stage in Harry Thaw's defense. His first witness, he announced, would be Benjamin Bouman, a former doorkeeper at the Madison Square Theatre, who would testify to an episode on or about January 2, 1904, in which Stanford White had made threats against the life of Harry Thaw.

Mr. Jerome was upon his feet immediately. He pointed out to Judge Fitzgerald that he had objected to Bouman as a witness only the day before; that no connection had been shown between the death of Stanford White and the conversation in question; that Judge Fitzgerald had sustained his objection only yesterday; that unless the defense intended to enter a plea of self-defense as the motive for the murder, the testimony of Benjamin Bouman was irrelevant.

"May it please Your Honor," Delmas countered, "we clearly stated in our opening that we would avail ourselves of all forms of defense under the laws of this state."

Delmas would not debate the relevancy of Bouman's testimony with Jerome, but with immense courtesy, and a feigned unfamiliarity with the procedures of New York State, neatly sidestepped the question of relevancy, pleading "the rights of a complete defense." He conferred at the bench with Judge Fitzgerald and prosecutor Jerome; he indicated to His Honor the nature of the testimony; and he won for his witness the opportunity to testify.

Before Justice Fitzgerald allowed the testimony of Bouman to begin he warned the court the conversations about to be repeated would include oaths and foul language, and any women who so desired should avail themselves of the opportunity to withdraw. The Countess Yarmouth and Mrs. George Lauder Carnegie rose and gathered their effects.

"Now then," said Mr. Delmas, "we will call Mr. Bouman."

On Christmas Eve, 1903, Bouman testified, Stanford White came to the stage door of Madison Square Theatre after a performance of *The Girl from Dixie*. White asked for Evelyn Nesbit, who was in the show. Bouman said he told White she had gone. Bouman said White replied, "That's a goddamn lie. Who did she go with?" Bouman said he told White she went with Mr. Thaw; that White then swore at him; that he told White to go backstage and look for himself; that as White came tearing back, he pulled a revolver out of his right-hand overcoat pocket; that as White passed he said, "I'll kill that son-of-a-bitch before daylight."

Mr. Jerome attempted a cross-examination of Mr. Bouman, but it was ineffective because whether Bouman's story was true or false was indeed irrelevant, and what the Napoleon of the Western Bar had accomplished was significant—Mr. Delmas had taken charge of the trial, and in doing so, he had succeeded in entering an indictment, and bringing to trial, the victim of the murder.

Mr. Delmas then called Martin Green, a feature writer for the New York *World,* and elicited from him a conclusion that Harry Thaw at the time of the murder appeared to be irrational. Mr. Jerome objected because witness Green, as a layman, was not qualified to give such a conclusion. Mr. Jerome cited the statutes; Delmas rephrased his questions, sidestepped Jerome again; and Green's testimony stood.

Delmas called Thomas McCaleb, and again ran over the events at the Café Martin leading up to the murder. He elicited from McCaleb testimony that Evelyn had written something on a piece of paper during dinner that night and handed it to her husband. Jerome objected, arguing that defense must produce the paper in question. Delmas answered by asserting that the piece of paper was in the possession of the District Attorney.

Jerome ignored him. Again Delmas asked the District Attorney to produce the note, and again Jerome sat with his back half-turned as if he had not heard. Delmas repeated the request a third time for its effect and then turned to the jury. "I presume that the learned District Attorney maintains his silence not so much from discourtesy as through a conception of his duty."

Jerome's cross-examination to discredit McCaleb stayed away from the piece of paper, but he failed: the piece of paper hung there, mysterious and unseen. Jerome failed to exclude another member of the audience of *Mamzelle Champagne* who testified that Harry Thaw appeared "irrational" on the night of the shooting. He even failed to exclude a reintroduction of Dr. John T. Deemar's testimony on the mental incompetence of some of Harry Thaw's relatives, testimony he had successfully excluded before as irrelevant. By the end of the afternoon, when attorney Delmas suggested an adjournment because his next witness would require considerable time, Jerome said he would agree if the identity of the witness were disclosed to the court. Mr. Delmas was only too glad to reveal that his next witness would be the defendant's wife.

The next morning a crowd estimated at ten thousand by the police milled about the streets outside the Criminal Courts Building, hoping to catch a glimpse of Mrs. Harry K. Thaw. When she walked to her place on the witness stand and took her oath to tell the whole truth and nothing but the truth, she was described by the newspapers as looking like a slim schoolgirl mounting the platform "on speaking day." She answered that she was Evelyn Nesbit Thaw; that she was the wife of the defendant; that she was born December 25, 1884. If she was twenty-two, reporters said, she looked no more than sixteen. She appeared to be tiny and helpless; her high, sweet voice was the voice of a child. She was described as "infinitely appealing," a "frail and delicate thing." She was "the most exquisitely lovely human being I ever looked at," said Irvin S. Cobb of the New York *Evening World*. "The slim, quick grace of a fawn, a head that sat on her faultless throat as a lily on its stem, eyes that were the color of blue-brown pansies and the size of half-dollars, a mouth made of rumpled rose petals."

"Not one particle of the mire through which she has passed has left a stain on her face," said another reporter who watched Mr. Delmas lead Evelyn through her testimony.

Delmas started by placing her with her husband at dinner at the Café Martin, a few minutes after eight o'clock on the evening of June 25, 1906. He asked her if she saw Stanford White coming into the restaurant from the Fifth Avenue entrance and if after seeing him enter, she had called for a pencil and written a note. She said she had.

Jerome objected to the missing note, and Delmas let the District Attorney object twice, with the result that Jerome again emphasized its importance.

As Delmas led Evelyn through her story, Evelyn answered for hours to an absorbed courtroom—gazing back in all innocence into hundreds of staring eyes. She told her audience that when she heard the shots she said to McCaleb, "My God, he has shot him!" She unfolded the drama of her private life. She said that her husband had first proposed to her in Paris in 1903; that she had refused him, because she had been on the stage; that he told her again that he loved her, that he would always take care of her, and he wanted to know why she could not marry him. "So I began by telling him how and where I first met Stanford White."

William Travers Jerome saw what was coming, and he was powerless to stop it. He made what objections he could. He insisted that testimony about Evelyn's relationship with Stanford White was not admissible, but he had to agree that as long as Delmas phrased his questions in such a way that Evelyn told the court what she had told her husband, her testimony was admissible because it bore on the possible mental condition of the defendant before the murder. Jerome knew Evelyn's testimony could not be examined for its truth, but only whether she had told such a story to Harry; indeed even if she had told Harry lies, they were lies that might possibly have led him to a temporary insanity.

She described to the jury a visit when she was sixteen years old to a studio of Stanford White's on Twenty-fourth Street. She said she and White had lunch, and she had played in his red velvet swing. She told how Stanford White had sent her to a dentist. In each instance she said she described the scene to Harry Thaw. She testified she had told Harry Thaw that Stanford White had given her a hat and a feather boa—and a long red cape; that she had gone to the Tower at Madison Square Garden for parties with other young ladies from the chorus; that her mother had left for Pittsburgh; that Stanford White had sent a carriage for her and that she had gone to a studio and her photograph was taken; that the next night she had gone again after the theater to the studio at Twenty-fourth Street; that she had sipped from a glass of champagne that Stanford White had urged her to drink; that a pounding began in her ears, and then the whole room seemed to go around, and that when she woke up she was in bed, and all her clothes had been pulled off, and she sat up and began to scream; and that she had related to her husband all that had transpired.

The reporters in the courtroom recorded that Evelyn's face "was contracted with a strained, agonized expression in her eyes. She clasped and unclasped her hands nervously, and finally cried."

Mr. Delmas could not have been more sympathetic to his distressed witness, but he had to remind her that it was absolutely essential for her to go on with her testimony. Evelyn remembered that when he had rehearsed her, he was exact in his instructions. He had said, "You must not say that you forgave Stanford White because he charmed you. That would be ruinous to your husband. And to you."

After he had put Evelyn's recollections of her seduction into the record, or at least that version of it which Evelyn said she had told Harry, Mr. Delmas led her through an account of her life—from Pittsburgh through her modeling days for James Carroll Beckwith and Charles Dana Gibson; her part in *Floradora;* her "appendicitis" at the DeMille School; her first trip to Europe with Harry Thaw "to recover from her illness" in 1903.

The court was spellbound. "The best emotional actress in America couldn't have done it as well," said the *World*'s reporter. As the court recessed for lunch on the first day of her testimony, she swayed as if she might faint. Assistant District Attorney Garvan caught her and helped her down.

After lunch she continued, and Mr. Delmas was able to get into the record letters written by Harry Thaw from Europe to his lawyer in 1903 about Mrs. Nesbit's daughter being kidnapped and drugged at fifteen by a "blackguard." The letter was sufficiently incoherent to serve as evidence of Harry's mental instability on the subject of Stanford White.

Evelyn testified throughout the next day. She testified about the affidavit she had drawn up against Thaw in Abe Hummel's offices in November, 1903—a dangerous subject for the defense. Mr. Jerome objected to the testimony because, he said, the witness was testifying to the contents of a written document that was not before the court. Mr. Delmas was ready for the objection, and he turned it aside by repeating once again that his witness was only recounting what she had told her husband.

Evelyn was able to describe her affidavit against her husband as something she had signed at White's insistence, something she had regretted. And she gave the impression that she had been pursued by White against her will, or at least she had told her husband something to that effect; which—whether what she said was true or not—was Mr. Delmas' point. The actual contents of the Hummel affidavit—the story of the Schloss Katzenstein—did not enter the record.

Finally Mr. Delmas led her through a description of her affair with John Barrymore, of White's management of its ending. The way the story was presented to the jury it seemed as if Stanford White was a middle-aged disrupter of romantic young love. After an adjournment for the weekend Mr. Delmas called his witness back to the stand on Monday morning to explain what she had written on the note she had given to her husband just before the murder—the note she had passed across the table at the Café Martin. Although District Attorney Jerome could have objected, because there was no note in evidence, Mr. Delmas was, after all, only asking Mrs. Thaw what she had told her husband. Evelyn testified that her note read, "That B— was here."

Mr. Delmas asked his witness with the utmost courtesy if she would explain to the jury the meaning of the letter *B*. Mrs. Thaw said that she and her husband regularly used the letter *B* as a designation for Stanford White, and, she claimed, it stood for "blackguard." Mr. Delmas soon had no further questions and delivered his witness to cross-examination by the District Attorney.

Jerome had few alternatives. He could try to shake Evelyn's story, but she might turn out to be adamant. He could try to discredit her as a witness, but to the extent that he dragged her through the details of her affair with Stanford White, he proved the points of the defense—if Evelyn had told her husband all that, it might very well have led to his temporary insanity. Nevertheless, Jerome proved she had letters of credit from White when she and her mother toured Europe with Thaw; that she had accounts at banks funded by White; that Barrymore had proposed to her. He suggested that perhaps she had not been "drugged" at all when White "ravished" her; that perhaps she had loved Stanford White, despite her denials for the sake of her husband's verdict.

There were those who believed Evelyn's story was a "magnificent lie"; and there were others who estimated from her testimony that she had appalled White by tales of abuse at the hands of her husband and simultaneously incensed her husband by her tales of seduction by White. Despite his reputation for rectitude, District Attorney Jerome called to the stand Mr. Abraham Hummel—a lawyer Jerome himself had disbarred for perjury. Through Hummel, Jerome entered into the record "the Hummel affidavit," which alleged to recount the story of the Schloss Katzenstein. Evelyn concluded, with considerable accuracy, that Jerome seemed so anxious to "wipe up the floor with me, he seemed to lose sight of Harry Thaw completely."

Evelyn knew that May Mackenzie and Mrs. J. J. Caine could have proved beyond doubt that the murder of Stanford White was premeditated, but she said Jerome "muffed his handling of us." When Mrs. Caine took the stand, said Evelyn, Jerome was so anxious to blacken Evelyn's reputation and defame her character that he failed to ask Mrs. Caine about the episode at the Saint Regis when Harry had threatened to shoot White.

Evelyn made Jerome lose his temper again and again. He soon was having frequent clashes with the judge. "And Mr. Delmas's calm, suave, lengthy, painstakingly polite replies," said Evelyn, "drove Jerome frantic." Evelyn had the ability to view the trial as a performance and to see the drama from the audience's—or jury's—point of view.

Jerome's efforts made the trial drag on. By April 5, 1907, the jurors had been sequestered in the Broadway Central Hotel for seventy-three days, and they heard District Attorney

Jerome begin to contradict his own case. Having denied that Thaw was insane and having refused testimony of experts on evidence of insanity, Jerome was forced to reverse his position after Evelyn's testimony. He attempted to pursue every angle of insanity.

To Judge Fitzgerald's surprise, Mr. Jerome interrupted the trial to ask that a lunacy commission be appointed. By then Thaw's attorneys estimated they could afford to object vigorously, but after a week of arguments over the District Attorney's motion, His Honor appointed a three-man panel to determine the defendant's sanity. Thaw issued a statement to the press: "I am perfectly sane, and everybody who knows me knows that I am sane. In fact, on second consideration of the matter, I am rather glad, on the whole, that the case has taken this turn, because I am satisfied the commission in lunacy is going to declare that I am sane at present, and after that you can guess for yourself what will happen."

His mother drew up an affidavit and issued a statement in support of Harry Thaw's satisfaction at the appointment of the commission. After seven days of testimony before the lunacy commission, including impressive testimony by Harry Thaw in his own behalf, the distinguished members of the commission issued their report to Judge Fitzgerald. They unanimously declared Harry Thaw mentally competent in every way.

By Monday, April 8, the jury could reconvene. They had heard testimony from expert witnesses examined by Mr. Delmas that perhaps Harry Thaw had "a brainstorm" when confronted by White, that Harry Thaw perhaps suffered from delusions. Jerome had done his best to remind the jury that "paranoia" was a form of insanity that was incurable; that the type of "melancholia" described by expert alienists to the court was a permanent form of insanity; that Harry Thaw's "mental depressions" might last for only a few days but would be more likely to last for long periods; that no patient could recover from an attack of mental depression in something like ten hours. But Evelyn had ruined William Travers Jerome before the jury, and if the jury was confused by the kinds of insanity that might excuse murder, they were going to listen to the explanations of the man who had presented a calm and consistent case.

To clear up the issues confusing the jury, on April eighth Mr. Delphin Michael Delmas rose to sum up the defense's case. He wandered through the evidence for eight hours, but he was summarizing for them the conflicting testimony they had heard for months. At the outset he put them at their ease. He said he would not appeal to anything so shadowy as the unwritten law. He said he would show them ample protection for the defendant's rights in the written law.

He paced back and forth before the jurybox. He spoke to them in the sonorous phrases of the good book: When Evelyn faced the consequences of a penniless life, "the tempter" came to her and guided her to a gilded den of Oriental luxuries. "Better that his eyes had never opened," he intoned in the heavenly cadences, "rather than that he should have heard the agonized shriek of his mangled, deflowered prey." He described Evelyn as a sweet little flower who was struggling toward the light and toward God.

"And if Thaw is insane," he roared in the voice of righteousness, "it is with a species of insanity known from the Canadian border to the Gulf. If you expert gentlemen ask me to give it a name, I suggest that you label it *Dementia Americana.* It is that species of insanity that inspires of every American to believe his home is sacred. It is that species of insanity that persuades an American that whoever violates the sanctity of his home or the purity of his wife or daughter has forfeited the protection of the laws of this state or any other state."

District Attorney Jerome summed up his case the next day, and he concluded to the gentlemen of the jury by asking, "Will you acquit a cold-blooded, deliberate, cowardly murderer because his lying wife has a pretty girl's face?"

CHAPTER TWENTY

TWENTIETH-CENTURY CELEBRITY:
Madman

WHEN DISTRICT ATTORNEY JEROME had concluded his summation Judge Fitzgerald instructed the jury: A person did not escape criminal liability on the ground of insanity unless his defect of reason was such that he could not understand his actions were wrong. Then he asked the jury to return to the court when they were ready to deliver their verdict.

Inside the jury room, after an initial poll, it soon became obvious they were being asked to make moral, as well as legal, discriminations between different kinds of insanity. They had heard, for example, distinctions made between temporary insanity and permanent insanity. They had heard testimony from learned doctors of medicine, sworn to the truth and buttressed by authority, that seemed to vary according to their employers. They had been asked to sift truth from a sequence of events described by witnesses they might easily guess were steeped in perjury. They had heard of luxury without stint, of moral conduct habituated to corruption, and then heard these acts defended in the cadences of Isaiah by Mr. Delmas. They had seen with their own eyes a hero of justice, Mr. Jerome, blown about by whirlwinds of contradiction.

For more than two months they had shifted in their seats, attempting to divine how to reach a verdict on the actors in the drama presented them. They did not imagine, at least in the beginning, that they were lacking in understanding. Their foreman, Deming B. Smith, manufactured umbrellas, and had learned something of the world. Henry C. Brearly was an advertising agent, Malcolm Fraser sold underwear, Bernard Gertsman managed a woolen mill, and Charles D. Newton had retired from the railroad at sixty. So also with the others: they knew from their own experience the consequences of a corrupt heart; that a soul who did not acknowledge an obligation to keep faith with others would shrivel; that when values ran false, men alternated between deadly lethargy and raving insanities; that if women were sold, or agreed to be sold, then every other value in society—all of them less dear—was corrupted, and "the general bond of love and nature's tie" was dissolved.

Yet as a jury they were being asked to weigh the tainted evidence presented to them and to decide for life or death. They had listened to stupidity, to braggarts, to scenes of senseless rage, to accounts of vanity, to nonsense, and to triviality dignified by pretense. Through it all, as one witness after another took his place on the stand, they had heard and seen money used—not as a storehouse of value nor as a means of exchange, but money as its own god, its own judgment, its own conclusion. And they were asked to decide whether Harry K. Thaw had acted rationally or irrationally, to render a verdict for the people of the State of New York on whether Harry K. Thaw was sane or insane, temporarily or permanently.

They reached no verdict on April 10. At eleven o'clock on April 11 they were reported still deadlocked. They returned to the courtroom at about four thirty in the afternoon of April 12, and Judge Fitzgerald asked: "Gentlemen, have you reached a verdict?"

Foreman Smith answered they had not. He said they could not reach any verdict. Their votes had varied throughout their deliberations, but their final tally deadlocked—with seven votes cast "guilty of first-degree murder," and five votes cast "not guilty by reason of insanity." The judge thanked the jury and dismissed them. There would have to be another trial.

When the jury announced its failure to agree Evelyn turned to kiss Harry, but he seemed hardly to notice her. She believed her testimony had kept her husband from the electric chair, and "her sacrifice would not be in vain." But now she would have to endure a second trial, and the endless hours on the witness stand. She issued a statement to the press: "My husband was justified in killing Stanford White. He will be tried again and triumphantly acquitted." She said she was his true wife and that she would be "with him in his fight."

Harry Thaw was returned across the Bridge of Sighs to the Tombs, where it was reported that he railed at Mr. Delmas for more than an hour, complaining that his defense had been mismanaged. His mother attempted to get Harry free on bail, offering to post as much as a million dollars, but William Travers Jerome refused. "Simply because this man has wealth is no reason, to my mind, why he should be turned out of jail."

Evelyn said that Harry was not entirely uncomfortable as a prisoner in the Tombs. He had bribed the guards and the sheriffs; he had arranged to have his food sent over from Delmonico's in metal containers kept hot by a little brazier of charcoal; Scotch whisky was delivered to him as "medicine"; and, he had almost everything he wanted when she visited him.

Although he would be perfectly comfortable in his private quarters, Harry would have to spend the year 1907 in jail. It was a year in which another Wall Street panic arrived. The stock market crashed in March, and by summer banks were unable to pay their depositors. At the handsome offices designed for them by Stanford White, the Knickerbocker Trust Company suffered a spectacular run, the crowd brawling in the street in its attempts to be first at retrieving their money, and the bank failed. The year 1907 was also the year the *Lusitania* arrived in New York on her maiden voyage; shirtwaists and bird-trimmed hats were in fashion; and the waltz had a brief revival thanks to *The Merry Widow* by Franz Lehár before it was finally overwhelmed by the popularity of the new "ragtime" dances—turkey trot, grizzly bear, bunny hug, one-step, and foxtrot.

After the trial Evelyn began to complain of being cooped up in the Hotel Lorraine. She was tired of hotel food, of never seeing anyone, and she said she was being worn thin by her difficulties with Mother Thaw over money. When she visited

Harry in the Tombs she complained repeatedly to him that she had no money. Harry instructed his new favorite lawyer, Daniel O'Reilly, to do what he could to help Evelyn.

Mr. and Mrs. O'Reilly took Evelyn motoring, then let her stay in their guest house at Long Beach for a vacation by the sea. Daniel O'Reilly helped Evelyn find a small house on Park Avenue between Fifty-sixth and Fifty-seventh streets, rented an electric brougham for Evelyn to use, and engaged servants for the house. But Evelyn discovered almost immediately that Harry had bribed her servants and paid them to spy on her, and O'Reilly admitted to Evelyn that Mother Thaw had hired detectives to report on everyone she saw.

As a matter of fact, the detectives reported to Mother Thaw that Evelyn was seeing a great deal of Daniel O'Reilly, Esquire, a report both Evelyn and Mr. O'Reilly easily discounted on the grounds that they were only busy at legal consultation. Then one night O'Reilly took a German girl and Evelyn to Frieda's Restaurant, and Mrs. O'Reilly appeared out of nowhere and started whacking Mr. O'Reilly over the head with an umbrella, demanding to know, "Which one of them are you in love with?" Unfortunately Mrs. O'Reilly's scene made its way into the papers, and difficulties with Mother Thaw increased. By Christmas, 1907, Evelyn had to fight for every penny she got, but she supposed they still needed her to keep Harry out of the electric chair.

The second trial of Harry K. Thaw opened on Monday, January 6, 1908, and once again Evelyn shared the spotlight with her accused husband. To the delight of the city's newspapers, most of the details of the first trial were serialized once again, with a few additional revelations added. District Attorney William Travers Jerome again conducted the prosecution, but Judge Victor J. Dowling sat on the bench, and Mr. Delphin Michael Delmas had disappeared—replaced by Daniel O'Reilly, Russell Peabody, and Martin W. Littleton for the defense. It took them only four days to select a jury.

Evelyn Nesbit Thaw was as beautiful as ever, but reporters sensed a change in her style—she appeared radiant, with an immense black hat topped by a lavender silk rose in a cluster of violets, and she was described as "no longer the wan, pinched girl of the first trial." When she spent a noon recess together with her husband and they were returning across the Bridge of Sighs, she was overheard asking him, "Aren't you going to make up, Harry?"

Mr. Jerome's case for first-degree murder was efficiently presented, but he no longer challenged the testimony of witnesses for the defense who detailed examples of Harry Thaw's history of irrationality. Dr. Robert H. Chase testified to the incompetence of Harriet Alice Thaw, a cousin of the defendant's father; Jerome let the testimony gather in the record, unchallenged as to its relevancy. Miss Amy Gosette said she had worked as a trained nurse in Monte Carlo between 1892 and 1897, and she had nursed Harry K. Thaw in a hotel room in 1897. She was impressed, she said, by the irrational behavior of the defendant when she attended him; Jerome let the testimony stand, undisputed as to its timeliness. Dr. John T. Deemar testified again that as a boy Harry K. Thaw was highly nervous. Charles F. Koehler of Winona, Minnesota, remembered Harry Thaw as a student at Wooster University and said Harry Thaw had an uncertain walk, stared, and was incoherent in speech. In cross-examination District Attorney Jerome asked witness Koehler how he was able to remember all those details for so many years but Jerome apparently was satisfied by the witness's response.

The defense put Alfred Lee Thaw on the stand to testify about the insanity of his brother Horace Thaw. Alfred and Horace were, it appeared, second cousins of the defendant. The defense asked the steward of the Whist Club to testify, and the steward said Mr. Thaw appeared very nervous on the afternoon of the murder. The defense asked permission of Mr. Jerome to introduce letters written by Mrs. William Thaw in 1882, showing that the defendant's mother was even then concerned with her son's stability. The letters said, "his mind is more or less unbalanced." Mr. Jerome had no objection.

Mrs. William Thaw, mother of the defendant, was called to the stand to testify in her son's behalf. She had to be helped to the chair by a nurse armed with smelling salts. As her testimony developed her head seemed to tremble constantly, and she blotted the perspiration from her face with a black handkerchief. She testified she had given birth to another child before Harry K. Thaw was born, that the child had lived only two days, and that she had discovered it dead in its crib. The shock of the child's death left her in a nervous state and in bad physical condition for a long time thereafter. She thought her whole nervous system must have been involved. She had not yet recovered when she was pregnant with Harry.

She said Harry seemed normal and healthy until he was three months old. After that he was very nervous. He would scream and throw up his hands and his limbs would twitch. Mother Thaw was often worn out by him, she said. The prosecution did not cross-examine Mrs. William K. Thaw.

When Mrs. Harry K. Thaw was called to the stand and identified herself once again as the wife of the defendant she repeated almost word for word her testimony at the first trial. Once again Mr. Jerome almost lost his composure, and once again his cross-examination of Evelyn became venomous. Evelyn added testimony of an attempt by Harry to commit suicide in Paris in 1904, which she had not offered in the first trial. Mr. Jerome wanted to know why she had not included it. Evelyn replied, "Mr. Delmas told me not to, because it would make Harry out to be too crazy."

The District Attorney of New York shouted at her, "Well, insanity was the defense at the last trial, wasn't it?"

Defense counsel immediately objected, and Judge Dowling sustained them. Defense attorney Littleton finally rose to protest the entire conduct of Mr. Jerome's cross-examination. "I contend that the District Attorney, by his attitude, his manner, and the very tone of his voice, is seeking to discredit statements of fact which, he knows, under the rulings of this court he cannot do."

Evelyn could not disguise her glee when Mr. Jerome pointed his finger at her, and "asked a breathless court to witness his public apology to me for the manner in which he had handled me on the witness stand during the first trial, especially as to my relations with Stanford White."

The final witnesses for the defense were three authoritative doctors. "Brain-storm" was the diagnosis of Dr. Britton D. Evans. According to Dr. Maurice Gauja from Paris, Evelyn's story of Harry's attempted suicide was true. Dr. Russell Wells, London, diagnosed Harry's difficulty as "acute insanity, or subacute mania, characterized by recurrent periods."

Then Mr. William Travers Jerome, friend of the common man, rose to sum up the case for the people of New York. There were those who guessed that he had given up any hope of convicting the defendant on charges of first-degree murder. But the spectators that day, in addition to the constant press, included actors and actresses, *beau gents* like Richard Harding Davis, and friends of Stanford White, and they came to hear Jerome have his say.

He did not attempt to exonerate White. He agreed that it was wrong for a man of White's years to have courted a girl of sixteen. Then he pictured Evelyn as a poor little waif of the theater, hunted by many men, breadwinner of her family, "who had never had a chance in her whole forlorn life." What did Harry Thaw do when this little girl refused to marry him because it would drag him down to her level? "I'll tell you what he did. This miserable creature, this pervert, this degenerate, took the poor little waif from her mother, and he flaunted her through the capitals of Europe as his mistress."

The prosecutor pointed his finger at the defendant and expressed his contempt. He continued his attack by commenting on the doctors who had testified to Harry Thaw's insanity. He said he was exhausted by the theories of alienists, and that they had brought shame and disgrace to the law. "Did you ever hear of a lawyer who couldn't get some expert to take any side of a question?"

But Jerome's case had long since foundered, because the courts in which he served had begun to make curious rulings —that murder, or any other lesser crime, could be excused provided the accused could be shown to have acted irrationally. Judge Dowling instructed the jury of Harry Thaw's peers that if "any reasonable doubt remains in your minds as to the defendant's sanity, he is entitled to the benefits of that doubt and to be acquitted upon this ground." He asked the gentlemen of the jury, when they had returned, if they had agreed upon a verdict.

The foreman said they had, and the clerk of the court called for their verdict, which the foreman then read. "We, the jury, find the defendant not guilty as charged in the indictment on the ground of the defendant's insanity."

A smile spread across Harry Thaw's face. Evelyn was hugged by Josiah Thaw, but she could not keep her teeth from chattering. District Attorney Jerome embraced defense attorney Littleton and generously said he was glad it had turned out the way it did. "It was a proper verdict."

Justice Dowling thanked the jury for their service and excused them and then read a statement he had prepared for the eventuality. "The jury having found a verdict that this defendant is not guilty of the murder of Stanford White on the ground of insanity, it now devolves upon the court to take certain action. . . . The court therefore orders that the defendant, being in custody and being a person dangerous to the public safety, the said Harry K. Thaw shall be kept in custody and shall be sent to the Asylum for the Criminal Insane at Matteawan forthwith."

Yet Judge Dowling's "forthwith" disguised some curious consequences. The verdict delivered by the jury on February 1, 1908, left Harry K. Thaw in a peculiar status with the law. Since he had been tried on charges of first-degree murder, he could not be tried for that crime again for the rest of his natural life without being subject to "double jeopardy." He was, therefore, free of murder. Thanks to the magnificent supply of his mother's Pennsylvania Railroad bonds, the abilities of his lawyers, and the testimony of his devoted wife, Harry Thaw was now merely a criminal lunatic suffering from "chronic paranoic schizophrenia." On his way to Matteawan he told reporters, "I'll be out in a few weeks."

The strangest result of Harry's trial was that the newspaper accounts of his wife's testimony and his mother's money, combined with his certifiable insanity, made Harry K. Thaw into a hero. As soon as Judge Dowling had committed Harry Thaw to Matteawan forthwith, the sheriff announced that his prisoner would be leaving on the four thirty-nine train for Fishkill.

A large crowd waited for Harry's appearance outside the Criminal Courts Building. When he did appear, they roared their approval. Accompanied by two of his lawyers, he drove in his own car to Grand Central Station in triumph, where an even larger crowd cheered him steadily while police attempted to clear a passage to the train gate.

For the trip to Matteawan, Harry Thaw had hired a private railroad car to be attached to the train. He had the car stocked with whiskey, and invited a mob of friends, including Charlie Sommerville, reporter for the New York *Evening Journal,* who took charge of the party. When the train arrived in Fishkill, Sommerville led the parade to the Holland House for an elaborate dinner, and champagne was ordered up by the case for the continuing toasts. It was nearly midnight before the deputy sheriff in charge finally had to insist that Harry drive over to Matteawan, and Harry finally agreed to go "so that no one would get into any trouble."

Evelyn soon went up to visit Harry at Matteawan. She asked Dr. Baker, one of the officials in charge of the State Institution, whether Harry had been kept with the other patients like those she saw suffering from schizophrenia. "No, indeed." Dr. Baker smiled. "You shall soon see he has very comfortable quarters." After the public excitement over Harry's verdict had died down and when the newspapers abandoned the Thaw story to pursue new insanities, Harry soon had a suite of his own. In the subsequent legal proceedings if newspapermen visited Matteawan, his privileges would vanish, "but the moment the coast cleared," said Evelyn, "he enjoyed virtual freedom."

Any doctors or attendants who dared deny the prerogatives Harry K. Thaw demanded were dismissed. When a Dr. Lamb of the State Lunacy Board opposed his release, Dr. Lamb was removed from the case. "Nocturnal motor rides to roadhouses were no rarity either," said Evelyn, and when she refused to take a cottage near Matteawan and move there, Harry flew "into paroxysms of rage."

In May, 1908—hardly three months after the end of the

second trial—attorneys for Harry K. Thaw secured a writ of habeas corpus for his release from Judge Morschauser. For three weeks the question of his sanity had to be argued again by opposing teams of doctors. Mr. William Travers Jerome opposed Harry's discharge, arguing that the public safety would be endangered. When Mr. Jerome asked Harry Thaw if he understood the purpose of the proceedings, Harry Thaw said he did. "It is to give me the ordinary rights of an American citizen."

During the first sanity hearings Harry lived in luxury in the Poughkeepsie jail. During later hearings Harry lived in "Sheriff Bob" Chandler's rooms in White Plains, and Harry was given every opportunity to escape, but he apparently thought he could win his release by legal maneuver.

His writ of habeas corpus was denied, and he was returned to Matteawan. He applied for transfer to a private sanitarium, the Homeopathic Institute for the Insane, but his application failed. In July, 1908, he demanded a jury trial to determine his sanity; the court refused him. On January 4, 1909, his indefatigable lawyers, still billing Mother Thaw for their services, appealed the decision that had turned down a jury trial for sanity; the appellate court denied the appeal. In August, 1909, his lawyers carried his appeal to the highest court in New York State, where it was denied, and then to the United States Supreme Court, where it was also denied at the end of 1909.

During the summer of 1909, his legal team had started a parallel series of habeas corpus proceedings, which also ended by being dismissed. In 1912 a third series of habeas corpus proceedings were also dismissed. Then Harry Thaw paid twenty thousad dollars to lawyer John N. Anhut to offer as a bribe to Matteawan Superintendent John W. Russell for a certificate of sanity. The scheme was exposed; lawyer Anhut was indicted, tried and convicted of fraud, and sent to prison—largely because of the testimony of Harry K. Thaw, offered to the court, he said, as a means of proving his sanity.

When a fourth series of habeas corpus writs failed in March, 1913, Harry Thaw walked through the gates of Matteawan into a waiting Packard touring car and was driven through

New England to the town of Sherbrooke in Canada. Upon reading the news, Evelyn called the New York police for protection. "Harry has threatened to kill me," she told them. He had told her, "I suppose I'll have to kill you next."

William Travers Jerome headed the delegation that set out for Canada to attempt extradition. He discovered his quarry in Sherbrooke being feted as a hero, driving through town in an open car, waving to the crowds who cheered him. Jerome's men discovered they were pariahs, that the waitresses in the Hotel Magog refused to serve them, and Jerome was trapped into a penny-ante poker game with waiting reporters and then arrested on charges of gambling. He was acquitted and given an apology by the Canadian magistrate, but Jerome's case for Thaw's extradition made slow progress in court against the defenses of Harry Thaw's lawyers.

Meanwhile Thaw occupied the entire second floor of the hospital ward of Sherbrooke's jail, surrounded by an entourage appropriate for a Caesar. One evening his adoring crowd offered to rush the jail to rescue him, but Harry appeared on the second-floor balcony and spoke to them, calming their fears for his safety. Each day as he rode in his car toward the tiny courthouse men and women nearly trampled each other to shake his hand. They would shout, "Here comes Thaw," and his face would beam back at them, "a perfect sunburst of joy and pride as he sweeps his hat in every direction and smiles his thanks."

But Jerome would not abandon his pursuit until finally, on instructions from Montreal, Canadian authorities took Harry Thaw to the border one night and shoved him across it, into the waiting arms of New Hampshire sheriffs. He was then driven to Concord and met again by another wildly cheering mob. He was assigned the "Throne Room" at the Eagle Hotel while Mr. Jerome argued with fresh battalions of New Hampshire lawyers on the niceties of extradition to New York. Jerome finally won his points, and Harry Thaw was returned to the city in December, 1914, after a year and a half on the legal road, and jailed in the Tombs.

He was tried once again on insanity, and on July 15, 1915, he was declared sane and acquitted of all charges. His first step as a free man was to order his lawyers to put through a divorce from Evelyn. He named John Francis, a newspaperman, corespondent for the only grounds admissible under New York law—adultery. He then proceeded to his home in Pittsburgh, where he was met by a crowd of over one thousand who turned his arrival into a victory parade for the drive to his mother's home.

On January 9, 1917, Harry K. Thaw of Pittsburgh, age forty-six, was arrested and indicted on charges of kidnaping Frederick Gump, Jr., of Kansas City. The charges stated that Thaw had met Gump, aged nineteen, at an ice-cream parlor in Long Beach, California; that he had enticed Gump with money to register at the McAlpin Hotel on Christmas Eve, 1916; that some time after Gump had retired to his room, Harry K. Thaw opened Gump's door, turned on the light, and proceeded to flog Gump into unconsciousness with a short whip.

To prevent his extradition from Pittsburgh to New York on the charges presented, Mother Thaw arranged to have a Pennsylvania commission on lunacy judge Harry Thaw insane and commit him to the Pennsylvania State Hospital in Philadelphia, where he stayed for seven years, until 1924. The damages claimed by the Gump family of $650,000 were settled in January, 1924, because Harry needed them out of the way before another sanity trial was held on his release. The Gumps settled for $25,000; the sanity trial was duly held; Harry K. Thaw was declared sane again; and the Pennsylvania State Hospital for the insane presented a bill of $75,000 "for board and lodging."

In 1925 Harry Thaw was in the papers again when Miss Fawn Gray, described as a New York nightclub dancer, announced her engagement to the Pittsburgh millionaire and displayed a $5,000 diamond bracelet as proof of his affections; Thaw denied her allegations of breach of promise. In 1926, at a party given by Earl Carroll for the backers of his *Vanities,* a girl took a bath in champagne, but none of the guests seemed impressed until about two o'clock in the morning when Harry Thaw appeared and drank from the bath to cheers and applause.

There were reports of Harry Thaw starting fights in nightclubs; of Harry Thaw touring Europe with a series of champagne suppers during the depths of the Depression; of Harry Thaw being barred from landing in England; of dissension among the Thaw family over his mother's will. In the late thirties he was sued for beating Miss Marcia Estardus, who gave her occupation as nightclub hostess. After three trials Miss Estardus was awarded $16,000 in damages.

In 1946 he rented a house for August in Saratoga, for the thoroughbred racing season. A local citizen of Saratoga paid a call to see the famous occupant. She found him on the second floor, in his bedroom, jumping up and down on the big fourposter bed the way a small boy would. To make conversation, she asked why he did not go over to the track to watch the horses run. He paused long enough to stare at his visitor. "Don't you know who I am?" He started to bite at his nails.

She shook her head.

"I am Harry Thaw of Pittsburgh," and he laughed and laughed, and started to jump up and down again on the bed. "I am Harry Thaw of Pittsburgh."

On February 21, 1947, he had a heart attack while living in a house he had rented on North Bay Road in Miami. He died the next day at seventy-six.

CHAPTER TWENTY-ONE

ILLUSIONS OF COMMUNITY

WHILE REPORTERS WERE COVERING Harry Thaw's second trial for murder in 1908, their editors filed obituaries to mark the death of Mrs. William Waldorf Astor. With the passing of Mrs. Astor, "society"—as it was understood in the nineteenth-century sense—also came to its end. No pretense could be maintained of any connections whatever between twentieth-century New York and the manners described in the novels of Henry James, Edith Wharton, and William Dean Howells. The systems of moral imperative that had been the style of Washington Square were abandoned.

During the nineteenth century the city was something more than the stage for national political ambition, more than the port of entry for hopeful immigrants: it had engaged itself in an effort to socialize the new rich, who seemed to have no other place to go. Philadelphia, the rich apparently believed, was a stage too narrow; and Boston, they discovered, was unfazed by money unless it was connected to Harvard or was in the possession of a near cousin. Except in New York, there seemed to be no place to exchange money for manners.

The late nineteenth century was described by Mark Twain as a "Gilded Age," but beneath the glitter was real gold. According to one estimate, after the Civil War 3,800 new millionaires appeared, every one of them with their gaze fixed on the possibility of being accepted on Fifth Avenue. To the city's business of money for its own sake, the Money Kings added what they thought might be the enjoyment of the arts, the maneuvers of civic virtue—largely efforts at making Presidents, and ceremonies and parades, feasts and dancings, and marvelous balls—all designed to accumulate social standing for their moneyed wives, and if that turned out to be impossible, at least for their wealthy daughters.

After all, the women were innocent of whatever crimes might have been committed in the gulches behind roaring Sierra mining camps. No wife could be held responsible for a sheaf of watered railroad bonds. No daughter had been accessory to the fact when recalcitrant coal miners were shot down in their pits. Beyond any shadow of a reasonable doubt, a jury would find the wives had done their best to sanctify their homes and raise daughters whose purity had never been violated.

Supplied by money in stupendous quantities, the delicate dances of courtship and the tough negotiations of marriage began to bubble with new energies, because it was self-evident that unless marriages were contracted, the success of money would be only temporary. Yet how could a suitable marriage be arranged when the social order was chaotic?

Thirty-eight hundred Money Kings, arriving almost simultaneously, constituted an unruly mob. There were not enough families of the old Washington Square aristocracy to teach them the canons of aesthetics and propriety, nor was Washington Square prepared to check ambition by contempt. Instead, the Money Kings were surrounded on every side by flattery; by shopkeepers with bolts of cloth to their elbows; by art dealers and architects with treasures ransacked from Europe; by dancingmasters with their hands waving elegant quadrilles into the fantasies of young girls.

Great, gruff weathered men, with big raw knuckles and calloused palms, men whose eyes had long ago learned to always squint, sent their wives and daughters to tutors in the poetry of Pope, to teachers of parlor-table etiquette and to masters in music appreciation. To insure the permanence of their victories, the lucky survivors of continental competition were asked to believe they might hire society, just as they did everything else, at so much per month, plus the cost of room and board on Fifth Avenue. And there were social advisors—a handsome supply of widows and young bachelors—who would explain to them the secret skills of gentility.

In these circumstances, Mrs. William Waldorf Astor took up the mace of social sovereignty. She was born a Schermerhorn in 1830, a descendant of one of the early Dutch families of New Amsterdam. She had married in 1853—the year Stanford White was born—a grandson of the original John Jacob Astor, fur merchant of the Upper Missouri trade. For the sake of her granddaughter, Caroline Schermerhorn Astor, Mrs. William Waldorf Astor had conferred legitimacy on the Vanderbilts, and their heirs, in a complicated but necessary social crisis in 1883. As a result of her maneuvers, the term *astorbilts* could be understood as a word defining any person who had, or pretended to have, social importance.

Mrs. Astor would reign as the "Queen of Society," in the sense that if there was no legalized aristocracy, she would attempt to create something like it. She owned regal jewelry, and she knew how to wear it. She had a sharp tongue, and she could use it. She kept heralds and pages at her side to announce her arrivals and departures and engaged Mr. Ward McAllister to choose who would be asked to her annual ball. Between Mr. McAllister and Mrs. Astor a list could be drawn up of young men who knew how to dance and could eat supper without using the back of their knives for their peas, and they might even have some on their list who would be able to talk cheerily about the new operas by Wagner.

Mrs. Astor's list and the list drawn from the National Horse Show for *The Social Register* were not dissimilar, but necessarily Stanford White's stockholders in Madison Square Garden were "men who counted in the city's affairs," while Mrs. Astor's list was arranged around the names of women whose grandchildren might be expected to continue a tradition. Mrs. Astor was a woman of great energy, the possessor of a perfect sense of timing, but owed her supremacy in the city's social life to her sense of noblesse oblige, and great patience, which was perhaps founded in real generosity.

Yet by 1904 she discontinued her annual ball—the ball that had been considered the certification of social acceptance to those who were invited. After 1906 she gave up her attendance at the Metropolitan Opera—the stage she often chose for social displays. After her death in 1908 there was no woman who would take her place, nor any woman who could be found to maintain any pretense of social distinctions. The village of Mrs. Astor's girlhood had become a metropolis with other concerns.

Just as Mrs. Astor's obituary marked the end of "society," the death of Charles F. McKim in 1909 marked the end of the nineteenth century's love affair with the *beaux arts,* or any "classical ideals." Afterward there would still be imitation of the work of Stanford White and Charles McKim, but the tendency of architects and artists was to express in permanent form the aesthetics of the machine; or if that had to be rejected, the surrealistic terrors that machines fostered. Both tendencies would be called Modern.

Richard Watson Gilder, editor of *Scribner's* and *The Century,* friend of McKim, of White, and model for Saint-Gaudens' legs of *Farragut,* died two months after McKim in 1909. John La Farge died the next year in Providence, Rhode Island, at the age of seventy-five. Their friend Henry Adams did not die until 1918, long after he had given up any hope for the twentieth century. William Dean Howells, editor for the *Atlantic* of the "smiling aspects of American life," and then novelist of dismay when the results of American success were examined realistically, died May 11, 1920. The generation of men born in the 1840's and 1850's, for which Henry Adams had said there would be so much hope, died, almost every one of them, appalled.

Of his generation, perhaps Saint-Gaudens was the most laconic in his explanation of what he called "all this turmoil, and sickness, and discontent." Absorbed by his work, Saint-Gaudens would say no more than he felt that "he had paid the city its price." Without naming what the price may have been, he moved out to Cornish, New Hampshire.

At first Mr. and Mrs. Saint-Gaudens had rented for the summer the remains of an old brick tavern in Cornish known as Huggins Folly from their friend and lawyer, Charles C. Beaman. During their first summer, in 1885, Gus worked in the hundred-year-old barn on his sketches for the *Standing Lincoln* and the *Seated Lincoln.* There were plenty of "Lincoln-shaped men" in New Hampshire to serve as models.

The next year, and the year after that, and then in successive years, they fixed up the old barn, and then the house, and a summer sojourn began to last well into November and finally all year around. Gus and Gussie had to admit they were spending every dollar Gus earned on the place. They bought it from counselor Beaman for five hundred dollars and a bust of Beaman in bronze.

Once the converted tavern was theirs, and as their son Homer began to grow, they decided it was a happier place than the city and continued to improve it. They transformed the old house, remodeling and adding rooms, building porches and verandas, rebuilding the barn completely with columns of Portland cement and enlarging it to contain Gus's accumulating works.

In addition, they had to provide housing for Gus's crews of assistants, apprentices, masons, and carpenters, who came and went depending upon the commissions. The crews could handle the model for Sherman's horse in the barn, but to build the model of the stele that was to stand behind the *Charles Stewart Parnell* in Dublin, they constructed a pillar seventy feet high in a field down from the house so that Gus could see how it would look. He said they could never have done that kind of thing in the city.

They were in Cornish Township on the New Hampshire side of the Connecticut River, situated on the rounded knoll of a hill between the Green and White Mountain ranges. To pick up his mail, Gus would ride his horse past Blow-Me-Down Pond, south along the banks of the Connecticut River for about a mile and a half, then across a covered bridge to the Vermont side and into the village of Windsor. There was a sign on the bridge that delighted him: "Walk your horses or pay two dollars fine."

For supplies he might have to take the wagon about twelve miles upriver to White River Junction, Vermont, which was still a fair-sized town, hanging on in a countryside of abandoned farms. He would ride through the lanes of old rock walls, lines of shale and bluestone that sometimes disappeared into the new grown forests—the fields that the walls had once marked instantly overgrown by the quick energies of balsam pine. Early in the fall country fires had to be started up again against the chill of the blue northerlies, which came whistling down out of Canada even before the hardwoods began to turn color. The smoke smell drifting down from the chimneys of the remaining farms could be identified as birchwood.

By Thanksgiving there would be ice on the pond, and skating, and Saint-Gaudens kept a square on the pond clear all winter long by shoveling the snow by hand. The neighborhood children drove over by sleigh to play hockey, and there was, Gus and Gussie agreed, a "joyousness" in the country. They were satisfied with the country calendar: the cycle of seasons marking their days, rather than the city's frenzied appointments; their golden falls, their snowbound winters, even the pleasures of the muds and rushing torrents of New Hampshire's miserable sudden spring.

Although he avoided them as much as he could, Gus had to keep open his studios in the city. He would go there by train to teach for the Art Students League, to work with White and McKim on their projects, to direct the meetings of the Society of American Artists, to check on the sites and the castings of his major works. During one winter he had an adventure with one of his models—she stood for Victory, leading Sherman's horse—and at the post office in Windsor, Gussie discovered the love letters. She said he should never come back.

Gus wrote her from the Player's Club, begging her forgiveness, admitting the affair and the child, but arguing that he had never scandalized their marriage the way MacMonnies or White had. Gussie forgave him, and they made it up in Cornish, because Cornish had become the center of their life.

A colony of other artists had grown up around them, buying and rebuilding abandoned farms, just as Gus and Gussie had done. On the summer solstice, June 23, 1905, Gus's friends organized an "outdoor masque" to celebrate the twentieth anniversary of "the founding of the Cornish Colony by Augustus Saint-Gaudens." The performance was also an excuse to celebrate the life of the greatest artist of nineteenth-century America: hundreds of guests arrived from the city, and at twilight when Saint-Gaudens and his family were seated before a gray-green curtain suspended between two pines, the overture was struck by the Boston Symphony Orchestra.

The figure of Iris appeared in diaphanous veils from behind the curtain. With a staff of fleur-de-lis in one hand, she held the script of the prologue in the other and began to read out the verses of tribute to Saint-Gaudens. At the end of the prologue the woodwinds of the orchestra took their cue, the curtains parted, and some forty actors and writers played out their parts on the stage nature had provided between the pines.

At the rear of the stage a little temple of Ionic columns stood as a centerpiece to the action. Its capitals were hung with laurel ropes. The temple was decked with flowers and flanked by classic benches. Behind it the murmur of the stream that fed Blow-Me-Down Pond could be heard. The script called for complications, local allusions, and tributes. Juno, Jupiter, Mercury, Pluto and his court, Venus, Diana, the wood gods, Apollo and the Muses—all had their parts. Smoke puffed up from the temple, and Fame appeared to choose the name of Saint-Gaudens from the golden bowl. Then the Graces locked arms with the Fates, and Cupid danced with Pan, and as the sun set over Mount Ascutney, shouts went up from both cast and audience, again and again: "Saint-Gaudens."

The temple, built of plaster and wood for the masque, was reworked in white Vermont marble after Saint-Gaudens died and his ashes kept there in an urn. Two years after the masque, on August 3, 1907, he lay on the porch of his house and watched the sun going down behind Mount Ascutney. He was fifty-nine. He spoke out of a long silence. "It is very beautiful," he said, "but I want to go farther away."

CHAPTER TWENTY-TWO

"I'M JUST A BROAD-MINDED BROAD FROM BROADWAY"

BEFORE HARRY'S SECOND TRIAL opened in January, 1908, Evelyn still believed she had a firm understanding with Mother Thaw's lawyers. She would testify again in his defense. As soon as the trial was over she could begin divorce proceedings against Harry and she would get a settlement that would amount to one million dollars. She was still only twenty-two, and she could imagine for herself the long, comfortable, secure life ahead of her.

During the months between the trials, however, Mother Thaw's detectives had been assembling a considerable dossier on Evelyn. It included the details of her affair with Harry's lawyer, Daniel O'Reilly—and the incident of Mrs. O'Reilly's attack on Mr. O'Reilly with an umbrella. It also included reports of midnight suppers in hideaway restaurants, afternoon sojourns aboard yachts cruising the Hudson River, and a trip by rail to Banff in the Canadian Rockies in a Pullman sleeper with an unnamed corespondent. During Harry's second trial Evelyn made headlines on her own by having a late supper with banker E. R. Thomas, a particularly indiscreet choice upon Evelyn's part because Mr. Thomas was involved in a notorious banking fraud. When newspaper reporters checked Mother Thaw for a quote, she said Evelyn's denial of supper with Thomas at the Knickerbocker Grill "sounded so much like other denials she has made."

Immediately after the second jury delivered its verdict of insanity and Harry was safely in Matteawan, Evelyn filed her papers in the County Clerk's Office in New York, asking for an annulment and charging that at the time of her marriage

"Harry Thaw was of unsound mind." But she soon discovered from Mother Thaw's lawyers that she had been trapped. If she annulled the marriage she had consummated, she had no title to Harry's estate; if she remained married to a man declared insane, she could not file for divorce to dissolve their marriage because Harry would not be "in his right mind" in any settlement he might contract. In any case, even if Harry should be declared sane, the estate from which he might pay a settlement for divorce was, by the terms of William Thaw's will, controlled by his mother.

When the jury had declared her son insane, Harry Thaw's mother no longer needed the evidence of Harry Thaw's wife. The price offered by Mother Thaw's lawyers for Evelyn's annulment dropped from $1,000,000 to $25,000. By arguing that the Thaws might still need her testimony in the hearings held to determine Harry's sanity, Evelyn got Mother Thaw's lawyers to agree to an allowance of $1,000 per month. Evelyn demanded that this time she be paid in advance, and Mother Thaw dutifully wrote out two checks of $15,000 each, "as insurance for the next two and a half years."

On her visits to Matteawan, Harry would grill Evelyn on how she intended to spend the money. He objected to his mother, arguing that she should not have given Evelyn any money at all. Evelyn soon had run through her "advance" and would visit Harry at Matteawan to wheedle, threaten, and beg for small checks. On one of her visits, Harry flew into a rage over money, grabbed her by the throat, and Daniel O'Reilly and a guard working together had a difficult time breaking his grip on her.

Faced with the realities of her situation, Evelyn was forced to abandon her pretty house and her servants on Park Avenue. She moved to the Prince George Hotel on Twenty-eighth Street, into two small dreary rooms, and hoped for some development in Harry's legal battles to turn up—something that would make her necessary again.

Instead, a lawyer of the Thaws, a Mr. Morschauser, appeared at the Prince George saying he had an unpleasant task to perform. Counselor Morschauser was a brother of the Judge Morschauser, to whom Harry had applied for a writ of habeas corpus. His instructions were "to advise you that from now on no more money will be paid you by your husband or his family."

She demanded to know how the Thaws expected her to live. She paced up and down and claimed she couldn't get work because the notoriety of the Thaw case had closed every avenue of the career her marriage had interrupted. What did they expect her to do?

Morschauser explained Mother Thaw's analysis: "Without money from the Thaws you will land in the gutter, and thereby gain sympathy for her son."

As he left, Morschauser seemed affected by her case. He told her he hoped she would fool them, but he had no alternatives for her because he had been given his instructions. To survive, Evelyn began selling her jewelry. She met and begged friends of Harry's to intercede with him on her behalf. One of them, Dr. Valdemar Sillo, talked Harry into giving her seventy-five dollars a week and her rent. Harry sent it for a while, and she moved to an apartment on Thirty-third Street, but then the checks stopped coming and Dr. Sillo seemed to be unable to get them started again.

From her apartment on Thirty-third Street Evelyn went out to dinner from time to time with some of her newspaper reporter friends. They made a trip to visit the Bronx Zoo, and at the zoo Evelyn won the heart of Dr. Raymond L. Ditmars, the curator. They shared with each other their passionate interest in snakes. On Christmas Day, 1908, her twenty-fourth birthday, she woke up alone in her apartment, gloomy and blue. Then an East Indian basket was delivered to her door with a card from Dr. Ditmars—"Merry Christmas, Mrs. Thaw!" In the basket Evelyn found a six-foot Florida king snake.

She named it "Tara," bathed it every day, let it swim in the tub in lukewarm water, let it curl up beside her in bed when she read or sewed. She fed Tara a live mouse, all it needed, once a month. She kept it in her white wicker sewing basket that stood on four legs in the corner. She had to put the *Century Dictionary* on the basket's lid to hold it down.

Harry Thaw was refusing to pay any outstanding bills because he imagined his creditors would constitute themselves as a committee to petition for his release from Matteawan. Instead they sued, and they soon discovered Mrs. Harry Thaw's new address on Thirty-third Street. Every time Evelyn stepped out of her apartment she would be surrounded by a half-dozen process servers. She accidentally discovered a marvelous cure for them when she walked out with Tara one day and let the snake begin to uncoil his length from around her arm. When they met Tara eye to eye, the process servers turned and ran.

Evelyn returned Tara to Dr. Ditmars and the snake house at the Bronx Zoo when Bobby Collier and his Racquet Club friends came to call. They had presented her with a black Pomeranian pup she named "Randy." At Thirty-third Street, she held "gatherings at her studio," on Sunday evenings. She broiled club steaks, served drinks, and supplied four other girls. Newspaper and Wall Street men and the Racquet Club "boys," began to drop by regularly. It was the kind of gathering she had learned was fun from Stanford White, and it might get her into circulation again.

Evelyn tried to make it seem all very Bohemian. She met Wilson Mizner, the producer, and Jack Francis, a newspaperman who wrote sensational magazine stories under a pseudonym. Jack Francis' girlfriend was Teddy Girard—she was in the chorus of *Havana*. Evelyn went with Wilson Mizner and Jack Francis to Teddy Girard's apartment to smoke opium. They worked out a lovely scheme to blackmail the son of a senior partner in a Wall Street firm for the love letters he had written Teddy. They thought they were playing a great joke, but to their surprise he actually paid for the letters, and because she needed it, Evelyn was allowed to split the money with Teddy and Jack.

In June, 1909, hearings were coming up on one of Harry's writs. Evelyn received a letter from Dr. Sillo, enclosing a two-hundred-dollar check and suggesting she use the money for "a little vacation" outside the State of New York. She refused to leave, cashed the check anyway, and turned the letter over to Mr. Jerome, who used it to show the court how the Thaw family was willing to tamper with witnesses. Evelyn's testimony in White Plains Courthouse helped Judge Mills decide that Harry Thaw should be returned to Matteawan to insure the public safety.

By Christmas, 1909, Evelyn had to admit she was pregnant again. She named Harry Thaw as father of the child, conceived, she argued to Mother Thaw's lawyers, during one of her visits to his private apartment at Matteawan. Harry Thaw denied his paternity, and she sensed in her negotiations that the Thaws might want to take the baby away from her. An offer Bobby Collier had made six years before came floating back to her. He had promised Evelyn then that anytime she wanted to go to Europe he'd send her, no strings attached.

When she asked Bobby Collier if his offer still held "he was as good as his word"; got her the boat tickets, promised to send her a thousand dollars a month, and even suggested Evelyn take along her friend from *Floradora* days, Lillian Spencer. "And if it's a boy," he said as he saw them off, "don't forget to send me a cable."

While Evelyn waited in Europe, Lillian Spencer decided she would return to New York. Jack Francis took Lillian's place as Evelyn's "companion." He was with Evelyn in Berlin, October 25, 1910, when a boy was born at four thirty in the afternoon. He weighed eight pounds at birth, and Evelyn named him Russell William Thaw and sent the cable to Bobby Collier.

She returned to New York with her baby and moved into the second-floor apartment of a small house on 112th Street. The floor above her was occupied by her newspaperman friend Jack Francis and his brother and unmarried sister. Jack's sister cared for the baby when Evelyn went out, but Jack became insanely jealous, and he and Evelyn began to argue. Jack Francis sold the story of "Evelyn Nesbit Thaw's Secret Baby" to the New York *Herald* for seventy-five dollars.

Evelyn had to move again, this time to a cheap studio apartment in the forties near Broadway. It was all she could afford, but it had a kitchenette where she could prepare her baby's food. She had the only living quarters in a loft building of music publishers, wigmakers, and agents. She sold her last jewels, her pearls, her Tiffany pins, until there were none left.

Because Harry was scheduled to have a third insanity hearing at White Plains Courthouse in 1912, Evelyn was able to get the Thaw lawyers to reinstitute a small allowance. At the hearings Mr. Jerome introduced into evidence one of Harry's whips—it had a greyhound's head in amethyst and a diamond collar. Jerome used the whip to support the contentions of Mrs. Susie Merrill, a witness he introduced as "the procuress who had provided girls for Harry Thaw's sadistic orgies." Evelyn testified that she recognized the whip as Harry's; that she herself had delivered it to Mr. Jerome; that Harry Thaw was a maniac. The hearings ended with Harry Thaw sent back once more to Matteawan, and Evelyn's allowance stopped.

Later the same year Evelyn met a Canadian lawyer at a party of Flo Ziegfeld's. He took her to dinner several times, and she decided she liked him because he was good company, well educated, and cultured, even though she admitted "he lacked sex appeal." After Christmas he offered to take her to Europe, where he had business to conduct, for three months. She let him know how delighted she was at the prospect of Europe but explained she would have to take her baby along, and her friend Lillian Spencer, too—as a chaperone.

They sailed together for Paris aboard the *Olympic* in May, 1913. By the time the ship had docked in Cherbourg Evelyn had turned her Canadian lawyer over to Lillian Spencer, and if he was miffed, there was little Evelyn could do about that because she had found other men on board whose acquaintance she needed to renew: Broadway impresarios Lee Shubert and Martin Beck; Albert de Courville, director of the London Hippodrome; and, H. B. Marinelli, the powerful international agent. While Lillian Spencer minded the baby and the Canadian, Evelyn concentrated on Marinelli. When the boat train arrived in Paris, Evelyn had won a contract to appear at the London Hippodrome in *Hello Ragtime*.

For the act Marinelli planned for her, she would need a dancing partner. Marinelli provided Jack Clifford, who had been teaching English society how to perform the ragtime dances—foxtrot and one-step. Because they needed time to rehearse in London, Evelyn left the baby and the lawyer with Lillian in Paris. *Hello Ragtime,* starring Evelyn Nesbit Thaw, opened at the Hippodrome to rave reviews. Evelyn took dozens of curtain calls, heaps of roses, and baskets of orchids. The publicity about "the woman in the case" did the show's bookings no harm.

Oscar Hammerstein saw the act in London and offered Evelyn $3,500 a week to open on August 3 at his Victoria Theatre in New York. To avoid the process servers who would inevitably swarm around the stage door, attempting to enforce court judgments for either her own bills or those of Harry Thaw, Mrs. Evelyn Nesbit Thaw declared bankruptcy in federal court before the curtain went up.

On opening night she stood in the wings with her partner Jack Clifford, waiting for her cue. She was back on Broadway, a star again, once more the toast of the town. Suddenly she was afflicted with an acute attack of stage fright. When her cue sounded, she could not go on. Fortunately, Flo Ziegfeld was standing with her in the wings. He gave her a healthy boot in the ass. Once she was out on the stage taking her one-step turns with Jack Clifford, she could charm them. The Victoria was packed for every show, and Ziegfeld announced he planned to star her in his *Follies.* Two weeks after she opened, Harry Thaw escaped from Matteawan. Evelyn asked the New York police for protection, but her fears evaporated when she learned Harry had fled to Canada.

The publicity did the dance act no harm. Instead of bookign her into *Ziegfeld's Follies,* her agent Marinelli booked her for a tour. She traveled across the country doing two-a-day on the vaudeville circuit. Crowds gathered to catch a glimpse of her in every city she played, mobs so unruly she could not stay in hotels but had to be secluded in a private railroad car, which had the advantageous name, *The Magnet.* In every city she broke records—$37,500 in one week in Chicago. In Los Angeles she was feted at dinner parties by D. W. Griffith, Mae Marsh, motion picture producers such as Fred Mace, and Mack Sennett's movie stars. In Pittsburgh, Mother Thaw attempted to get a court order to prevent Evelyn's appearance, the injunction claiming that ragtime dances were immodest and immoral. Mother Thaw failed in the courts, and in reply the Pittsburgh audience gave Evelyn a fifteen-minute standing ovation. In Richmond, Virginia, Mother Thaw organized and financed a group of ministers who arranged in their turn to have Evelyn arrested for immoral dancing, but the charges had to be dropped. The results of Mother Thaw's efforts seemed to be that she added to the publicity and increased the size of adoring crowds.

Evelyn took pride in the distance she had gained from the gutter Mother Thaw had prayed she would reach. Evelyn sailed for Paris in the summer of 1914 with no immediate cares, no entanglements, and money of her own to spend as she pleased. Producer Fred Mace arrived in Paris from Hollywood. He said they would use Paris as the background for the scenes for Evelyn's first motion picture; he shot hundreds of feet of film of Evelyn walking, running, and mugging on the grounds of the Cluny Museum. They would fit the scenes into the story later. While she posed for reels of silent film, Marinelli booked her for a month at the Folies-Marigny Theatre on the Champs Elysées. On the night of the Grand Prix, Evelyn opened again to roaring success. She was the toast of Paris, and Marinelli booked the dance act into Copenhagen, Vienna, and Berlin.

She was still in Paris on the evening of August 3, 1914. She had gone to dinner with her dancing partner, Jack Clifford, her producer Fred Mace, and his actress "Lovey" Marsh. They were at an Italian restaurant with a balcony overlooking the Place Boileau, and they saw the square begin to fill with screaming, cheering men and women. *"Vive la guerre! Vive la guerre! A bas les Boches!"* To get back to their hotel they had to make their way through streets jammed with cavalrymen and soldiers forming battalions. All Paris was giddy at the prospect of war, happy with the honor and the glory that would be won. Marinelli said he would have to cancel her European tour and she should return to New York at once.

In boarding the *Olympic* at Cherbourg the next day, there was a good deal of confusion. Evelyn lost her purse with several thousand francs of gold and $60,000 worth of jewelry. She didn't think it would matter, because back in New York she made a picture called *Threads of Destiny,* and Marinelli sent her out again on the Keith-Albee vaudeville circuit. She one-stepped across America again with Jack Clifford, and their act continued to do well enough throughout the war years.

There was nothing really wrong with the act except perhaps that the publicity that had once surrounded "the woman in the case" was fading in comparison to the news of murders by the million in the trenches of Europe. Evelyn was on the road in 1915 when Harry Thaw was declared sane and served her with divorce papers. She didn't bother to contest them, yet they hardly made any news at all. In the summer of 1915 she married Jack Clifford, which made news in *Variety,* but the daily papers had more fascinating reports about the effects of machine guns, artillery and poison gas.

They worked the tour as husband and wife, but her billing was always as Evelyn Nesbit Thaw. In 1919 the United Booking Office announced they wanted a new partner for her act for the next season—a fresher face, someone who could sing as well as dance. Because they insisted, she began to rehearse with Bobby O'Neil. Jack Clifford was furious, but Evelyn tried to explain there was really nothing she could do about it. They argued endlessly, until Jack "lapsed into a most annoying sulkiness. Finally, I packed my trunks and left for New York."

Evelyn noted with smug satisfaction that Jack Clifford tried to make it on his own with a new partner, a pretty little thing, Agnes Dunne. Their act was good, but not a success. Evelyn's performances with Bobby O'Neil continued to draw, and she saw no more of Jack Clifford. Even though "Evelyn Nesbit Thaw" doing one-step turns and a few songs no longer broke records, she still possessed a name that could be exploited. She made two pictures for Joe Schenck and six pictures at the Fort Lee, New Jersey, studios of Fox. Movies were the coming thing, she said.

There was always some truth in everything Evelyn said, and the facts of any story she ever told always made a coat of many colors, because she knew nothing less would delight an audience. She said, for example, that she had gone for a long drive in an open car in cold weather, which had caused her to suffer from "facial neuralgia." She could not sleep, she could not even lie down, pain stabbed at her nose and at her ears, and she was unable to reach her doctor, Jesse Heiman, by phone. She called an ex-*Follies* girlfriend, who claimed she knew how to relieve Evelyn's agony and would be right over to Evelyn's apartment. The *Follies* blonde gave Evelyn an injection.

Instead of calling Dr. Heiman the next time an attack of facial neuralgia occurred, she phoned the *Follies* blonde. "The attacks began to assail me with an alarming regularity," and she regularly called her blond friend. The night came when she couldn't sleep without a call "to this girl and a dose of her medicine." Evelyn said she finally understood the phrase "hooked with a habit."

She did not take care of herself and her beauty began to fade. She failed to show up for curtain calls, and the agents stopped booking her. She was paying for heroin at forty dollars an ounce and buying several ounces at a time. She knew she had to try to give it up. She went to a "milk farm" in New Jersey where the cure was six weeks of no food, drinking milk all day long, reducing the heroin slowly to a small daily dose, "but I could not dislodge that craving altogether."

Evelyn decided to open a tearoom near Broadway because it might be some time before her "health should permit a return to the stage." To go into business she raised $1,500 by pawning a $6,000 Tiffany marquise diamond ring and diamond laveliere "worth at least $3,000." Despite the discount she had to accept on her remaining capital, it was enough to open the tearoom on West Fifty-second Street. Old friends and new from Broadway were her steady customers, but she made very little money. She lived alone on the top floor of the building, and the drug dealers easily found her there.

Stories about Evelyn Nesbit Thaw began to appear again in the newspapers, but there was a new tone to the reports. To keep her company and do odd jobs around the tearoom, Evelyn took in a "pansy" named "Jackie." In attempting to get evidence of adultery for divorce under the laws of New

York, Jack Clifford broke into Evelyn's apartment one night with a crowd of witnesses, "scaring Jackie half to death."

Clifford and his witnesses were somewhat nonplussed by Jackie's fit of hysterics: he was screaming at them that his friends would accuse him of having an affair with a woman; his reputation would be ruined. Then in shrieking midflight, he suddenly fainted. Clifford's witnesses had to revive him. When Clifford finally filed for divorce there was no mention of Jackie, and he named instead as corespondent Eugene Strong, described as a movie actor. In Evelyn's counterclaim she named Ann Luther and Juanita Hansen, movie actresses.

There were reports of an attempted suicide by the once famous Evelyn Nesbit Thaw. Actually, Evelyn said there was no suicide attempt at all—a friend gave her an overdose, and by giving her a heart stimulant and keeping her awake and making her walk all night, her doctor saved her life. Within days of the overdose she admitted she was back on the habit.

The newspapers reported a robbery at Evelyn's tea shop; that a receiver had been appointed to liquidate it; that she was evicted; that she would marry Baron Sander de Windt as soon as her divorce from Jack Clifford was final; that Evelyn Nesbit Thaw was named as corespondent in the divorce action filed by the wife of Harry Schneider, a taxi driver; that letters signed with her name asking for drugs had been seized in a drug raid.

In 1924, she was thirty-nine years old; she weighed less than one hundred pounds, her looks were ruined, and she could not shake off a mood of deadly inertia. At that moment Harry Katz, owner of an Atlantic City nightclub, came to New York and made her an offer for the summer: one-half of the cover-charge receipts and free hotel accommodations. She turned over her heroin supply to a doctor and left for Atlantic City. The doctor put her on a scale of diminishing doses. She went on a diet of milk and cream, mixed half and half, consuming as much as three quarts a day. She strolled the length of the boardwalk every day, over and over, back and forth. On the beach she exercised with a medicine ball and swam in the Atlantic. She began to feel better, and even some of her beauty began to return.

In Harry Katz's nightclub she put together a cabaret act, which included a song the men at the tables loved:

> "I'm just a broad-minded broad from Broadway,
> And conventions never bother me . . ."

She had to learn how to sit down with the customers and get them to buy drinks. Two wealthy Germans from South America wandered in one night and were delighted to find a woman who could speak to them in French. They came every night for a week and left her tips of two crisp one-hundred-dollar bills. Their last night they left her three hundred dollars.

Later that summer two men appeared in Mr. Katz's office and asked to interview her in private. When Katz had left, they dumped two thousand dollars in bills on the desk, saying "it was a little gift from Harry Thaw, and there was more to come." They explained that a Mr. Frank Johnston, who was one of Mr. Thaw's lawyers, would be around to see her in a few weeks. As soon as her visitors had left, Harry Katz presented her with a staggering bill for her hotel accommodations. Despite her pleas, she was forced to pay.

Evelyn quit, and went across the street to Martin's; left Martin's, and went to work at The Palais Royal, where she discovered they were cheating her on her percentage of the cover price. Then she found a backer and opened her own place, El Prinkipo. Atlantic City during Prohibition was a wide-open town, with the treasury agents on the payrolls of the nightclubs and the clubs selling illegal booze brought to the New Jersey shore by mobs of "rum runners." Evelyn redecorated El Prinkipo in rose, black, and silver, with subdued rose-colored lamps, and sang for the customers that she was "a broad-minded broad from Broadway." She was coining money, she said, but she was backed by the wrong mob, and rival clubs arranged to have her raided.

Not long after the raid Mr. Frank Johnston appeared to explain that Harry was involved in a hearing to determine his sanity, which could result in his release from the Pennsylvania State Hospital in Philadelphia. She might be asked to testify, and Harry wanted to be sure "she felt right about it."

Evelyn told counselor Johnston she wanted her own home, income sufficient to live on, and the bills paid for her son Russell at his school. Johnston said he was sure something could be worked out. He bought Russell a bicycle.

At the sanity hearing in Philadelphia, Evelyn arrived in the courtroom in a bright yellow sport dress, but the judge barred her appearance as "unsuitable." She returned the next day in a duller costume to file a petition to have her son made party to the proceedings, because Russell William Thaw "has an expectant interest in the estate of Harry Thaw." When her petition for her son was denied, her deposition was that "Harry Kendall Thaw had not fully recovered his normal mental condition . . . and that if he should be freed from restraint and his estate restored to him, he would dissipate and probably destroy the interests the said Russell William Thaw has as aforesaid." Despite sufficient evidence to the contrary, Harry Kendall Thaw was found judicially sane.

As a free man, Harry Thaw began to take "a warm interest in Russell," according to Evelyn. Harry bought Evelyn a fifteen-thousand-dollar house in Atlantic City and told her the house "would be held in trust for the boy." He started an allowance for Russell's education. But Harry's interest soon lost its focus, and he stopped an allowance to Evelyn of ten dollars a day. Then Evelyn discovered that Harry had actually contributed only five thousand dollars cash for the house. Since she could not meet the mortgage payments, she had to sell it.

She went back to work in the winter of 1925, was booked into The Moulin Rouge in Chicago, and sang "I'm a Broad-Minded Broad from Broadway" until she was fired. The newspaper reports claimed she had attempted suicide by drinking six ounces of Lysol; that her apartment was littered with whiskey bottles; that Harry Thaw had appeared in Chicago and had inquired at the hospital on the progress of her recovery. In the summer of 1926 she had recovered sufficiently to open again in Atlantic City at The Folies Bergères. After an argument over percentages she took her act down the boardwalk to Martin's.

During the summer Harry Thaw came to see her, and she

and Russell and Harry had a quiet dinner in Harry's hotel. Within weeks lawyer Johnston reappeared with a check of two thousand dollars, explaining that Mr. Thaw wanted to do the right thing and that if Evelyn would give up working in speakeasies, Mr. Thaw would arrange an income of three hundred dollars a month. Evelyn agreed to Harry's propositions; she hated the work in the clubs, and she found a bungalow on Ventnor Avenue. Lawyer Johnston made the down payment and told Evelyn to go ahead with the necessary remodeling. When the bills began to mount Harry Thaw refused to pay them.

Mr. Johnston explained to Evelyn that she would have to forget the house on Ventnor Avenue, but she could pick out another, provided it was already furnished and ready to move into. The house she found was in Northfield, a few miles from Atlantic City, over on the mainland. She had hardly moved in when she discovered that Harry had not bought it in her name at all but in his own. He had decided to charge her one hundred dollars a month rent, which she could not meet because the checks he had promised would be three hundred dollars per month dwindled to two hundred dollars, then to one hundred, then stopped altogether.

She went back to work in nightclubs. Again she found backers who had booze, and she opened a speakeasy called Chez Evelyn on West Fifty-second Street in New York. In Chez Evelyn she sang "You Are My Song of Love" and "I'm Nobody's Mamma Now" and saw Harry Thaw for the last time. He came in one night with his bodyguard and several showgirls. He ran up a tab for more than two hundred dollars. When Evelyn presented him with his bill, he flew into a rage, turned over the table, smashed bottles and glasses and anything else he could get his hands on. "It was one of Harry's mild tantrums," she told inquiring reporters. "You know what he is."

Chez Evelyn soon had to be closed when her backers could not arrange the necessary payoffs to the Treasury men in New York. She went back to Atlantic City and opened The Evelyn Nesbit Club on Pacific Avenue. It had a revue with "Eight Ravishing Girls," and the newspapers said Evelyn had designed the costumes herself. They also reported that mobster Jerry Daniels was her backer, and he was found murdered in some petty jurisdiction dispute between the gangsters of New Jersey.

Evelyn Nesbit seemed undaunted. She opened The Uptown Club in New York; there were headlines when it was raided, and Evelyn arrested. She reopened The Evelyn Nesbit Club in Atlantic City, but she must have picked the wrong backers again, and she was raided and closed. She took her cabaret act to Chicago and played The Club Alabam' and then played clubs wherever she could get a booking.

She was playing a seedy roadhouse club in Biloxi, Mississippi, when she got a call from Mrs. Mamie Kelly of New Orleans. Mrs. Kelly met Evelyn at the New Orleans railroad station and took her to a fabulous apartment over the Absinthe House "to talk over a proposition." Mamie Kelly was famous because she owned and operated one of the most famous whorehouses in the world: The Kelly Ritz in Panama City, Panama. Although Evelyn was forty-five years old, she would still be an attraction in Panama, especially "if her act was dressed up." While Mrs. Kelly and Mrs. Thaw discussed the terms of their deal, it was Mardi Gras week in New Orleans, and they went to one party after another. Wherever they went, the girls in New Orleans would warn Evelyn, "Don't go there whatever you do. You will have to sit and drink with Chinks, Hindus, Turks, all sorts of men."

Despite the girls' warnings, Evelyn sailed for Panama aboard a United Fruit steamer, accompanied by a black maid, a pair of Belgian griffons, "The Three Dancing Jay Sisters," and "The Singing Thornton Sisters." On March 15, 1929, newspapers back in the States reported her arrest in Panama on charges of gambling: "Attired in a red hat and trailing an evening dress, Evelyn Nesbit was arrested yesterday morning at 3:30 A.M. with eleven other Americans, five of them cabaret girls." Mother Thaw died the same year, and the stock market crashed.

Evelyn wrote the story of her life and had it published in 1934. Nothing much more was heard from her for a while. In 1955 Charles Brackett wrote a screenplay and produced a

Technicolor movie, *The Girl in the Red Velvet Swing,* starring Ray Milland as Stanford White and young Farley Granger as Harry K. Thaw. Evelyn's part was played by Joan Collins. After the initial distribution, the movie began to appear on television, endlessly, in reruns at nine in the morning or in the dead of night. The story of Evelyn Nesbit, or at least one version of it, became a permanent landmark of the national imagination.

She had lived in a roominghouse in Hollywood for a while after the Second World War, apparently supported by her son, Russell William Thaw. In Hollywood a young man who was shipping around the world as a merchant seaman fetched up for a while in the same boardinghouse and fell into frequent conversations with a woman there who said she was a theosophist and was studying all the great religions past and present. She invited the itinerant seaman to spend a Sunday picnic with her and her son Russell. She showed him the work she was doing in her room—modeling in clay and painting. She wore glasses, her hair was gray, and she admitted she was Evelyn Nesbit. "She was," her admirer would recall, "one of the most attractive women I have ever met."

Early in the nineteen sixties she had to be moved to a nursing home, where a reporter interviewed her and came away with a quote that ran: "Stanny was lucky, he died. I lived." Whether she meant what she said, it was apparent that she could still draw from the curved, soft, interior spaces of her experience a quote with the thrust hard news required. She died not long afterward in 1966 in Hollywood at the age of eighty-one.

CHAPTER TWENTY-THREE

CATAFALQUES

To SOME OBSERVERS, the meaning of Evelyn Nesbit's life would remain opaque—an eternal question, as Charles Dana Gibson had captioned it. According to many critics, she had played the whore; according to others, she was the virgin wronged. A few moralists used her career to draw an easy parable: the life guaranteed a pretty fifteen-year-old Pittsburgh girl upon Broadway's wicked stage was a fate worse than death—an interpretation that always brought a smile to the sophisticated. Nothing, they could demonstrate, left so little evidence of its passage as Evelyn's virtue.

Perhaps all these exegeses were true simultaneously. Evelyn Nesbit's mysterious fascination apparently derived from her ability to reflect whatever illusion happened to appear in her lovers' eyes. Her charm consisted precisely in her inability, or unwillingness, to deny any dream. When she was asked to play innocence, she soon had the pose perfected. When she was required to act out scenes of perversion, she was quick to learn her lines. If she often seemed to lie, surely she did so because she was anxious to please. If there were times she appeared to give in to self-pity, she had justification: she certainly might have expected better treatment from Fifth Avenue's Mr. White, and Pittsburgh's Mr. Thaw, and the Racquet Club boys, and the Broadway agents, and the movie producers, and the nightclub owners, and Mrs. Mamie Kelly, and all the others. If it appeared that she had exchanged her beauty for money, the city in which she had played her parts could not imagine any reward but money for her glories.

When she died in 1966 the city might have seemed to have changed considerably from the stage on which she had answered illusion's demands, but it had not. The city continued to heave up gigantic thrusts, arches and concatenations of stone and steel, but they were consecrations of the same thrusts she had known. They were still focused in more or less the same place—on Manhattan Island, 74 degrees west, 40 degrees, 42 minutes north. The salt tides of the Atlantic continued to swirl along the faces of the city's rock walls, flooding in every six hours, then out again on the ebb. The significant materials of the city's consumption were still being mined from the earth's blackest depths and then burned. The quantities of coal and oil consumed had increased by staggering amounts, and the velocity of their fires improved to vertiginous speeds, but the residues of decayed organic materials continued to leave a yellow haze and a slightly sulfuric odor in the streets during the day and provided the city with a magic glow at night, just as they had at the turn of the century. Beneath the sufuric pall and the glow of perpetual fires, fraud or violence constantly absorbed every citizen's whole attention.

Yet there were some changes—new variations, nuances, on the central doctrines of the city's theology. Money, for example, was rarely worshiped for its own sake, and the Money Kings had entirely disappeared. If an historian could trace the emanations from a residual mass of money in the way twentieth-century physicists traced the energies of radium from the tracks left by speeding matter, if some inheritance was examined and traced back through consortiums and marriages, through wills, codicils, and trust instruments, through years of administration without fault by pallid fiduciary officers, the energy of any of the Money Kings who had once called Fifth Avenue their own would have to be calculated as negligible.

Despite the folly of heirs, there might still exist residual incomes to descendants of Henry Villard, William Collins Whitney, various Astors or various Vanderbilts, but because Mrs. Astor's "society" had fallen into disarray, the marriages she had hoped would guarantee permanence were entered into haphazardly, and the heirs of the Gilded Age could not be distinguished from the heirs of yesterday afternoon. A half-century after Mrs. Astor abandoned her ball, the emissions from Fifth Avenue were faint, and when the half-life of Fifth Avenue's energies was calculated, the social power that remained was inconsequential.

Curiously, a few families of the merchant aristocracy from Washington Square—the predecessors of what Mark Twain had called the prophets of Mammon—continued to be active. Since the merchant aristocrats had never derived their strength from money but rather from manners, their half-lives could still be traced in some of the city's better clubs, might still be found working on the side of Reform, still allied with the ministers of their remnant faiths, as they applied their efforts to what they imagined were "good works." They could usually be identified as cold but noble and reasonable men and women whose voices the city politely ignored. The community they once represented—the village port with a Bowling Green and the Washington Square with its Arch—could be examined in the city's museums, whose administration seemed to be the old aristocracy's chief occupation.

Yet they endured, whereas the Money Kings had disappeared. The case of Mother Thaw was typical: No heir of hers could be discovered as influential, nor any heir of any other great fortune. The original sources of the Thaw's Pittsburgh power—bonds issued against the franchises of the Pennsylvania Railroad—were worthless. To support more than a hundred years of bonds issued in the name of the franchise, the directors of the Pennsylvania Railroad merged, acquired, and reorganized repeatedly. They joined forces with the directors of Vanderbilt's system, then finally declared their bankruptcy. The Thaws and the Vanderbilts took the income from the bonds while they could. They then turned over their railroads' frauds to regiments of lawyers who would defend them, and let the power they had once exercised slip from their hands. As a sign and seal of the new portents, the city wrecked Pennsylvania Station by McKim, Mead and White and dumped its remains in a New Jersey swamp.

The influence Money had once exerted was concentrated in the political system the Money Kings most abhorred—Tweed's invention of power through population. To Tweed's scheme of spoils for the party, others had added sophistication and applied his influence on a national scale. This continental system was often fostered by slogans with the word *new* as part of its appeal: New Freedom, New Deal, New Society. The franchises for city and national services, which had been the Money Kings' bonanza and Tweed's delight, were expanded. But the expansion appeared under political rather than personal jurisdictions: railroads, subways, elevateds, docks, ships, bridges, tunnels, housing for the poor, even office buildings—all of which multiplied and filled the city's landscape. These were franchises, too, against which bonds could be issued, just as bonds had been issued to build railroads. It was, therefore, not long before city and nation discovered how to issue money called bonds, spend it for whatever delights were deemed necessary to continue the privileges of power, and then declare bankruptcy just as railroad corporations had always done. As the city combined under its sole jurisdiction Tweed's system with the Money Kings' former tastes in rapacity, the opportunities for fraud multiplied geometrically and were attended by surging crowds of lawyers.

There were objections to such magnificent fraud, of course, particularly by the good middle-class citizens, like William Dean Howells' Mr. and Mrs. Basil March. They were angered by their discovery that the money they had saved for their children's future had been made worthless. From time to time, they would rush to oppose the politics of power, attending the revival meetings of Reform with an admirable fervence. They would then have to be reminded that the majority ruled—winner take all, just as Boss Tweed had said—and the courts, judges, police and tax collectors stood ready to use force if necessary to apply the decisions of duly elected officials. If Mr. and Mrs. Basil March complained and if an annual raise of five thousand dollars a year would not hold them, they were allowed the freedom to leave the city, and go to the suburbs.

Many left, and the space they occupied in brownstones along the city's avenues and streets was absorbed steadily by those mythical persons invented by Senator Roscoe Conkling of New York in his draft of the Fourteenth Amendment, the corporations—persons like angels, thousands of which could dance across the desks of the same lawyers absorbed by the city's jurisdictions, but persons never troubled by any city taxes, nor by judges, courts, police, nor even by any dainty moral considerations that might have inhibited the behavior of humans. They were capable of every crime without quaver.

Besides replacing the brownstones of the Marches, for example, the corporations that took their place systematically destroyed in fifty years more exquisite architecture, according to one estimate, than all the barbarian invasions of Rome by Goths, Huns, and Vandals. As might be expected, the corporate sacking of the city was carried out in each instance in the name of progress. The magnificent houses of the Vanderbilts at 666 Fifth Avenue were replaced by an office tower that displayed the new uses of aluminum. The palace of William Collins Whitney at 871 Fifth Avenue was said to rival in its beauty and detail any Renaissance palace ever built, but it went down in dust to wrecking balls because the corporation that sacked it needed tax advantages from the property. Stanford White's magnificent Tiffany house was vandalized "to make better use of the space available." The Herald Building that White created for James Gordon Bennett, Jr., must have been equally inefficient, for it too was wrecked. The Villard houses still stood when Evelyn Nesbit died in 1966, but they were scheduled for defacement.

Those examples of the work of McKim, Mead and White that survived did so almost by accident or because no corporation had yet found their site necessary to its ambitions. Most of the clubs survived, including the University, the Metropolitan, and the Century, because they were inhabited by the residual representatives of Washington Square, still unmoved by either money or power, and devoted to the practice of manners. In addition, the Arch on Washington Square stood, because it was in the park. Similarly, *Admiral Farragut* still presided over Madison Square, and Saint Gaudens' *Victory* continued to lead *General Sherman*'s horse toward the Plaza.

McKim's Library for J. P. Morgan survived. Joseph Pulitzer's soundproof mansion was converted into apartments. The Payne Whitney house at 972 Fifth Avenue was occupied by the cultural staff of the French Embassy. The townhouse of Charles Dana Gibson at 127 East Seventy-third Street was occupied by the tax-exempt Scandinavian Foundation. In Great Barrington, Massachusetts, the fairyland castle White created for Mrs. Mark Hopkins was used to train salesmen of the Home Insurance Company. In Harlem two rows of brownstones by White were declared city landmarks because black lawyers, doctors, songwriters, and artists maintained them handsomely against repeated assaults of city fraud.

But making lists of what survived and what did not gave few clues to the city's fascination with destruction because the violence displayed could not be understood by simple categories. For example, when Pennsylvania Station was wrecked its ruins were trucked to the Secaucus meadows in New Jersey, where sections of its magnificent columns were dumped. Some of the sections included Grecian goddesses designed by McKim on a gigantic scale—big enough to diminish the mass of the Pennsy's immense train sheds. As a result, the swamps of Secaucus contained for a short time the upper torso of young women carved in stone, draped in the folds of flowing Dionysiac gowns, resting on their backs in Jersey mud. Then a corporation pulverized McKim's huge examples of classic virgin energies in rock-crushing machines and spread the pulverized materials as fill, offering the site for development. Under the circumstance, the significance of the goddesses' style, their grandeur, their delicate values, was difficult to determine—unless destruction itself was the ultimate meaning.

The place where the goddesses once stood looking down on Seventh Avenue was taken by the new Madison Square Garden, and towering above it a new tower—the Garden Corporation's skyscraper of office space—an absolutely blank, monumental object. Just as McKim's goddesses were expressions of his classic ideals, just as the old Garden was an example of White's titanic gamboling, the new Garden's office tower was a container of the latest nuances in the city's devotions. Its owners had built what they adored, expressed themselves in the forms they thought appropriate, consecrated by structure the energies they admired—bland, impersonal, and banal. If the meaning of such a tower were to be understood, it would have to be approached cautiously—by sidling up to it as mourners do when passing an empty coffin, not at all sure of what spirits it might contain.

Such a catafalque must have cost enormous sums of money, but the immense wealth assembled by the Money Kings was more conveniently measured, and the influence their money carried more easily understood. When some Pittsburgh idler such as Harry Thaw had used money to outrage the moral law, criminal penalties might not always be the consequence of his crimes, but if he escaped jail he would probably be committed to some place like Matteawan. Obviously the corporate office tower represented some other kind of money: the scale of its construction was too grand for those who controlled its powers to be sent to any jail or insane asylum.

As to the powers represented by forty stories of steel and glass, the political powers of Tweed and Reform seem small and human by comparison. When some "Boss" attempted to pursue the logic of his power to its conclusion, defeat by hastily assembled majorities might not be an immediate deterrent to his manias, but the city's preference for anarchy had eventually always asserted its claim. Besides, when men had abused power in the past they had usually done so to the accompaniment of folly—a pretty woman had caught their eye, or they hoped a daughter married successfully, with the result that power's excess was usually diminished by laughter or at least scandal.

But the corporations for which skyscraper towers were the appropriate forms never dallied. They combined money, influence, and power—as Henry Adams had predicted—in a person who was the figment of legal imaginations. At the outset, corporations were irrational, unaffected by any code of manners, untested by any democratic ceremonies of popularity, never subject to any moral law of any kind, nor indictable for any fraud or any violence, nor confinable to jails or asylums. Only under the very worst circumstances would the corporation need to pretend it had moved to New Jersey, or Delaware, or perhaps as far as Panama.

A mass of such corporations, a landscape of their towers, a horizon of skyscrapers, made the scale of life on the streets below them seem insignificant. At a distance it appeared as if the corporations had built for themselves cathedrals, one after another, street by street, avenue by avenue; shining towers thrust up toward heaven, just as Paris and Chartres had once done, but in New York crowded against each other, jostling for attention. Curiously, the new cathedrals were also sheathed in stained glass from top to bottom, but they were never multicolored like the glass in the old cathedrals. Instead each tower chose for itself some monochrome—blues, greens, browns, and often an ominous gray-black. If these catafalques meant anything at all by their example, they seemed to consecrate in permanent form the theology of power—not the power of money or the power of politics, but the continuous worship of power for its own sake, an eternal dispensation of fraud and violence. Mrs. March was wrong when she said that New York forgot death. The evidence of the new cathedrals suggested that New York worshiped death.

CHAPTER TWENTY-FOUR

THE NEW CATHEDRALS

ACCORDING TO HISTORIANS of style, form must follow function. Without any reasonable doubt, it was the function of the new corporate cathedrals to house, on an efficient floor plan, the endless celebration of the city's illusions: for the poor, the illusions of opportunity; for the middle class, the illusions of progress; for the rich, the illusions of gaiety; for Society, the illusions of community; for Democracy, the illusions of Reform; for Capital, the illusions of money; for the faithful, the illusions of instant revelation dispensed by newspaper editors.

The new dispensation was preached every day, in morning and evening editions, brought up to the minute in relentless detail, but always reported with a vague tolerance, as if the miracles cited should neither be approved nor condemned, because no decision need ever be final. With these cautions attached, circulations attracted howling crowds. Each new revelation could be cheered for its truth and then abandoned just as quickly in the rush to follow the banners of the next fashion. Gorgeous lusts were reported, like those attributed to Stanford White, and then the pages iridescent with luxuries could be used to wrap tomorrow's fish.

Voluptuous passions were marched past the amazed imaginations of the citizens; recipes for exact gluttonies strung out in long columns; reports completed on how men and women had preyed upon one another or amassed incredible piles of worldly goods; investigations were pursued on how foods were adulterated, or machines constructed with fatal flaws, or how perjuries were sold as dreams to the unsuspecting, or how larcenies were worked on the hopeful; but all these entertainments passed in such profusion, few could distinguish one horror from the next.

Suicides were recalled with compassion; panders and seducers made into celebrities; flatterers consulted for their advice; thieves honored by city commissions; and liars blessed with the chair on their hostess's right. Savage revenge gurgled from the throats of judges as they sentenced the opponents they had replaced in the administration of justice, while the sentences of those convicted of assault, murder, and rape were suspended because there were too many crimes for justice to administer. Anyone who sowed discord was assured the attention of a chanting mob, until he was abandoned for the next hero who could raise a clenched fist.

The flames of hatred were always being newly fanned, and wars great and small waged to vent some fury; but vicious enemies were soon happy allies once millions had been savaged. After scalding destruction had been visited on some other city, the reasons for ferocity were forgotten, new contracts entered into, and a dismal sulkiness taken up to replace the pleasures hatred had once provided.

In a landscape of such constant terror Harry K. Thaw exercised a more perfect logic than many supposed. He understood exactly that in the kingdom of the dead a madman and murderer could go about as a prince, provided his dementia could be certified by competent psychiatric authority. Such authorities were always available.

Against the city's tendency to chaos Stanford White had attempted by his designs to redeem disorder by Grace, and White's life argued that Beauty was one of the Graces. Unfortunately, the city did not care to preserve most of his effort. It would remember him principally because he had loved a pretty woman and been murdered for doing so.

Evelyn Nesbit arrived in the city as a child and might easily have given in to dismay, but she called up from the labyrinth the threads of feminine understanding. From the maze of ancient memories she met the necessities always required of virgins. It could be said that she did no more than receive communion as a saint would in the city's dispensation, the eternal covenant, the ancient mystery of fraud and violence.

ACKNOWLEDGMENTS AND SOURCES

IN STUDYING THE STORY of Evelyn Nesbit and Stanford White, and in composing a catechism of the city's illusions, I have accumulated a long schedule of personal and intellectual debts. Unfortunately, it is impractical to acknowledge all who contributed. After absolving even the unnamed for any errors, which are wholly mine, I can do no more than single out some companions and sources in an abbreviated way, much as guidebooks do—highlighting the accommodations a traveler might expect, providing a list that might serve as a map for others, but telling nothing of the delights of the journey, nor anything about most of those who helped along the way.

I am indebted, for example, to *The Comedy of Dante Alighieri,* translated by Dorothy Sayers, Penguin Classics edition, London, 1949, not only for the quotes that appear in the text but for instruction in the topography of illusion. To understand the biographies of Evelyn Nesbit, Stanford White, and Harry K. Thaw I had to synthesize, but I came to depend upon certain sources, each in its peculiar way. *The Traitor,* by Harry K. Thaw, Philadelphia, Dorrance and Company, 1926, claimed to be "The Untampered With, Unrevised Account of the Trial and All That Led to It"—an autobiography full of precise details, and at the same time almost unintelligible. I took the details as probably correct and ignored the lunacies. *Prodigal Days,* by Evelyn Nesbit, New York, Julian Messner, Incorporated, 1934, claimed "to tell for the first time" Evelyn's own "untold story," although it was not at all either the first time, or untold. It was valuable to the extent that it corroborated, or added shading, to all the other stories told by her or about her. *Glamorous Sinners,* by Frederick L. Collins, New York, Ray Long and Richard R. Smith, Incorporated, 1932, is one of the more colorful accounts of the affair. *The Murder of Stanford White,* by Gerald Langford, Indianapolis, the Bobbs-Merrill Company, Incorporated, 1962, is the most accurate account of Thaw's many trials.

To these versions I added or subtracted as it seemed necessary from: the New York *Evening World* and the New York *Sunday World* (particularly the reports of Irvin S. Cobb), the New York *Evening Journal,* and *The New York Times.* In addition, I used or synthesized from: *The Great Harry Thaw Case,* Benjamin H. Atwell, Chicago, Laird and Lee, 1907; the Robinson-Locke Collection of Dramatic Scrap Books, maintained at the New York Public Library; *Turn West on 23rd,* Robert Baral, New York, Fleet Publishing Corporation, 1965; *Painted Veils,* James Huneker, New York, Liverwright Publishing Corporation, 1920; "McKim, Mead and White," John Jay Chapman, *Vanity Fair,* September, 1919; *The Girl in the Red Velvet Swing,* Charles Samuels, New York, Fawcett Gold Medal Books, 1953; and, *The Story of My Life,* by Evelyn Thaw, London, J. Long and Co., 1914.

Throughout, I have depended upon and I am indebted to: *Our Times,* Mark Sullivan, Volumes I-III, New York, Charles Scribner's Sons, 1930; *Stanford White,* Charles C. Baldwin, New York, Dodd, Mead and Company, 1931; *The Life and Times of Charles McKim,* Charles Moore, Boston, Houghton Mifflin Company, 1929; and *The Reminiscences of Augustus Saint-Gaudens,* edited and amplified by Homer Saint-Gaudens, New York, the Century Company, 1913.

It seemed to me that the biographies of White, McKim, and Saint-Gaudens were both reliable and interesting but the social necessities of their era widely interpreted. Their generation created a period of history that has been called by as many names as there are historians. Among dozens of other interpretations, the years in which "America came of age," has been described as: the Lost Generation, the Dreadful Decades, the Age of Big Business, the Rise of Modern Capitalism, the Tragic Era, La Belle Epoque, the Mauve Decades, the Days of the Idle Rich, the Big Spenders, the Splendor

Seekers, the Robber Barons, the Magnificoes, the Elegant Eighties, the Age of Reform, the Naughty Nineties and the Gay Nineties. When a history is open to so many interpretations, its consequences must be undigested and its issues still a subject of argument.

To meet the difficulties inherent in such diverse understandings, I adopted both the description by title and the attitudes of Mr. Samuel Clemens—*The Gilded Age: A Tale of Today,* by Mark Twain and Charles Dudley Warner. In addition, Mark Twain gave better instruction in the significant issues than any historian, particularly in: *The Innocents Abroad,* 1869; *A Connecticut Yankee in King Arthur's Court,* 1889; *Personal Recollections of Joan of Arc,* 1896; *The Man That Corrupted Hadleyburg,* 1899; *Extract from Captain Stormfield's Visit to Heaven,* 1909. Most critics have noted Mark Twain's sense of increasing dismay after 1886. His novels record the significant reasons.

Similarly, after the Haymarket strike, William Dean Howells abandoned his insistence on the "smiling aspects" of American life. He moved from the evergreen optimism of Boston to New York—a city of desolations. His grim but realistic portraits of middle-class couples like Mr. and Mrs. Basil March provide better understanding of the city's unresolved issues than all the standard histories combined. I am particularly indebted to *A Hazard of New Fortunes,* not only for the quotes from Mrs. March, but also for its descriptions and definitions. The evidence suggested by Howells in his *Letters* is that most writers and artists of his generation were appalled after 1886—Mark Twain, Henry James, Edith Wharton, Augustus Saint-Gaudens, and Henry Adams. The generation that succeeded them was not only dismayed but angry. I have drawn from *A Book About Myself,* Theodore Dreiser, Boni and Liveright, 1922.

Perhaps the most pessimistic reporter of the American scene was Henry Adams—the leading historian of the nineteenth century and a prophet of the twentieth equal to Mark Twain. In the text I have quoted from *The Education of Henry Adams,* Houghton Mifflin Century edition, 1961, and from *Chapters of Erie,* Charles Francis Adams, Jr., and Henry

Adams, Cornell Paperbacks, Cornell University Press, 1966. In addition to his work as an historian, Henry Adams considers for his countrymen the alternatives in social arrangements they might have chosen: he measures sex as a force, compares the forces of the Virgin and the Dynamo, explains the relations between form and energy. For the beginner, therefore, Adams is the primer on theologies and architecture, and on the significance of poets, writers, sculptors, artists, and architects. I am indebted to *Mont-Saint-Michel and Chartres,* Anchor Books edition, 1959.

After considering the evidence of fraud and violence assembled by novelists and prophets, the choices available for the pursuit of detail begin to multiply. I have no alternative but to select from many sources an abbreviated list from which I drew, upon which I depended, and which I recommend: *The Memoirs of Henry Villard,* two volumes, Houghton Mifflin, 1904; *The Robber Barons,* Matthew Josephson, Harvest Book, Harcourt Brace and World, Incorporated, 1962; *The Politicos,* Matthew Josephson, Harvest Book, Harcourt Brace and World, Incorporated, 1938; *The President Makers,* Matthew Josephson, Harcourt Brace and Company, 1940; *The Boss and the Machine,* S. P. Orth, Yale University Press, 1919; *History of the Great American Fortunes,* Gustavus Myers, three volumes, Charles H. Kerr and Company, 1910; *Society As I Have Found It,* Ward McAllister, Cassell Publishing Company, 1890; *The Rise of New York Port,* Robert Greenhalgh Albion, Charles Scribner's Sons, 1939; *The Pentagon of Power,* Lewis Mumford, Harcourt, Brace Jovanovich, Incorporated, 1964/1970; *The Death and Life of Great American Cities,* Jane Jacobs, Vintage Books, 1961; *The Economy of Cities,* Jane Jacobs, Vintage Books, 1969; *A City Destroying Itself,* Richard J. Whalen, William Morrow and Company, 1965.

On social history: *The American 1890's,* Larzer Ziff, Viking Compass edition, 1966; *The Richard Harding Davis Years,* Gerald Langford, Holt, Rinehart and Winston, 1961; *The American Mind,* Henry Steele Commager, Yale University Press, 1950; *Paths of American Thought,* edited by Arthur M. Schlesinger, Jr., and Morton White, Sentry edition, Houghton

Mifflin Company, 1970; *Great Issues in American History,* edited by Richard Hofstadter, Vintage Books edition, 1958/1969; *The Age of Reform,* Richard Hofstadter, Vintage Books, 1955; *The American Scene: 1860 to the Present,* edited by William J. Chute, Bantam Matrix edition, 1966; *Popular Culture and Industrialism, 1865-1890,* edited with an introduction by Henry Nash Smith, Anchor Books, Doubleday and Company, Incorporated, 1967; *The Big Change,* Frederick Lewis Allen, Harper and Row, 1952; *Crisis of the American Dream,* John Tipple, Pegasus, 1968; *The End of the American Era,* Andrew Hacker, Atheneum, 1970; *The New Industrial State,* John Kenneth Galbraith, Houghton Mifflin Company, 1967; *The Concept of the Corporation,* Peter F. Drucker, the John Day Company, Incorporated, 1946/1964; *The Principles of Organization,* James D. Mooney, Harper and Brothers, 1939/1947.

On the dynamics of social organization and architecture: *The Architecture of America,* John Burchard and Albert Bush-Brown, American Institute of Architects/Little Brown and Company, 1961/1966; *Will They Ever Finish Bruckner Boulevard?* Ada Louise Huxtable, a New York Times Book, the Macmillan Company, 1963 to 1970; *A Cartoon History of Architecture,* Osbert Lancaster, Sentry edition, Houghton Mifflin Company, 1964; *AIA Guide to New York City,* New York Chapter, American Institute of Architects, Norval White and Elliot Willensky, editors, the Macmillan Company, 1967/1968; *Fifth Avenue Old and New, 1824-1924,* Henry Collins Brown, the Fifth Avenue Association, 1924; *Fifth Avenue,* Theodore James, Jr., Walker and Company, 1971; *New York Landmarks,* edited by Alan Burnham, AIA, the Municipal Art Society of New York/Wesleyan University Press, 1963; *Architecture in New York,* Wayne Andrews, Icon editions, Harper and Row, 1969; *Lost New York,* Nathan Silver, Schocken Books edition, 1971; *This Was New York!* Maxwell F. Marcuse, LIM Press, 1965.

To these sources I would like to add acknowledgments and thanks to William C. Shopsin, AIA, for his teaching, his extraordinary collection of photographs of the history of New York architecture, and for his bibliographies. I am grateful to Lewis

Lapham, friend and companion, for his generosity: when he abandoned the project himself, he turned over his notes and bibliography as if they were a minor gift. I am in debt to the New York Public Library for the facilities and privileges of the Frederick Lewis Allen Room; to the New York Historical Society; the librarians of the Naugatuck, Connecticut, Library, of the East Hampton Free Library, and of the New York State Intra-Library System. Librarians all: I thank you for your searches and your courtesies.

Finally, my thanks go to Hillel Black, patient editor; to Alan P. Mooney, William C. MacMillen, Clarkson N. Potter, and Roberta Pryor for a thousand kindnesses; and to Anne Sears Mooney, my wife.

MICHAEL MACDONALD MOONEY

Wainscott, 1976

INDEX